Making Our Democracy Work

ALSO BY STEPHEN BREYER

Active Liberty

Breaking the Vicious Circle

Regulation and its Reform

Making Our Democracy Work

A Judge's View

Stephen Breyer

ALFRED A. KNOPF NEW YORK 2010

THIS IS A BORZOI BOOK
PUBLISHED BY ALFRED A. KNOPF

 Published in the United States by Alfred A. Knopf, a division of Random House, Inc., New York, and in Canada by Random House of Canada Limited, Toronto.

www.aaknopf.com

A portion of this work previously appeared in *The New York Review of Books.*

Library of Congress Cataloging-in-Publication Data
Breyer, Stephen G., [date]
Making our democracy work : a judge's view / by Stephen Breyer.
p. cm.
Includes bibliographical references.
ISBN 978-0-307-26991-1
1. Judicial review—United States. 2. Judicial review—United States—History. 3. Political questions and judicial power—United States. 4. Separation of powers—United States. I. Title.
KF4575.B73 2010
347.73'12—dc22 2010016839

Manufactured in the United States of America
Published September 14, 2010
Reprinted Four Times
Sixth Printing, December 2010

To my grandchildren—

Clara, Ansel,

Eli, Samuel,

and Angela

Contents

Author's Note

My objective in writing this book is to increase the public's general understanding of what the Supreme Court does. The Constitution's framers and history itself have made the Court the ultimate arbiter of the Constitution's meaning as well as the source of answers to a multitude of questions about how this vast, complex country will be governed, and thus it is important that the public understands how the Court carries out its role. I try to facilitate that understanding by explaining how the Court first decided that it had the power to hold a federal law unconstitutional, by showing how and why it was long a matter of touch and go whether the public would implement the Court's decisions, and by explaining how, in my view, the Court can, and should, help make the Constitution, and the law itself, work well for contemporary Americans.

This book is the work of a judge, a member of the Court, and it essentially contains my own reflections about the Court and the law. When I read a case, including those decided long ago, I can try to imagine how its author might have felt or reasoned, but I cannot speak as a historian, a political scientist, or a sociologist. Thus, my historical descriptions rely on only a few, but well-accepted, historical sources.

Because I believe it important for those who are not lawyers to understand what the Court does and how it works, I have tried to make the book accessible to a general audience. A few chapters involve more complicated and technical matters, but there too I have tried to make the discussion accessible even to a non-lawyer who can grasp the general themes without following every detail. And, in discussing cases, I have often simplified considerably, abstracting from the many factors that enter a judge's decision-making calculus, to highlight a few factors that I believe are key. I hope some readers will want to understand the cases more fully and read the cases themselves. They are easily obtainable on the Supreme Court's Web site, www.supremecourt.gov. (In discussing the cases, I have drawn what I say solely from the written record.) For those curious about how these opinions came to be, I have included in Appendix B a brief description of the Court's work, as well as a few essential points about our Constitution. I would urge all but expert readers to look through that Appendix before reading Parts II and III. I hope this book manages to be both interesting and informative to members of the public, lawyers and non-lawyers alike.

Introduction

Day after day I see Americans—of every race, religion, nationality, and point of view—trying to resolve their differences in the courtroom. It has not always been so. In earlier times, both here and abroad, individuals and communities settled their differences not in courtrooms under law but on the streets with violence. We Americans treasure the customs and institutions that have helped us find the better way. And we not only hope but also believe that in the future we will continue to resolve disputes under law, just as surely as we will continue to hold elections for president and Congress. Our beliefs reflect the strength of our Constitution and the institutions it has created.

The Constitution's form and language have helped it endure. The document is short—seven articles and twenty-seven amendments. It focuses primarily on our government's structure. Its provisions form a simple coherent whole, permitting readers without technical knowledge to understand the document and the government it creates. And it traces the government's authority directly to a single source of legitimizing power—"We the People."

Words on paper, however, no matter how wise, are not sufficient to preserve a nation. Benjamin Franklin made this point when, in 1787, he told a Philadelphia questioner that the Constitutional Convention had created "a republic, Madam, if you can keep it." The separate institutions that the Constitution fashioned—Congress, the executive, the judiciary—were intended to bring about a form of government that would guarantee that democracy and liberty are not empty promises. But what would enable the Constitution to work not only in theory but also in practice? How could the nation make sure that the Constitution's limits are respected, that our citizens enjoy its important protections, that our legal system resolves disputes fairly and impartially, and that our courts dispense justice?

Alexander Hamilton, along with many of the other constitutional framers, thought that a Supreme Court would provide part of the answer. The Court would interpret the law, thereby enforcing the Constitution's limits. It would help ensure a democratic political system, and it would safeguard individual constitutional rights and liberties. Indeed, as the historian Gordon Wood has pointed out, "by protecting the rights of minorities of all sorts against popular majorities," the Court would "become a major instrument for both curbing [American] democracy and maintaining it."[1]

In the framers' eyes, then, the Court would help to maintain the *workable democracy* that the Constitution sought to create. I have previously written about the Court and democracy, explaining the ways in which that constitutional concept critically affects judicial interpretation of much of the Constitution's language and also how the Constitution's democratic objective assumes a public that actively participates in the nation's political life. The present book focuses on the Supreme Court's role in maintaining a *workable* constitutional system of government. It discusses how the public and the Court can help make the Constitution work well in practice. And it shows why the Constitution necessarily assumes that the typical American learns something of our nation's history and understands how our government works.[2]

In particular, this book considers two sets of questions. The first concerns the public's willingness to accept the Court's decisions as legitimate. When the Court interprets the law, will the other branches of government follow those interpretations? Will the public do so? Will they implement even those Court decisions that they believe are wrong and that are highly unpopular? Many of us take for granted that the answer to these questions is yes, but this was not always the case. Part I uses examples from our nation's history to show how, after fragile beginnings, the Court's authority has grown. It describes how the Court was given the power to interpret the Constitution authoritatively, striking down congressional statutes that it finds in conflict with the Constitution. And it goes on to describe several instances where

Supreme Court decisions were ignored or disobeyed, where the president's or the public's acceptance of Court decisions was seriously in doubt. These examples of the Court's infirmity—perhaps startling today—demonstrate that public acceptance is not automatic and cannot be taken for granted. The Court itself must help maintain the public's trust in the Court, the public's confidence in the Constitution, and the public's commitment to the rule of law.

Part II considers how the Court can carry out this constitutional responsibility. The key lies in the Court's ability to apply the Constitution's enduring values to changing circumstances. In carrying out this basic interpretive task, the Court must thoughtfully employ a set of traditional legal tools in service of a pragmatic approach to interpreting the law. It must understand that its actions have real-world consequences. And it must recognize and respect the roles of other governmental institutions. By taking account of its own experience and expertise as well as those of other institutions, the Court can help make the law work more effectively and thereby better achieve the Constitution's basic objective of creating a workable democratic government.

My argument in Part II takes the form of examples drawn from history and from the present day, illustrating the Court's relationships with Congress, the executive branch, the states, other courts, and earlier courts. Part of my aim is to show how the Court can build the necessary productive working relationships with other institutions—without abdicating its own role as constitutional guardian.

The Court's role in protecting individual liberties presents special challenges to these relationships, some of which are discussed in Part III. I describe how this protection often involves a search for permanent values underlying particular constitutional phrases. I describe a method (proportionality) useful in applying those values to complex contemporary circumstances. And I discuss the Japanese internment during World War II as well as the recent Guantánamo cases to illustrate the difficulty of finding a proper balance between liberty and security when a president acts in time of war or special security need.

Throughout, I argue that the Court should interpret written words, whether in the Constitution or a statute, using traditional legal tools, such as text, history, tradition, precedent, and, particularly, purposes and related consequences, to help make the law effective. In this way, the Court can help maintain the public's confidence in the legitimacy of its interpretive role.

The various approaches that I discuss in Parts II and III fit together. They constitute a set of pragmatic approaches to interpreting the law. They provide a general perspective of how a pragmatically oriented judge might go about deciding the kinds of cases that make up the work of the Supreme Court. I do not argue that judges should decide all legal cases pragmatically. But I also suggest that by understanding that its actions have real-world consequences and taking those consequences into account, the Court can help make the law work more effectively. It can thereby better achieve the Constitution's basic objective of creating a workable democratic government. In this way the Court can help maintain the public's confidence in the legitimacy of its interpretive role. This point, which returns full circle to Part I, is critical.

At the end of the day, the public's confidence is what permits the Court to ensure a Constitution that is more than words on paper. It is what enables the Court to ensure that the Constitution functions democratically, that it protects individual liberty, and that it works in practice for the benefit of all Americans. This book explores ways in which I believe the Court can maintain that confidence and thereby carry out its responsibility to help ensure a Constitution that endures.

PART I

THE PEOPLE'S TRUST

PART I ADDRESSES THE ISSUE OF DEMOCRATIC LEGITIMACY—how the Supreme Court has come to gain public trust even when its decisions are highly unpopular. The Constitution's efforts to ensure a *workable* constitutional democracy mean little if the public freely ignores interpretations of the Constitution that it dislikes. We simply assume today that when the Court rules, the public will obey its rulings. But at various moments in our history, the Supreme Court's decisions were contested, disobeyed, or ignored by the public and even by the president and Congress.

This part describes the important power of judicial review—how the Supreme Court first came to assume the powers it now has to interpret the Constitution authoritatively and to strike down as unconstitutional laws enacted by Congress. Subsequent chapters present historical snapshots of how, in fits and starts, the Supreme Court came to be accepted and trusted as a guardian of the Constitution. The cases presented include an example in which the president and the State of Georgia refused to implement a Court decision protecting the Cherokee Indians; the example of *Dred Scott,* where the Court itself, misunderstanding the law, its own authority, and the likely public reaction, refused justice to an individual because of his race; and an example in which the president had to send troops to Little Rock, Arkansas, because so many people there, including the governor, refused to comply with the Court's decision, in *Brown v. Board of Education,* holding segregated schools unconstitutional. These examples help us understand the importance and the value, the uncertainty and the pitfalls, that predate today's widespread acceptance of Court decisions as legitimate. They help demonstrate that public acceptance is not automatic, and that the Court and the public must work together in a partnership of sorts, with mutual respect and understanding.

Chapter One

Judicial Review: The Democratic Anomaly

The Supreme Court can strike down statutes that violate the Constitution as the Court understands it. Where did the Court find this power of judicial review? The Constitution itself says nothing about it. One can easily imagine a Supreme Court without the power to patrol constitutional boundaries.

Canada's Supreme Court, for example, can strike a statute down as unconstitutional, but it does not necessarily have the final word on the matter. The legislature, without amending the constitution, may in certain instances overturn the result and restore the statute. Similarly, the courts in Britain and New Zealand are charged with interpreting parliamentary statutes so as to ensure their compatibility with their nations' constitutional traditions and, more recently, bills of rights (in Britain's case, the European Convention on Human Rights). If a court in either country is unable to interpret legislation consistently with the bill of rights, the court can make a "declaration of incompatibility." But doing so does not invalidate the legislation. After a court makes a declaration of incompatibility, it is up to Parliament to decide whether to amend or repeal the legislation that the court found violated citizens' rights. Parliament could choose to leave the legislation in place, notwithstanding the court's ruling.[1]

Many commentators, scholars, and ordinary citizens have viewed the U.S. Supreme Court's power of judicial review as out of place in a democracy. Why should a democracy, a political system based on representation and accountability, entrust the final or near-final making of such highly significant decisions to judges who are unelected, independent, and insulated from the direct impact of public opinion?

There are several partial answers to these questions. Some decisions *must* be made undemocratically—for example, the criminal trial of an unpopular defendant. The defendant's rights are rights the defendant can assert against the majority's will, and other constitutional rights also have this characteristic. Our system of democratic government is not pure majoritarian democracy, but majoritarian democracy with boundaries set by our constitutional structure and by rights that the Constitution ensures to individuals and minorities against the majority's desires. Moreover, most people understand that democratic governments, like all governments, need stability; and stability is inconsistent with a legal system whose content varies daily and directly with changes in popular opinion. Modern government also requires delegation of decision-making power, which means that the content of treaties, administrative rulings, even statutes, will not always mirror the views of the whole electorate or even a significant part of it. Instead, they mirror the more expert knowledge that the delegation of power has allowed. Thus most of us are aware that any actual democracy contains a host of institutions and procedures that are not purely democratic.

People also understand that the power to interpret a statute will sometimes resemble the power to interpret the Constitution. Delay, lack of legislative time, lack of public interest, and public hesitance to change a judicial result all mean that legislatures are not often able to overturn judicial interpretations of statutes as a practical matter, even though they may have the power to do so. This legislative reluctance, along with the unpopularity of overturning decisions that are intended to protect human rights, has meant that legislatures in Canada, for example, have overturned few, if any, of their courts' constitutional decisions, despite their legal power to do so.[2]

These answers are not completely satisfactory, however. The point remains that the Court's power to give binding effect to a constitutional interpretation is virtually ironclad. This power often concerns matters of great importance to the nation, and it can well place the

Court and other governmental institutions at loggerheads. Consider the Court's reapportionment decisions, which radically changed previous methods for drawing election district boundaries and consequently changed election results in many states; or its "affirmative action" decisions, which limited the use of race as a criterion for, say, assigning students to a secondary school to increase racial diversity there; not to mention its abortion decisions, which struck down laws that prevented women from obtaining abortions. Consider the Court's decisions finding prayer in public schools unconstitutional—decisions that have shaped the public debate about the relation of government and religion. Consider how its "search and seizure" decisions changed the way in which many police departments operate. Consider how its desegregation decisions changed what previously amounted to a caste system in the South.

In a word, the Court's application of judicial review has brought about important and often long-lasting changes. Judicial review has resulted in significant limits on the actions of other government bodies, on the terms of public debate, and on the ways in which Americans lead their lives. Hence, it still makes sense to ask why the judiciary does, or should, possess this power, a far stronger power than the power to interpret a statute.

Some have found an answer in the need to ensure a workable *democratic* system. Free speech helps the voters exercise an informed democratic choice, for example, by helping citizens obtain access even to extreme and highly unusual points of view. Equal protection of the laws helps ensure that government will not improperly weigh one citizen's voice more heavily than another's. Thus, to exercise a power that seeks to ensure a well-functioning democracy is not anomalously undemocratic.

Others find answers in the Constitution's dispersion of power among so many different government bodies. This dispersion, they believe, calls for a referee. Still others find justification in the need to protect minority rights. Democracy, they argue, refers to the will of a majority that may or may not act consistently with equal respect for minorities. Given the history of a twentieth century during which democratically elected governments mistreated minorities and then abandoned democracy altogether, one might see judicial review, here and abroad, as a kind of institutional ballast, helping to stabilize the kind of democracy that respects minority rights and helps to prevent the "people drunk" from undoing the will of the "people sober."[3]

These answers may help explain the anomaly, but they cannot fully explain why the Court has the power to find, say in the Constitution's word "liberty," certain rights that have little to do with the preservation of democracy or even the protection of minorities. We may still ask why the framers wrote a document that gave the Court the last word as to the constitutionality of virtually any congressional statute. Why did that document let the Court assume the power to strike down a statute as contrary to the Constitution?

The Framers' Response

Many framers, Federalists and even some Republicans, expected the undemocratically selected Court, at least on occasion, to strike down statutes it believed were in conflict with the Constitution. James Madison, for example, pointed out that the Bill of Rights would protect individuals from abuse by a majority. And he immediately added:

> Independent tribunals of justice will consider themselves in a peculiar manner the guardians of those rights; they will be an impenetrable bulwark against every assumption of power in the legislative or executive; they will be naturally led to resist every encroachment upon rights expressly stipulated for in the constitution by the declaration of rights.[4]

Alexander Hamilton wrote the same in *The Federalist Papers*—a series of newspaper articles in which he, James Madison, and John Jay advocated adoption of the Constitution. Hamilton said that the Constitution's limitations

> can be preserved in practice in no other way than through the medium of courts of justice, whose duty it must be to declare all

> acts contrary to the manifest tenor of the constitution void. . . . [Otherwise] all the reservations of particular rights or privileges would amount to nothing.[5]

The Constitutional Convention and ratification process resounded with similar language. Among those who expressed support for the power of judicial review were Elbridge Gerry of Massachusetts ("[The judiciary possesses] a power of deciding . . . [on a law's] constitutionality"); Rufus King, another delegate from Massachusetts ("[The judiciary needs no veto power, for] they will no doubt stop the operation of such [laws] as shall appear repugnant to the constitution"); and James Wilson, speaking at Pennsylvania's Ratification Convention ("[When the judges] consider [a law's] principles, and find it to be incompatible with the superior power of the Constitution,—it is their duty to pronounce it void"). One present-day scholar reports that "apparently no delegate" to the Constitutional Convention "questioned the repeated references to the power of the judiciary to ignore unconstitutional laws." Nor was anyone "surprised by the repeated references to judicial review—precisely the opposite reaction one would expect if judicial review had not yet been generally embraced."[6]

How did the framers explain this expectation of judicial review? Hamilton, in *The Federalist* numbers 78 and 81, argued that the Constitution must trump any ordinary federal law. The Constitution is fundamental, it represents the will of the people, and it is the source of lawmaking authority. A statute, by contrast, represents the exercise of constitutionally delegated authority and reflects the will of the people only indirectly, through their legislators. Thus, says Hamilton, "where the will of the legislature, declared in its statutes, stands in opposition to that of the people, declared in the Constitution, the judges . . . ought to regulate their decisions by the fundamental laws, rather than by those which are not fundamental."[7]

Hamilton, then, assumed that conflicts between statutes and the Constitution could not be resolved by leaving the matter to the public. Some members of that public would recognize the need to strike down a statute that violates the Constitution. After all, those whom unconstitutional laws help today may be hurt tomorrow. But others might well favor immediate self-interest over constitutional principle. Indeed, public instability in the 1780s such as Shays's Rebellion pointed directly to that risk.

Hamilton argued against placing final authority to interpret the Constitution in the hands of the president, because the president could then become too powerful. After all, the "executive not only dispenses the honors but holds the sword of the community." He also argued against placing final authority to interpret the Constitution in the hands of the legislature, because the legislature would too rarely enforce the Constitution if this invalidated a law it had recently passed. How, he asked, can it "be expected that men who had infringed the Constitution in the character of legislators, would be disposed to repair the breach in the character of judges?"[8]

That left the judiciary. The "interpretation of the laws," said Hamilton, "is the proper and peculiar province of the courts." Judges enjoy comparative expertise in the matter. They frequently reconcile apparently conflicting statutes; they study precedents; they are "skill[ed] in the laws," whereas legislators are "rarely . . . chosen with a view to those qualifications which fit men for the stations of judges." Indeed, "there is no liberty" unless the "power of judging" be "separated from the legislative and executive powers."[9]

Moreover, to place the power to resolve constitutional/statutory conflicts in the judiciary's hands would not threaten the public. That is because the judiciary, lacking both "purse" and "sword," is the "weakest of the three departments of power." Hamilton said the "nature" of the judicial power, how it is exercised, the comparative weakness of the judges, and their inability to "support" any "usurpation[] by force," reduced the "supposed danger of judiciary encroachments on the legislative authority" to a "phantom."[10]

Hamilton saw a greater risk in the opposite tendency, namely, that judges would fail to faithfully guard the Constitution when "legislative invasions of it had been instigated by the major voice of the community." To stand up against the force of public opinion would require an "uncommon portion of fortitude." It would require that judges be appointed for lengthy terms and receive constitutional guarantees as to their compensation. For all these reasons, the judiciary was the safest as well as the most natural place to lodge the power of judicial review.[11]

Another member of the founding generation, the Supreme Court justice James Iredell, elaborated on Hamilton's argument. In a concurring opinion written in a 1798 case, *Calder v. Bull,* Iredell assumed the need for an institution that would have the power to strike down an unconstitutional law. Otherwise the legislature could simply ignore the Constitution.[12]

Iredell must have recognized that the people themselves might help to keep the legislature within constitutional bounds. They could elect new members, petition for repeal of an unconstitutional law, and refuse to carry out such a law. But even if we ignore the instability inherent in such a system, these methods could at most "secure the views of a majority." What if the legislature enacts a law that is unconstitutional but popular? As Iredell explained in a letter he wrote in the 1780s, every citizen

> should have a surer pledge for his constitutional rights than the wisdom and activity of any occasional majority of his fellow-citizens, who, if their own rights are in fact unmolested, may care very little for his.[13]

Thus, as between court and legislature, it is the court that must have the last word. Individual liberty "is a matter of the utmost moment." If there be

> no check upon the public passions, it is in the greatest danger. The majority having the rule in their own hands, may take care of themselves; but in what condition are the minority, if the power of the other is without limit?[14]

Iredell concluded that the courts must have the power of judicial review. They may abuse that power, but one can find safeguards against abuse in the transparency of the judicial process, which allows the public to assess the merits of a judicial decision, and in the judges' own desire to maintain a strong judicial reputation.[15]

Still, what if the Court abuses that power? Or what if the Court simply gets it wrong? The Court certainly got it wrong in *Dred Scott* (see Chapter Four). Franklin Roosevelt believed the Court abused its power when it invalidated New Deal legislation he thought essential to the nation's recovery from the Great Depression. And many believe that a wide variety of individual decisions are very wrong indeed.

When the Court proceeds down a wrong track too long, as the pre–New Deal Court did in the early twentieth century, the public can become aware and react. The reaction can take the form of legislation, say if the Court has misread a statute. Or voters can elect a president and senators who will appoint and confirm judges who have different basic attitudes from the judges with whom they disagree. In President Roosevelt's case, he pushed for legislation that allowed him to "pack" the Court, a battle he lost. But he ultimately won by virtue of being in office long enough to appoint eight of the nine justices on the Court.

And although judges are guaranteed life tenure in order to withstand the force of public opinion, they cannot help but be aware of the public mood. Criticism of judges and judicial decisions traces back to our founding. It is a healthy thing in a democracy. Judges read the newspaper, they read academic critiques of their decisions, and they read briefs urging them to decide a case one way or the other. They realize they can be wrong. That is why they sometimes reconsider earlier decisions and in rare cases overrule them.

Nonetheless, we Americans have, over the past two hundred plus years, absorbed the notion that in order to be protected by the rule of law, we must follow the law even when we disagree with it. And many, perhaps most, Americans would now likely agree with Hamilton that it is better to give independent judges, rather than the executive or legislative branches, the power of judicial review.

The arguments for judicial review, as Hamilton and Iredell set them out, come down to saying that some power of review is necessary, particularly to protect unpopular minorities; judges are reasonably well qualified to undertake review, which is basically a legal job; and the review power is less dangerous and more effective if lodged in the judicial branch than if lodged elsewhere. One can find widespread support for this view among the founding generation. But questions remain.

For one thing, what exactly does "judicial review" mean? The term refers generally to the fact that the Court has the power to strike down a statute as incompatible with the Constitution in a particular case. But does that mean that Congress or the president must agree with the Court in later, similar instances? Do other institutions have an independent obligation to determine whether a statute is consistent with the Constitution? Can they ignore a Supreme Court decision to the contrary? These matters remained ambiguous for many years, not resolved until the mid-twentieth century.

More important, the arguments for judicial review do not answer the puzzling question of why the public would accept as legitimate and follow the decisions made by the inoffensive, technical, and comparatively powerless body that Hamilton and Iredell described. Where political emotions run high, few accept a technician's choice as clearly valid. Where public feelings are strong, a technician lacking "purse" and "sword" may find it difficult to assuage them. Why doesn't the public just ignore a constitutional decision that a majority believes is both important and wrong? And if they do ignore the Court's decisions, has the whole objective of Hamilton's argument not been rejected? None of the framers answers that question. Yet it is a question that, during our nation's history, has cried out for an answer.

In Shakespeare's *Henry IV,* Hotspur listens to Owen Glendower boast, "I can call spirits from the vasty deep." Hotspur then replies, "Why, so can I, or so can any man, *but will they come when you do call for them?*"

This basic question unites and underlies this book's discussion.

Chapter Two

Establishing Judicial Review: Marbury v. Madison

IN 1803 IN *Marbury v. Madison,* Chief Justice John Marshall established the Court's authority to invalidate laws that conflict with the Constitution through a judicial tour de force. Marshall wrote the Hamiltonian theory of judicial review into law. And in doing so, he overcame major institutional and political obstacles.[1]

The federal judiciary was a weak institution, and the number of lower-court federal judges was small. State courts enforced federal law, but there was no guarantee they would follow federal court interpretations of that law. Nor was there any guarantee that local officials would carry out federal court orders. The Supreme Court itself had little to do. Its caseload was unimportant, and its judges badly paid, and they had to spend considerable time "riding circuit"—traveling over bad roads to hear cases arising throughout the new nation. The first chief justice, John Jay, resigned in 1795 to become governor of New York; he later refused reappointment because the position lacked "energy, weight and dignity." A major newspaper referred to the position as a "sinecure." Lacking its own courtroom, the Court met in the Senate clerk's office.[2]

The position of the judiciary also became an important and controversial issue between mobilized political parties. The Republicans, led by Thomas Jefferson, had beaten the Federalists in elections, winning the presidency (in 1801) and taking control of Congress. Party rivalry was fierce. The Federalists feared Jefferson as a dangerous radical "visionary" intent on undoing Federalist efforts to create a strong federal government. The Republicans thought the Federalists were seeking a central government so strong as to threaten ordinary citizens' liberties. And the Republicans particularly disliked the judicial branch, with its judges, appointed by presidents of the opposition party, who had enforced unpopular laws forbidding seditious libel; had found ways to prosecute popular rebels such as the leaders of Pennsylvania's Whiskey Rebellion; and had, from time to time, spoken out against the Republican Party and in favor of the Federalists. As far as Jefferson was concerned, the less powerful the Supreme Court, the better for the country.[3]

Furthermore, Jefferson was less willing than was Hamilton to give judges ultimate power to resolve constitutional/statutory conflicts. As he later wrote,

> each of the three departments has equally the right to decide for itself what is its duty under the constitution, *without any regard to what the others may have decided for themselves under a similar question.*

Other Republicans went further, denying that the Court had any power to overturn an act of Congress as contrary to the Constitution.[4]

Moreover, the Republicans correctly understood that the judiciary was the only branch of government that after 1801 would remain in Federalist hands. And they feared that the Federalists would make use of their control of the presidency and Congress during the 1801 lame-duck period between the elections and the March swearing in to reinforce their judicial power. Their fears proved justified when the Federalist Congress passed the new Judiciary Act, which cut the number of Supreme Court justices from six to five on the next resignation (thereby putting off the evil day when Jefferson might be able to make a Court appointment). The act extended federal court jurisdiction, making it easier for litigants to bring cases in federal court as opposed to state court; abolished the requirement that justices ride circuit; and created new judgeships, including sixteen new lower-court judgeships, thereby permitting John Adams, the lame-duck president, to make new appointments.[5]

Once in office, the Republicans began a legislative counterattack. They repealed the 1801 Judiciary Act, thus withdrawing new federal court powers to hear more cases and abolishing the new circuit courts of appeals. Once again the Supreme Court justices had to travel across the country to hear cases. Eventually, the Republicans tried to use the power that the Constitution gave Congress to impeach federal officials to rid the government of Federalist-appointed judges—for example, John Pickering, a New Hampshire federal judge (who had a drinking problem and was convicted), and Samuel Chase, a Supreme Court justice (whom the Republicans opposed primarily on philosophical grounds and who was acquitted by a narrow vote). Congress also postponed the Supreme Court's next meeting time until 1803—thereby delaying the Court's consideration of the constitutionality of their actions.[6]

But had the counterattack come too late? To what extent did the Constitution protect the actions of an earlier Federalist-controlled Congress from later legislative change? President John Adams, a Federalist, sent that question on the road to resolution before leaving office. Acting almost immediately after the Federalist Congress (in mid-February 1801) passed its judiciary-strengthening laws, he began filling the new judicial vacancies by appointing the "midnight judges."

In most instances, Adams successfully nominated and secured Senate confirmation of his new appointees before March, when his term expired. But he did not act quickly enough in the case of William Marbury, nominee for justice of the peace in the District of Columbia. On the evening of March 3, 1801, the day before Jefferson's inauguration, Adams signed Marbury's commission. He gave the commission to John Marshall, who had recently been appointed chief justice of the United States but had remained as secretary of state for a last few days. Marshall affixed the great seal to the commission. But in the last-minute hubbub, the commission was not actually delivered to Marbury. When Jefferson took office, he found the commission and refused to deliver it.[7]

That is how the great case of *Marbury v. Madison* began. Marbury initially wrote to the new secretary of state, James Madison, asking what had happened to his commission. Madison ignored him. Marbury then considered suing Madison to force him to deliver the commission. But where should he bring that lawsuit? A state court might well have had reservations about getting involved in a dispute about a federal commission, and the Republicans had begun to "purge" state judges with Federalist sympathies. If he sued in a District of Columbia court, he would have to face a Republican chief judge (and, in any event, Congress had given lower federal courts like this authority to hear only a narrow category of cases that might not have included Marbury's case, and Congress might have abolished the lower court in which he brought suit).

Marbury then found a federal statutory provision that apparently provided an answer. The statute said that the Supreme Court could "issue . . . *writs of mandamus,* in cases warranted by the principles and usages of law, *to any* courts appointed, or *persons holding office,* under the authority of the United States." Perfect—perhaps. A writ of mandamus was a legal order that compelled an officeholder to perform a routine task. James Madison was a person holding office under the authority of the United States. The delivery of a piece of paper, namely, the commission, was just such a routine task. And so Marbury filed a lawsuit directly in the Supreme Court, asking it to issue a writ of mandamus compelling the secretary of state to deliver his commission.[8]

The court case highlighted the political, legal, and constitutional controversies of the day. Jefferson feared that his bitter political enemies, who included John Marshall, would force him to accept one of their Federalist appointees. He doubted that the Court could review the constitutionality of statutes; he hoped it lacked the power to review the validity of presidential actions as well. And he consequently told James Madison simply to ignore all the Court's proceedings, not even to file a response.[9]

As a result, Jefferson forced John Marshall and the Court onto the horns of a critical dilemma: On the one hand, if the Court held that the law did *not* entitle Marbury to his commission, it would radiate institutional weakness. It would fail to force an executive branch official to perform a purely routine act, thereby making clear that courts, and perhaps the law itself, could not stand in the way of a determined president. On the other hand, if the Court held that the law *did* entitle Marbury to his commission, then Jefferson (who saw the judges as enemies and thought his own conduct exemplary) might continue to ignore the Court. By ignoring the Court's decision, Jefferson would answer Hotspur's question in the worst possible way. When the Court called, the president would not come. Whatever the Court might say, it would have failed to act effectively.

As it happened, Marshall, writing for a unanimous Court, brilliantly escaped the dilemma. The Court held that the law *did* entitle Marbury to his commission. And the opinion also adopted Hamilton's theory of judicial review. Yet at the same time, the Court held that *Jefferson won the case* on constitutional grounds. Jefferson had no problem enforcing this decision—he simply continued to withhold Marbury's commission. Thus the Court avoided the practical problem of enforceability.

How did the Court accomplish this legal feat—worthy of the Great Houdini? It began by posing the case's ultimate question as follows: Should the Court issue a writ of mandamus directing the secretary of state to deliver to Marbury his commission? It then pointed out that Marbury had a legal right to a copy of the commission. A statute made clear that once appointed as justice of the peace, Marbury had a legal right to the position for a term of five years. And once the president signed Marbury's commission, he was legally "appointed." The acts of affixing a seal to the commission and recording it were routine, that is, "ministerial act[s]," which another statute specifically required the secretary of state to undertake. And, once Marbury showed he had satisfied these legal obligations, the secretary could no more refuse to give Marbury a copy of the commission than a recording officer today could refuse to give a copy of a public document to someone who requests it and pays the copying fee.

But the fact that Marbury has a legal right to the commission is not enough. Does the law give him the power to enforce that right, that is, does Marbury have a legal *remedy*? Again the Court answered yes, and for reasons that are not entirely technical. The United States is a "government of laws, and not of men." Under such a government, "where there is a legal right, there is also a legal remedy." Indeed, the "very essence of civil liberty certainly consists in the right of every individual to claim the protection of the laws, whenever he receives an injury."[10]

The Court noted some exceptions to this rule, and they are important. In particular, a "*political act*" of the president (or one of his "political or confidential" executive branch "agents") was not "examinable in a court." But whether such an act escaped judicial review "must always depend on the nature of that act." The political acts that a court could not examine were at the least acts where "the executive possesses a constitutional or legal discretion." Here neither president nor secretary possessed discretion. Indeed, "the law in precise terms directs the performance of an act, in which an individual is interested." If a specific duty was assigned by law and individual rights depended on the performance of that duty, then the person who considered himself injured must be able to "resort to the laws of his country for a remedy."[11]

Still, not even the fact that Marbury had both a legal right and a legal remedy was sufficient. The Court still had to ask whether it had the power to grant Marbury that legal remedy. That is, did the law entitle Marbury to have the *Supreme Court* issue a writ of mandamus, that is, an order that would require a government official, namely, Madison, to deliver the commission to Marbury? Chief Justice Marshall quickly answered that the federal jurisdictional *statute* to which Marbury pointed—a statute that defined the kinds of cases the Court could hear and that seemed to offer the "perfect" jurisdictional solution—answered this question yes. The statute said that the Supreme Court may "issue . . . *writs of mandamus,* in cases warranted by the principles and usages of law, to . . . persons holding office, under the authority of the United States." Thus, Marshall concluded, the statute gave the Court jurisdiction to issue the writ that Marbury sought (mandamus) to the person responsible for giving the commission (Madison), as long as the issuance was "warranted by the principles and usages of law." And the issuance arguably was warranted because courts have traditionally issued writs of mandamus to compel government officers to carry out legally required ministerial duties such as delivering a document like the commission.[12]

But the Court was still not finished. It went on to ask whether the Constitution allowed Congress to enact a statute like this, which grants the power to issue a writ of mandamus in Marbury's favor. The Court's answer made the case famous.

Recall that Marbury did not originally file his case in a lower court and then appeal the case to the Supreme Court. Rather, he originally filed the case in the Supreme Court itself. Now, here is Marshall's tour de force: whatever that "perfect" statute might say, the Constitution itself says that

> in all Cases affecting Ambassadors, other public Ministers and Consuls, and those in which a State shall be Party, *the supreme Court shall have original Jurisdiction.* In *all* the other Cases before mentioned, the supreme Court shall have *appellate* Jurisdiction.

But this case did not affect ambassadors, public ministers (that is, representatives of foreign governments), or consuls. It was not a case in which a state was a party. Nor did it invoke the Court's *appellate* jurisdiction. Hence, if the statute gave the Court the power to hear Marbury's case as an *original* matter, the statute conflicted with the Constitution. Thus, the Court had to decide "*whether an act repugnant to the constitution can become the law of the land.*"[13]

Chief Justice Marshall said this question was "deeply interesting to the United States; but, happily, not of an intricacy proportioned to its interest." For one thing, the American Constitution, unlike the English constitution, was a *written* constitution. And an "act of the legislature repugnant" to that written Constitution must be "void." Otherwise, the Constitution's provisions would not be "fundamental," "supreme," and "permanent." Otherwise, the Constitution would create a federal government of unlimited, not limited, power. By enforcing a law that is "entirely void," the Court would grant the legislature legal and practical "omnipotence."[14]

The opinion next pointed out that resolving conflicts among different laws by determining, for example, which law prevailed was "the very essence of judicial duty." Here is the heart of the matter: an invalid law could not bind the courts because it "is emphatically the province and duty of the judicial department to say what the law is."[15] The Constitution is law and is our country's supreme law, so the Court must follow the Constitution and override a conflicting statute if a case presents that conflict.

Finally, various provisions of the Constitution itself seemed to foresee that courts would have the power to authoritatively interpret and enforce the Constitution. Article III says that the "judicial Power" of the United States includes the power to decide cases "arising under" the "Constitution." It also says that the government may not convict a person of treason on the testimony of only one witness. Article I says that states may not impose an export tax. And Article VI says that the Constitution "shall be the supreme Law of the Land" and provides that "all . . . judicial Officers . . . shall be bound by Oath . . . to support this Constitution." (Congress had added that judges must promise to "discharge" all their duties "agreeably to the Constitution.") Surely this meant that if a state (violating what the Constitution said) tried to prosecute someone who had failed to pay an export tax, a court ought not "close [its] eyes on the constitution, and only see" the tax. Nor, if the legislature should "declare one witness . . . sufficient for conviction" of treason, could a court be expected to allow "the constitutional principle [to] yield to the legislative act." No, "this is too extravagant to be maintained." In these instances and elsewhere, "the language of the constitution is addressed especially to the courts," and, therefore, "it is apparent, that the framers of the constitution contemplated that instrument as a rule for the government of courts, as well as of the legislature." Thus, Marshall reasoned, when an ordinary law conflicts with the Constitution, it is the Court's duty to apply the Constitution, not the ordinary law.[16]

The Court's conclusion: The statutory provision that granted the Court the power to hear Marbury's case as an original matter was unconstitutional, and so the Court could not give it effect. Therefore the Court could not hear the case (and it never did). As a result, it obviously could not issue a writ of mandamus. Marbury lost. And Madison, in effect representing Jefferson, won.

Marshall's legal reasoning was strong, although it is open to criticism, as are all opinions. A judicial opinion cannot logically prove that its result is correct; it can only explain the judge's own reasons for having reached a particular conclusion, often in a case where much can be said on both sides. Still, one criticism is particularly striking. Numerous critics, including Thomas Jefferson, have pointed out that a court that lacks the legal power (that is, jurisdiction) to decide a case should not then go on to decide the merits of that case. How could Marshall, having ultimately found that the Court lacked the power to hear Marbury's case, also have decided the merits of the case (that is, that Marbury was entitled to the mandamus even if the Court did not have jurisdiction to give it to him)?[17]

One possible modern answer to the criticisms is this: Had Marshall simply followed the ordinary jurisdictional rule, jumping directly to, and exclusively discussing, the constitutional issues, critics at the time might have wondered whether he really had to decide the great constitutional question of judicial review. They could reasonably have asked whether Marshall had reached out *unnecessarily,* that is, for political reasons, to claim that power for the Court.

To show that the Court had acted not from political expediency but out of judicial necessity, Marshall had to make clear that Marbury's claim satisfied each and every one of the statute's requirements. Only then would it be *necessary* to move on to the great constitutional question of judicial review in order to avoid a legally incorrect decision (that is, a decision in Marbury's favor). Marshall could not both show that he *had* to reach the constitutional questions and decide *nothing but* the constitutional questions. He could not follow what has become one canon of judicial decision making, namely, "try to avoid making constitutional decisions by deciding nonconstitutional matters first," without ignoring a different canon of judicial decision making, namely, "where a court lacks jurisdiction, do not decide the merits of the case."

In a political world suspicious of Marshall's efforts to expand the

Court's power, a world where the Court's basic judicial review power was itself yet undetermined, Marshall's choice is understandable. By explaining why he could not rest his decision on nonconstitutional grounds, he would diminish the public's concern that courts, armed with the power to decide constitutional questions, would reach out and decide them unnecessarily, thereby needlessly limiting the power of the legislature. They would decide constitutional questions only when they had to.

In a sense, both the criticisms and response are beside the point, for consider what Marshall did. He made clear that courts will ordinarily protect the legal rights of individuals, will ordinarily review the lawfulness of executive branch activity, and will themselves determine whether the "political" nature of an executive branch decision precludes court review and, above all, that a federal statute contrary to the Constitution cannot bind the courts. He supported these conclusions with strong legal arguments, including considerations similar to those set forth by Hamilton and Iredell, namely (1) the Constitution's "fundamental" and "superior" legal role, (2) the nature of judicial expertise, and (3) the need to avoid an all-powerful legislature. *And because Jefferson won the case, Marshall did not have to worry whether the government would enforce his decision.*[18]

For present purposes, the last-mentioned fact is particularly important. Faced with circumstances that threatened to demonstrate, and would thereby reinforce, the Court's institutional weakness, Marshall avoided the enforcement issue while holding that the Court had the power to declare an act of Congress unconstitutional and refuse to apply it.

Consider too what Marshall did not do. He did not decide that the Court had an *exclusive* power to interpret the Constitution or a power superior to that of other branches. Indeed, he wrote that the "courts, *as well as other departments,* are bound by" the Constitution. Nor did the case of *Marbury v. Madison* answer Hotspur's question: Would the public follow an unpopular Court decision with which it strongly disagrees? Marshall feared a negative answer; and the next case shows how right he was to worry.[19]

Chapter Three

The Cherokees

ALTHOUGH *MARBURY* GAVE the Court the power to refuse to apply an act of Congress on the ground that it violated the Constitution, the Court did not again exercise that power until its decision in the *Dred Scott* case more than fifty years later. This hesitancy to find a federal statute unconstitutional, like Marshall's strategic view of *Marbury,* suggests a Court deeply uncertain as to whether the president, the Congress, or the public itself would accept the Court's views about the Constitution—at least when they strongly disagreed with those views. And without assurance that other government officials and the public would follow the law, how could the Court successfully exercise its review power? How could it help to protect, say, an unpopular minority? How could it help make the Constitution more than words on paper?

Today judges from all over the world ask similar questions. A chief justice of an African nation struggling to maintain an independent judiciary recently asked me directly, "Why do Americans do what the courts say?" What in the Constitution makes this likely? What is the institutional device that makes court decisions effective? What, she wondered, is the secret? I answered that there is no secret; there are no magic words on paper. Following the law is a matter of custom, of habit, of widely shared understandings as to how those in government and members of the public should, and will, act when faced with a court decision they strongly dislike.

My short answer to the chief justice's question was to say that history, not legal doctrine, tells us how Americans came to follow the

Supreme Court's rulings. My longer answer consists of several examples that illustrate different challenges the Court and the nation faced as gradually, over time, the American public developed those customs and habits.

The Cherokee Indian cases of the 1830s provide an early example of enforceability put to the test. The Cherokee tribe sued to protect its legal rights to its ancestral lands in northern Georgia. The U.S. Supreme Court held in its favor. What happened next is an unhappy story.[1]

IN THE FIRST part of the nineteenth century, a dispute developed between the Cherokee Indians and their neighbors, settlers in the state of Georgia. The dispute was simple. The Indians owned land, rocks, and minerals that the white Georgia settlers wanted, and the Indians did not want to give them up. The Georgians had tried hard for two decades to convince three presidents (James Monroe, John Quincy Adams, and Andrew Jackson) to remove the Indian tribes from Georgia and send them to the West. But they got nowhere. Monroe, for example, told the Georgians that he would use only reasonable, peaceful means to convince the tribe to move.[2]

The Cherokees, who had lived in northern Georgia far longer than the Georgians, had moved on from their purely hunting/fishing life to become farmers and landowners. They had developed an alphabet, established a printing press, and built a capital called New Echota. Under the leadership of their great chief John Ross, they had also adopted a constitution. They had no reason to leave their own land. And they told President Monroe that "it is the fixed and unalterable determination of this nation never again to cede one foot more of our land." They added that they were not foreigners but the original inhabitants of America, who "now stand on the soil of their own territory" and who will not "recognize the sovereignty of any State within the limits of their territory." And they would later tell President Andrew Jackson that when they moved, they would not go west but, instead, would only go "by the course of nature to sleep under *this* ground which the Great Spirit gave our ancestors."[3]

Then, in 1829, gold was found on the Cherokee lands, and the Georgians decided to break the stalemate. They entered the Cherokee territory and began to work the gold mines. They passed laws that nullified all Cherokee laws, prohibited the Cherokee legislature from meeting, and ordered the arrest of any Cherokee who argued against moving to the West. Furthermore, the Georgians found an ally in a new president, Andrew Jackson, who announced his support for Georgia, refused to keep federal troops in the mining area to enforce the Indians' rights, and urged the Indians to move west.[4]

Some in the federal Congress opposed removing the Indians from their homes, churches, and schools to send them to a "wilderness." That minority pointed out that the "evil . . . is enormous; the violence is extreme; the breach of public faith deplorable; the inevitable suffering incalculable." But a congressional majority felt differently. And Congress enacted a removal bill that was intended to enforce the president's position.[5]

Lacking sufficient support in the elected branches of the federal government, where could the Cherokees turn for help? Could they look to the law? After supporting the British during the Revolution, the tribe had signed treaties with the new United States in which the United States promised to protect the Cherokees' land and guarantee its boundaries. The Constitution specifically says that not only the Constitution and laws made thereunder but also "*all Treaties* made . . . under the Authority of the United States shall be the supreme Law of the Land; and the Judges in every State shall be bound thereby, any Thing in the . . . Laws of any State to the Contrary notwithstanding."[6]

Although the Cherokees' legal case seemed ironclad, the same political circumstances that led them to put their hopes in the law made it difficult to get that law enforced. The Georgians would not protect them. A majority in Congress apparently did not care. And Andrew Jackson had refused the Indians' request to enforce their treaty. Hence, the Cherokees could look only to the courts for protection.

But the tribe's unpopularity and political weakness made bringing a lawsuit more difficult than one might think. The tribe found a lawyer, William Wirt, a former attorney general of the United States and one of the greatest lawyers of his day. Wirt thought that "the Supreme Court would protect" the tribe. But Wirt could not be certain that Georgia would follow the law, even if embodied in a Supreme Court decision. After all, some years earlier, when John Quincy Adams was president, the Georgians had seized land belonging to the Creek tribe, passed resolutions declaring they owned it, sent surveyors to map the territory, and said they would "resist to the utmost" any federal effort, including any Supreme Court effort, to stop them. After all this, the Creeks just gave up.[7]

Moreover, how was Wirt to get his case to the Supreme Court? He hesitated to bring a case in Georgia's own courts—for example, by suing Georgians for trespass. He feared that Georgia state judges might indefinitely delay matters by raising problems of state property law. He thought for a time that he might represent a Cherokee Indian—Corn Tassel—whom the Georgians had arrested for committing a serious crime in Cherokee territory. Wirt would appeal Corn Tassel's case to the Supreme Court, arguing that Georgia did not have the power to enforce its laws in the Cherokees' territory. But Georgia's governor and legislature announced that they would pay no attention to the Court's decision and would resist with force any effort to enforce a Supreme Court order. To make certain a Court order would have no effect, Georgia executed Corn Tassel before the Supreme Court could hear the case.[8]

Wirt next tried suing Georgia directly in the Supreme Court, in the case of *Cherokee Nation v. Georgia.* He thought the Court would hear and decide the case. After all, the Constitution said that the Supreme Court had "original Jurisdiction" over cases "in which a State shall be Party." And as to enforcement, he told the Court that it should not assume that the president or a state would not do its "duty." There was a "moral force in the public sentiment," he said, that would "constrain obedience."[9]

The Court, however, apparently decided not to place its faith in "public sentiment." In an opinion written by Chief Justice Marshall, a divided Court (4 to 2) set forth a highly dubious interpretation of the Constitution, as allowing the Court "original Jurisdiction" only in those cases where a state is a party *and* the case involves another state, a citizen of a different state, or a foreign state. Because the Cherokee tribe was none of these but, rather, a "domestic dependent nation[]," the

Court dismissed the case on technical, jurisdictional grounds. The Georgians were delighted. Georgia's governor wrote that the state "must put an end to even the semblance" that the Indians could constitute "a distinct political society."[10]

After this setback, Wirt finally found the case he had been looking for. Georgia law required "all white persons residing within the limits of the Cherokee Nation" to take an oath to support Georgia's laws. A New England missionary, Samuel A. Worcester, refused. (He sent the governor a hymnbook instead.) The governor ordered Worcester arrested, and a Georgia court convicted him of violating the law and sentenced him to four years of hard labor. Georgia would not free Worcester, but it was unlikely to execute him. Furthermore, the Judiciary Act of 1789 gave the Supreme Court the authority to hear cases in which a state court had rejected a party's claim that a state's criminal law violated federal law, which the Constitution made "supreme." Thus the law made clear that Wirt could appeal Worcester's case to the Supreme Court, making the argument that application of Georgia's criminal law in Cherokee territory violated treaties made by the United States, treaties that the Constitution made "supreme."[11]

The Court heard the case, *Worcester v. Georgia,* and by a vote of 5 to 1 found in Worcester's favor. Again Chief Justice Marshall wrote the Court's opinion. He pointed out that a federal statute empowers the Court to review a final state court judgment that upholds a state statute and that also rejects a claim that the statute is repugnant to the Constitution, treaties, or laws of the United States. Furthermore, another federal statute requires the Court to hear such an appeal. In Marshall's words, the Court therefore has "the duty, . . . however unpleasant," to hear the case.[12]

Moreover, the Court held that Worcester was clearly right about the merits of his case. Neither Britain nor the colonies nor the United States ever extinguished the Cherokees' independence. All had treated the Indian tribes as "nations capable of maintaining the relations of peace and war." The United States specifically promised that it would guarantee the Cherokees all lands "not . . . ceded" and would regulate trade for their "benefit and comfort." Congress too had recognized that Indian tribes are "distinct political communities" with a right to all the lands within their boundaries. Thus Georgians could not enter the Cherokee lands without the Cherokees' consent, and Georgia could not apply its state law there.[13]

Because the state statute used to prosecute Worcester "is consequently void," Georgia had to release him. After all, if Georgia had taken property under the authority of an invalid law, it would have to return the property to its owner; the same principle applied when the state invalidly deprived Worcester of his "personal liberty."[14]

In a well-aimed aside, the Court referred to the enforceability problem. It pointed out that Georgia had "seized" Worcester and "carried [him] away" while he was under the "guardianship of treaties" of the United States, indeed while he was "performing, *under the sanction of the chief magistrate of the union,* those duties which the humane policy adopted by congress had recommended." Perhaps President Jackson would get this hint. Perhaps he would understand that his own authority and the authority of the entire federal government were at stake.[15]

Justice Joseph Story, Marshall's colleague, felt relief. He wrote to his wife, "Thanks be to God, the Court can wash their hands clean of the iniquity of oppressing the Indians and disregarding their rights." A few days later, he wrote to another correspondent: "The Court has done its duty. Let the Nation now do theirs." But he added, "Georgia is full of anger and violence. . . . Probably she will resist . . . and if she does, I do not believe the President will interfere."[16]

Story was correct. On March 5, 1832, the Court issued an order requiring Georgia to release Worcester. Shortly thereafter, when Worcester's lawyers asked the state judge to release him, the judge refused. The governor then told the state legislature that he would meet the Supreme Court's "usurpation of Federal power with the most prompt and determined resistance."[17]

The president also refused to help enforce the Supreme Court's decision. On the contrary, Jackson's secretary of war stated that the president, "on mature consideration," believed that state legislatures have the "power to extend their laws over all persons [that is, Indian tribes included] living within their boundaries." Consequently, the president, he said, has "no authority to interfere" in Georgia's dealings with Samuel Worcester. Furthermore, in Jackson's view the president and the Congress had as much authority "to decide upon the constitutionality" of statutes as do "the supreme judges," who, he added, "must not . . . be permitted to control the Congress, or the Executive, when acting in their legislative capacities." The *New York Daily Advertiser* told its readers that the president "has said . . . that he ha[s] as good a right to order the Supreme Court as the Court ha[s] to require him to execute its decisions." And popular wisdom attributed to Jackson the famous phrase "Well, John Marshall has made his decision, now let him enforce it." As Worcester languished in jail, John Marshall wrote to Joseph Story, "I yield slowly and reluctantly to the conviction that our Constitution cannot last."[18]

Marshall obviously feared the power of example. If the states could ignore the Court's decision favoring the Indians, why could they not similarly ignore others they did not like? Why should states or their citizens follow federal law at all? Why pay federal taxes? Why enforce federal customs law? Indeed, only a few months after the *Worcester* decision, South Carolina published a "Nullification Ordinance." This ordinance made it unlawful to pay (within South Carolina) any duties imposed by certain federal statutes. It required all state courts to follow state, not federal, law in these matters; it forbade taking an appeal to the Supreme Court and punished with contempt of court anyone who tried to do so.[19]

Suddenly Jackson understood the political power of Georgia's example. Many in the South had long thought that states need not follow federal laws with which they disagreed. But Jackson as president now saw the threat to the Constitution posed by such a theory. If states could nullify federal law willy-nilly, then the Union might well become not the federation that the Constitution foresaw but a voluntary, and perhaps temporary, association of independent states.

Seeing the folly of his earlier position, Jackson reversed course. On December 10, 1832, he issued a statement: "I consider . . . the power to annul a law of the United States, assumed by one State, incompatible with the existence of the Union." Then he acted. Allying himself with Daniel Webster, a strong opponent of the nullification principle, he secured enactment of the Force Bill. This new federal statute explicitly gave the president the legal authority to use federal troops to enforce federal law. Its sponsors had South Carolina in mind. And South Carolina, understanding this, gave in to the threat of force. It repealed its Nullification Ordinance.[20]

Just as Georgia's example affected South Carolina, so the South Carolina example affected Worcester. The general public understood the need for similar treatment of similar instances as a universal tenet of the rule of law. The newspapers wrote that "no person but a Jackson or Van Buren man can see any essential difference between the case of Georgia and South Carolina." Wirt filed papers to take Worcester's case back to the Supreme Court for a further order, and Jackson, hinting at the use of troops, said he would enforce that order. Georgia saw what had happened in South Carolina and began to look for a settlement. The governor offered a pardon. The Board of Foreign Missions, Worcester's employer, urged Worcester to accept the pardon and withdraw the motion pending before the Supreme Court. Worcester did so, and in January 1833 he was released from prison. Thus, the Court's order ultimately was enforced. Or was it?[21]

Wasn't the original point of Wirt's judicial effort to secure legal protection for the Cherokee tribe? Didn't the Court's decision explicitly state that Georgia could not seize the Cherokees' land, that the land belonged to the tribe, not to Georgia? What happened to the Cherokees' effort to keep their land?

That effort failed. President Jackson sent federal troops to Georgia, not to enforce the Court's decision, but to evict the Indians. In early 1835, without the authorization of Chief Ross and the Cherokee government, federal representatives arranged for a handful of the tribe's members to meet in Washington to negotiate a treaty. There they reached an agreement providing for the removal of the tribe to the West. Jackson proclaimed victory.[22]

Horrified, the remaining seventeen thousand members of the tribe—including Chief Ross and the Cherokee government—immediately protested, but it was too late. Jackson submitted the "treaty" to the Senate, which ratified it by a one-vote margin. The secretary of war then informed Chief Ross that the "President had ceased to recognize" his government. And Jackson's federal troops ensured the Cherokees' removal. General John Ellis Wool, in command of the federal troops, wrote to his superiors in Washington that the Cherokees were "almost universally opposed to the Treaty." He reported that the great majority of the tribe were "so determined . . . in their opposition" that they had refused to "receive either rations or clothing from the United States lest they might compromise themselves in regard to the treaty," they "preferred living upon the roots and sap of trees rather than receive provisions" from the federal government, "thousands . . . had no other food for weeks," and many "said they will die before they leave the country."[23]

But Jackson ordered Wool to enforce the treaty. Jackson forbade the Cherokees to assemble to discuss the treaty, and he ordered Wool to show his letter to Chief Ross, after which he was to have no further written or oral communication with Ross on the subject.[24]

Wool obeyed. He described the subsequent scene as "heartrending," adding that, were it up to him, he "would remove every Indian tomorrow beyond the reach of the white men who, like vultures, are watching, ready to pounce upon their prey and strip them of everything they have." "Yes sir," he later said, "ninety-nine out of every hundred" of the Cherokees "will go penniless to the West." And that they did. Their route, called the Trail of Tears because so many died, led them to Oklahoma, where descendants of the survivors live to this day.[25]

This sad story has a few positive aspects. Despite the tragic outcome, it helped establish a principle—namely, that like cases need to be treated alike. The perceived unfairness of treating similar cases differently led to press articles demanding Worcester's release. The case also underlined the importance of the Supreme Court's power to strike down state laws that are inconsistent with the Constitution or treaties or federal statutes. South Carolina's ordinance made clear, even to President Jackson, the threat that "nullification" posed to national union.

Still, the predominant lesson the story tells us is not a happy one. A president used his power to undermine a Court decision and to drive the Cherokees from their native land. Moreover, Story's and Marshall's concerns about injury to the Court were well-founded. As far as the Court was concerned, the popular account of Jackson's attitude revealed the Court's weakness. The chief justice "has made his decision, now let him enforce it." Georgia was prepared to hang anyone who entered that state to enforce the Supreme Court decision. The president of the United States saw no problem with Georgia's attitude—at least not initially—and he ended up subverting the Court's basic holding. Would the president, the Congress, the states, and the public enforce, support, and follow a truly unpopular Court decision? The case suggests a strong likelihood that they would not.

IN ANY EVENT, during the next half century the Court, perhaps aware of its limitations, did not meaningfully test its power of judicial review. The next great constitutional confrontation after *Marbury* took place in 1857, when the Court decided the infamous *Dred Scott* case, to which we now turn.

Chapter Four

Dred Scott

IN THE *DRED SCOTT* decision, the Court held that a former slave *was not* a citizen entitled to sue in federal court, and it held that a slave could *not become* free simply because his owner took him into a free state or territory. In the process the Court also held, for the first time since *Marbury*, that a federal statute (in this case the Missouri Compromise) was unconstitutional. When the Court decided the case in 1857, the country was deeply divided over slavery and on the brink of civil war. Given the timing and political circumstances, one could wonder whether the country would have implemented the *Dred Scott* decision had war not broken out.[1]

We should be aware that the *Dred Scott* decision has long been considered one of the Court's worst. It may well have helped to bring about a war, which was the very political result it hoped to avoid. As an example of judicial review, it is the opposite of the kind of Constitution-protecting review that Hamilton hoped the Court would undertake. What went wrong? The decision was unworkable and unenforceable because the Court itself made a legal and practical mistake. In other words, in this case the Court, not the president, Congress, or the general public, deterred Americans from following the law.

Background

DRED SCOTT WAS born a slave on a Virginia plantation around 1800. His first owner, Peter Blow, took him to St. Louis, Missouri, where he sold him to an army doctor, John Emerson. Emerson took Scott with him from base to base, including Fort Armstrong in the free state of Illinois and Fort Snelling in the free territory of Wisconsin (now in the state of Minnesota). During his two-year stay at Fort Snelling, Scott married Harriet, a slave who also lived there. Emerson then returned to St. Louis with Scott, Harriet, and their newly born child, Eliza. After Emerson died, Scott and his family became the property of Emerson's wife and, eventually, of his wife's brother, John Sanford. Scott, or perhaps Harriet, was not satisfied with this arrangement, so the couple brought a lawsuit, first in state court, then in federal court. They argued that their lengthy stay in free territory had made Scott legally a free man.[2]

Roger Taney, chief justice of the United States, wrote the majority opinion in the *Dred Scott* case. Taney was born in Maryland in 1777 to a family of tobacco farmers. A longtime supporter of Andrew Jackson, he became attorney general in the Jackson administration and was appointed chief justice in 1836. He was an excellent lawyer, possessing what William Wirt (who had represented the Cherokees) called a "moonlight mind," a mind that gave "all the light of day without its glare." Taney had argued for a gradual end to slavery, an institution he viewed as "evil" and a "blot on our national character." He had represented abolitionists and had freed most of his own slaves. On the other hand, as attorney general, Taney had advised the secretary of state that the "African race . . . even when free . . . hold whatever rights they enjoy" at the "mercy" of the "white population."[3]

Benjamin Curtis wrote the main dissent in *Dred Scott.* Curtis was a native of Massachusetts whom President Millard Fillmore had appointed to the Supreme Court in 1851 partly because of his reputation as a "moderate" on the slavery issue. He served on the Court only six years, resigning after the *Dred Scott* decision, saying that he doubted his usefulness on the Court in its "present state" (and perhaps for financial reasons as well).[4]

In *Scott,* the Court was faced with an issue that the Constitution's framers had postponed and that was reaching an explosive state. Aware that the South would not join a Union that prohibited slavery, the framers in effect postponed the question of slavery's continued existence by writing into the Constitution a series of compromises. They included language that said Congress, prior to 1808, could not prohibit the "Migration or Importation" of slaves into the United States. They prohibited any amendment affecting that bar. And they apportioned legislators (in the lower house of Congress) among the states according to population as determined by "adding to the whole Number of free Persons . . . three fifths of all other Persons," that is, slaves. This method of counting (allowing the South additional representatives based on its slaves while understanding that the South would forbid its slaves to vote) meant that the South was overrepresented in the lower house of Congress and in the vote count for president. That overrepresentation initially gave the South sufficient political power to block abolitionist efforts.[5]

During the first half of the nineteenth century, however, population grew more rapidly in the newly acquired territories of the Northwest, rather than in the Southwest as the South had expected. That fact cost the South the political advantage it had been relying on to resist abolitionist legislation. Nonetheless, the North continued to fear that the South would use every political and legal device within reach to extend slavery into the new territories, thereby helping the South to maintain its political power once those territories became full states.[6]

In this atmosphere Congress had to decide how to treat new territories. In 1820, Congress had enacted the Missouri Compromise, forbidding slavery in territories north and west of Missouri. In 1845 it admitted Texas as a slave state, and in 1850 it admitted California as a free state. In 1854 it departed from the principles of the Missouri Compromise by permitting two territories north and west of Missouri—namely, Kansas and Nebraska—to choose for themselves whether to become slave states or free states.

In 1854, the year Dred Scott's appeal reached the Supreme Court, the legal status of slaves in the territories was of enormous political importance. The South feared that new states, if free, would soon produce a Congress that abolished slavery. It wanted the Supreme Court to hold that individuals had a constitutional right to own slaves, even in the territories. The North, of course, wanted the Supreme Court to hold that Congress could prevent the spread of the South's evil institution throughout the nation. The *Dred Scott* case would give the Court the opportunity to justify the legal hopes of one region or the other by clarifying the legal status of slaves brought by their owners into free territory.

The Legal Issues

Once back in St. Louis, Dred Scott initially brought his case against his then owner, Mrs. Emerson, in a Missouri state court. He pointed to earlier Missouri cases holding that a slave who resided for a time in free territory became a free man. The Missouri Supreme Court, however, rejected his claim, noting that "times are not now as they were when the former decisions on this subject were made." Before the Missouri court's decision was final, Scott brought the same suit (now against Sanford, his new owner and Mrs. Emerson's brother) in a lower federal court. That court, stating that it must accept Missouri's decision, rejected Scott's claim. Scott then appealed to the U.S. Supreme Court.[7]

The case attracted considerable attention. A prominent attorney, later a member of President Lincoln's cabinet, represented Scott. So did Benjamin Curtis's brother. Two prominent lawyers, both U.S. senators, represented Sanford. The case presented two issues: First, a jurisdictional question concerning the Court's authority to hear the case. The lawsuit was properly in federal court only if a "citizen" of one state was suing a "citizen" of another state. Sanford was a citizen of New York. Was Scott a citizen of a different state, namely, Missouri? Second, if Scott was a "citizen" and jurisdiction was proper, did the law make Scott a free man?[8]

The lawyers argued the case over the course of four days in February 1856. On May 12 the Court asked for reargument on the jurisdictional question. Court notes reveal that a majority had agreed to a compromise: Justice Samuel Nelson would write a short opinion rejecting Scott's claim that he was free simply on the narrow ground that the Court, as a matter of comity, would follow the state courts. When two justices said they would write a dissent, however, that compromise unraveled. Chief Justice Taney reassigned the opinion to himself. On March 6, 1857, Taney read his lengthy opinion from the bench. The next day Curtis read, and then released, his dissent. Taney then took the unusual step of rewriting his opinion, releasing his final version in May.[9]

The Decision

The Court initially considered the first issue: Does the Court have the power to decide a case of this kind? If not—that is, if it lacks "jurisdiction"—then in principle Dred Scott must lose even if he is right about his other legal contentions, for the Court lacks the authority to help him. The chief justice, writing for the Court, described the jurisdictional question as whether "a negro, whose ancestors were imported into this country, and sold as slaves," is "entitled to sue as a citizen in a court of the United States." The chief justice, and the majority, held that the answer to this question was no. Even if Dred Scott was a free man, he was not a "citizen."[10]

The Court's reasoning was highly legalistic: The Constitution allows the suit only if the case arises "between Citizens of different States." The word "citizens" was limited to "citizens of the several States when the Constitution was adopted." And that group, said Taney, could not possibly have included freed slaves because public opinion would not have allowed it. Writing in language that has since become infamous, Taney explained that public opinion at that time considered Africans "so far inferior" to the "white race" that they had "no rights which the white man was bound to respect." Even northern states where abolitionist sentiment was strong and slavery had been outlawed forbade slaves to serve in the state militia, limited their educational opportunities, and forbade interracial marriage. Moreover, many of the founders, themselves slaveholders, could not have intended the "equality" they preached to extend to slaves or former slaves. Furthermore, some contemporaneous federal statutes distinguished between "citizens" and "persons of color," showing that the latter were not included among the former. Indeed, some attorneys general of the United States had expressed that view.[11]

Finally, Taney wrote that the Constitution guarantees to "citizens of each State . . . all privileges and immunities of citizens in the several States." In 1789, no one could have thought that the South would have granted "privileges and immunities" to former slaves whom the North considered free. The Court, Taney concluded, must not "give to the words of the Constitution a more liberal construction in their favor than they were intended to bear when the instrument was framed and adopted. . . . [I]t must be construed now as it was understood" then.[12]

Curtis issued a powerful dissent. "[E]very free person born on the soil of a State, who is a citizen of that State by force of its Constitution or laws, is also a citizen of the United States," and consequently can sue a citizen of a different state in federal court. One reason Curtis thought this way was that at the time of the Constitution's ratification, five states—New Hampshire, Massachusetts, New York, New Jersey, and North Carolina—included freed slaves among their citizens. Granted, these states may have imposed some disabilities on those freed slaves, but their laws permitted freed slaves to vote. Indeed, the North Carolina Supreme Court had explicitly held that slaves who were freed in North Carolina became North Carolina citizens if they had been born in the state. How can one understand the Constitution, which did not then define "citizen," as excluding some of the very people who as citizens were allowed (in those states) to vote on the Constitution's ratification? Moreover, the very purpose of allowing federal courts to hear "diversity of state citizenship" cases was to extend federal jurisdiction to cases where local feelings or interests might cloud the issues and "disturb the course of justice." That purpose was the same whether a party to the case was of "white" or "African descent."[13]

Saying that he would not "enter into an examination of the existing opinions of that period respecting the African race," Curtis wrote that a "calm comparison" of the assertion in the Declaration of Independence that "all men are created equal" with the "individual opinions and acts" of its authors "would not leave these men under any reproach of inconsistency." This comparison would show that the authors wanted to make the "great natural rights" asserted in the Declaration of Independence effectual wherever possible.[14]

Curtis also mercilessly destroyed the majority's remaining arguments. Its statutory claim proved nothing, for, if the language of some old federal statutes suggested that freed slaves were not "citizens," the language of other old federal statutes suggested the precise opposite. Nor was its "privileges and immunities" argument convincing once one learned that that constitutional provision simply repeated an older guarantee in the Articles of Confederation that entitled "free inhabitants of each of these States . . . to all privileges and immunities of free citizens in the several States." This language did not suggest that a freed slave was not a citizen. To the contrary, the drafters of the articles explicitly rejected by a vote of eight states to two (with one state divided) a South Carolina amendment that would have inserted the word "white" between the words "free" and "inhabitants." This strongly suggested that the privileges and immunities clause protected *all* free citizens, not just white citizens.[15]

The Court, however, rejecting Curtis's views, held that it had no power to hear the case or decide the merits of Scott's claim (because Scott was not a citizen). Nonetheless, it went on to do just that. The Court majority held that Dred Scott's three-year sojourn in the free territory of Wisconsin and in the free state of Illinois did not emancipate him. The majority might have reached this conclusion by simply relying on the fact that Missouri state courts had reached it and that federal courts should follow state courts on matters of state law. But in the 1850s that was not always so; federal courts often second-guessed state courts on state law matters, particularly where the matter concerned judge-made common law, not statutory law.[16]

In respect to slavery, both the common law and foreign law were uniform and clear. As Curtis pointed out in his dissent, when a master took a slave into free territory and lived there indefinitely, participating in the territory's "civil or military affairs," the slave became free. This was certainly the case when the slave married and had children in a free territory. Indeed, important federal statutes—the Missouri Compromise, for example—made this clear, by insisting that the law of the Wisconsin Territory, the jurisdiction in which Fort Snelling was located, did not permit slavery. It therefore gave Dred Scott his freedom.[17]

The Court majority countered that the laws of Congress, such as the Missouri Compromise, did not apply because, in its view, Congress lacked the power to make those laws. The Court had to concede that the Constitution's territories clause says that Congress "shall have Power to dispose of and make all needful Rules and Regulations respecting the Territory or other Property belonging to the United States." But, the majority said, the language, history, and structure of the Constitution made clear that this clause applied only to those territories that existed as territories in 1789, namely, certain land belonging then to Virginia, North Carolina, and a few other states, which those states intended to cede to the federal government. Congress, the majority conceded, had an implied power to hold territory for the sole purpose of turning it into new states. But it could not interfere with the rights of citizens entering or living within that territory—any more than if they were citizens of states. And were they such citizens, the Constitution would forbid the federal government to interfere with their rights to own slaves. This (and here lies the heart of the majority's pro-slavery position) is because the Constitution forbids Congress to deprive a person of property without due process of law. The Constitution, wrote the majority, recognizes the "right of property of the master in a slave." And nothing gives Congress "a greater power over slave property . . . than property of any other description." The opposite is true: The fugitive-slave clause requires that slaves who escape into other states be returned to their owners. This clause, read together with the due process clause's prohibition on the deprivation of property without due process of law, the majority reasoned, meant that the Constitution insisted that the federal government "guard" and "protect" the "[slave] owner in his rights."[18]

Thus, the Court's conclusion: "The act of Congress which prohibited a citizen from holding and owning property of this kind . . . is not warranted by the Constitution and is therefore void; and . . . neither Dred Scott himself, nor any of his family, were made free by being carried into this territory; even if they had been carried there by the owner, with the intention of becoming a permanent resident."[19]

Curtis replied to the majority's argument as follows: First, the territories clause certainly gave Congress the authority to hold territory acquired from a foreign nation, to make all necessary rules for governing that territory, and to include among those rules a prohibition against slavery. Congress had acted on that assumption since the nation was founded, enacting ordinances and laws excluding slavery from various of the territories (for example, the Missouri Compromise). Curtis counted eight distinct instances, "beginning with the first Congress, and coming down to the year 1848," where Congress had explicitly excluded slavery from the territory of the United States. The acts by which Congress had regulated slavery in the territories "were severally signed by seven Presidents of the United States, beginning with General Washington, and coming regularly down as far as Mr. John Quincy Adams, thus including all who were in public life when the Constitution was adopted." And when one interprets the Constitution, Curtis wrote, a "practical construction, nearly contemporaneous with the adoption of the Constitution, and continued by repeated instances through a long series of years, may always influence, and in doubtful cases should determine, the judicial mind."[20]

Curtis replied to the Fifth Amendment due process argument by pointing out that a slave is not ordinary "property." Rather, slavery is a "right existing by [virtue of] positive law [for example, statutes]." It is "without foundation in the law of nature or the unwritten common law." Nor could "due process of law" mean that a slave remained a slave when his master moves from, say, slave state A to live permanently in free state B. What law would then govern the slave, the slave's wife, his house, his children, his grandchildren? State B has no laws governing slavery. Its judges could not manage a proliferating legal system under which each slave, coming into free state B, brought with him his own law, whether from A or from C or from whatever other slave state he happened to be from.[21]

More important, said Curtis, the phrase "due process of law" comes from the Magna Carta. When Congress passed the Northwest Ordinance in 1787, it did not think that law violated the Magna Carta. Moreover, numerous states, including Virginia, had passed laws prohibiting the importation of new slaves. Under these laws, any slaves imported in violation of the prohibition would be set free. And, Curtis wrote, "I am not aware that such laws, though they exist in many States, were ever supposed to be in conflict with the principle of Magna Charta incorporated into the State Constitutions." If those laws did not violate the Magna Carta, then Congress's prohibition of slavery in territories could hardly violate the due process clause of the federal Constitution.[22]

Despite the strength of Curtis's arguments, however, the majority still held: (1) Scott could not bring his case in federal court because freed slaves are not citizens of the United States; (2) many congressional anti-slavery-spreading statutes, including the Missouri Compromise, were unconstitutional; and (3) the Fifth Amendment's due process clause protected the ownership rights of slaveholders even when they took their slaves into free territories and free states to live for extended periods.

The Aftermath

The Court issued its decision in early March 1857, and the chief justice issued his written opinion later in the spring. The South and southern sympathizers reacted favorably. President Buchanan (perhaps forewarned) favorably referred to the opinion in his March inaugural address and again in his December State of the Union address. But the northern reaction was vehemently negative. Horace Greeley's *New York Tribune* described the holding as "wicked" and "atrocious." "If epithets and denunciation could sink a judicial body," another observer wrote, "the Supreme Court . . . would never be heard of again."[23]

A joint committee of the New York legislature reported that the decision had "destroyed the confidence of the people in the Court," predicted that it would be overruled, and described Taney's statement that people of African descent had no rights as "*inhuman, unchristian, atrocious,*—disgraceful to the judge who uttered it and to the tribunal which sanctioned it." The committee said the opinion paved the way for slavery's spread to free states. If "a master may take his slave into a Free State without dissolving the relation of master and slave," then "some future decision of the Pro-Slavery majority of the Supreme Court will authorize a slave-driver . . . to call the roll of his manacled gang at the foot of the monument on Bunker Hill, reared and consecrated to freedom."[24]

The case had increasing reverberation. The abolitionist Frederick Douglass offered a slightly different analysis. In a New York lecture he remarked that despite this "devilish decision" produced by "the slaveholding wing of the Supreme Court," the Court could not make "evil good" or "good evil." The decision, he concluded, "is a means of keeping the nation awake on the subject. . . . [M]y hopes were never brighter than now."[25]

Indeed, the decision did keep the nation awake. Northern supporters widely circulated the Curtis dissent in pamphlet form. Abraham Lincoln, then a Republican candidate for Senate, spoke often about the decision, describing it as an "astonisher in legal history" while arguing that Taney's "whites only" views had turned "our once glorious Declaration" of Independence into a "wreck" and "mangled ruin." In February 1860, Lincoln based his Cooper Union speech—a speech that helped make him a national political figure—on Curtis's dissent. Lincoln fed the North's fear of spreading slavery by asking, what "is necessary for the nationalization of slavery? It is simply the next *Dred Scott* decision. It is merely for the Supreme Court to decide that no State under the Constitution can exclude it, just as they have already decided that under the Constitution neither Congress nor the Territorial legislature can do it."[26]

Although historians debate the precise role of *Dred Scott* in bringing on the Civil War, the decision at least energized the anti-slavery North. It became the Republican Party's rallying cry and contributed to Lincoln's nomination and election as president. These circumstances together with others helped bring about that most fierce War Between the States. After the war, the nation added the Thirteenth, Fourteenth, and Fifteenth amendments to the Constitution, ending slavery while guaranteeing equal treatment, voting rights, and basic civil rights for the newly freed slaves.

On a more personal level: Benjamin Curtis resigned from the Court immediately after the *Dred Scott* decision. Chief Justice Taney remained on the bench until his death. Dred Scott and his family were bought by a son of his original owner, Peter Blow, who set them all free. Within little more than a year, however, Scott died of tuberculosis.[27]

Lessons

Modern critics describe the *Dred Scott* case as "infamous," "notorious," "an abomination," "odious," a "ghastly error," and "judicial review at its worst." Chief Justice Charles Evans Hughes said the decision was a "self-inflicted wound" that almost destroyed the Supreme Court. *The Oxford Companion to the Supreme Court of the United States* says that "American legal and constitutional scholars consider the *Dred Scott* decision to be the worst ever rendered by the Supreme Court." These judgments reflect the immorality of the decision. What can people today learn from it? By reading with care, we can draw certain lessons about the Court that remain relevant. I suggest five.[28]

The first lesson concerns judicial rhetoric. Today, as in 1857, the language a judge uses to set forth his or her reasoning matters. Taney's words about Americans of African descent having "no rights which the white man was bound to respect" are lurid and offensive, more so than can be found in other Supreme Court opinions, including other opinions that Taney wrote. An experienced Supreme Court justice would not write such a phrase without being aware of the fact that others will repeat it and emphasize its judicial origin in order to make the sentiment appear legitimate. Taney's effort to attribute his words to others, such as political officials or citizens, does not help. The public simply ignores the attempt to put moral distance between the sentiment and the author. Taney could not have thought otherwise, for the language was morally repugnant even then, as Curtis seemed to acknowledge when he refused to "enter into an examination of the existing opinions of that period respecting the African race," calling instead for a "calm comparison."[29]

The second lesson reinforces the optimistic judicial view that when a judge writes an opinion, even in a highly visible, politically controversial case with public feeling running high, the opinion's reasoning—not simply the author's conclusion—can make all the difference. A strong opinion is principled, reasoned, transparent, and informative. And a strong opinion should prove persuasive, make a lasting impression on the minds of those who read it, and (if a dissent) eventually influence the law to move in the direction it proposes.

Curtis's opinion was one of two dissents. Its language is not the most colorful, but its reasoning is by far the strongest. Indeed, it paints the Taney majority into a logical corner from which it has never emerged. For example, what is the answer to Curtis's claim that five states treated slaves as citizens (hence they were American citizens) at the time the Constitution was written? He supported the claim by pointing to a state supreme court decision (explicit on the point) and to the fact that five states allowed freed slaves to vote. Taney, in reply, referred only to racially discriminatory marriage and military service laws, but these laws are actually consistent with citizenship and hence do not significantly undercut Curtis's argument.

What is the answer to Curtis's jurisdictional argument? If Dred Scott was not a "citizen," then the Court lacked jurisdiction to hear the case. If it lacked jurisdiction, it had no business deciding the merits of the case, holding the Missouri Compromise unconstitutional, and depriving Congress of the power to maintain slavery-free territories in the process. In *Marbury* itself one could find a countervailing legal principle—the need to explain why the law did not permit the Court to avoid constitutional questions—and this principle helped to explain, if not excuse, Marshall's decision to address the merits. Here there is no such excuse. The Court reached out, without legal justification, to decide the constitutional question itself.

And what sound response can the majority make to Curtis's explanation of the scope of the Constitution's due process and territories clauses? That explanation was the only one that proved workable going forward, taking account of a nation that was continuously changing. How could judges of a single free state or territory, say Wisconsin, administer a legal system under which different slave state laws (for example, Alabama law, Georgia law, or Virginia law) would have to govern well into the future the relationships of different slave families brought permanently to live in that single free state?

Given the strength of Curtis's reasoning, it is not surprising that those opposed to slavery circulated his dissent in pamphlet form throughout the nation or that Lincoln's speeches, abolitionist lectures, and informed northern reaction reflected Curtis's analysis.

A third lesson concerns the relation between Court decisions and politics. The kindest view of the majority's opinion is that it had a political objective. Many in Congress had asked the Court to "umpire" the great political issue dividing the nation. Taney and his majority might have thought that by reaching out unnecessarily to decide a politically sensitive legal question—that is, by settling the constitutional status of slavery in the territories—the Court would promote a peaceful resolution of the slavery question (perhaps even through eventual abolition).

If that is what Taney believed, he was wrong. The Court's decision did not heal the nation. Rather, it reinforced the North's fears of southern dominance, solidified the case for abolition, and promoted the political standing of the anti-slavery Republican Party. The Court was more an instigator of the Civil War—or at least a contributing factor—than a mediating force. Moreover, as a purely legal matter the anti-slavery constitutional amendments resulting from the Civil War effectively reversed the *Dred Scott* decision.

There are, of course, strong institutional, jurisprudential, and ethical arguments against judges of a constitutional court holding their fingers up to the political winds. A court that acts "politically" plays with fire. For one thing, at a minimum, it undermines the confidence of that portion of the political public that favors the opposite result. More important, Hamilton's writings make clear that the very point of granting such a Court the power of judicial review was to offer constitutional security where doing so is politically unpopular. To such reasons *Dred Scott* adds another, purely practical consideration. Judges are not necessarily good politicians. Their view about what is politically expedient could well turn out to be completely wrong. Such, as history shows us, was the case in *Dred Scott.*

The fourth lesson concerns the Court and the Constitution. The Court's *Dred Scott* opinion can find its justification only by viewing the Constitution in a particular way—as requiring a consensus among slave states before the nation could embark on a course that would lead to abolition. Thus, Taney's decision essentially treats the Constitution as no more than a political compact among independent states, with its central focus on compromise about slavery in particular.

Yet the Constitution's language does not support such an interpretation. The protection it provided the slave trade expired in 1808. The constitutional guarantees of equal state representation in the Senate and the census-related supermajority status of slave states in the House of Representatives were written in terms that permitted the political destruction of the protection they offered the South. The preamble says that "We the People of the United States . . . ordain and establish this Constitution," language broad enough to cover Dred Scott.

One cannot easily reconcile Taney's vision with the expressed abolitionist hopes of, for example, Benjamin Franklin and many other framers. Nor, most important, can one reconcile this vision with the Constitution's most basic objective, the creation of a single nation. The Constitution does so by creating political institutions strong enough to permit the "people" to govern themselves, determining policies and resolving problems ranging in subject from defense to territorial expansion to commerce, while protecting basic personal liberties across (the framers hoped) the centuries. The concept of a political treaty among sovereign and independent states focusing primarily on slavery is not compatible with this more basic constitutional objective. (And, of course, if the *Dred Scott* majority doubted that fact in 1857, the post–Civil War amendments to the Constitution ending slavery, guaranteeing voting rights, defining citizenship, assuring individuals equal protection of the laws, and protecting basic individual liberty from state interference overturned the legal precedent they created.) Taney's vision was not of a Constitution that created a central government but of a treaty that linked states.

A fifth lesson concerns the harm the Court worked upon the Hamiltonian cause. The Court placed those who saw the need to follow the law in a dilemma that Lincoln himself expressed well in his first inaugural address:

> I do not forget the position . . . that constitutional questions are to be decided by the Supreme Court; nor do I deny that such decisions must be binding in any case, upon the parties to a suit, as to the object of that suit, while they are also entitled to very high respect and consideration in all parallel cases by all other departments of the government. And while it is obviously possible that such decision may be erroneous in any given case, still the evil effect following it, being limited to that particular case, with the chance that it may be over-ruled, and never become a precedent for other cases, can better be borne than could the evils of a different practice. At the same time, the candid citizen

> must confess that if the policy of the government upon vital questions, affecting the whole people, is to be irrevocably fixed by decisions of the Supreme Court, the instant they are made, in ordinary litigation between parties, in personal actions, the people will have ceased to be their own rulers, having to that extent practically resigned their government into the hands of that eminent tribunal.[30]

That is to say, the other departments of government, while bound to carry out the Court's decision in a *particular* case, owe that Court only "high respect and consideration" in respect to its interpretation of the Constitution. And sometimes the "people" rightly can themselves decide "vital" interpretive "questions" irrespective of the Court's views. If Abraham Lincoln has begun to sound like Andrew Jackson, is the *Dred Scott* Court itself not to blame?

Finally, *Dred Scott* tells us something about morality's relation to law. When discussing *Dred Scott* at a law school conference, I asked the audience to consider a hypothetical question. Suppose you are Benjamin Curtis. Imagine that Chief Justice Taney comes to your chambers and proposes a narrow ground for deciding the case. He asks if you will agree to a single-paragraph unsigned opinion for the entire Court, in which the Court upholds the lower court on the ground that the matter is one of Missouri law in respect to which the Missouri Supreme Court must have the last word. He will agree to this approach provided there is no dissent.[31]

Should you agree? If you do, the majority will say nothing about citizenship, nothing about the Missouri Compromise, nothing about slavery in the territories and the due process clause. As a result, the Court will create no significant new law; it will not diminish its own position in the eyes of much of the nation; it will not issue an opinion that increases the likelihood of civil war; and because no one knows who would win such a war (after all, the North almost lost), the prospects for an eventual abolition of slavery will be unaffected, perhaps increased.

Not a bad bargain, but the audience was uncertain. Then a small voice came from the back of the room. "Say no." And the audience broke into applause. That applause made clear the moral nature of the judge's legal obligation in that case.

A close examination of the *Dred Scott* opinion, the Court's "worst case," can teach us through negative example about the important relation between the way the Court fulfills its obligation to maintain a workable Constitution and the way the public carries out theirs. It also can help us understand the importance of solid reasoning, the dangers of reliance on rhetoric, the need for practical constitutional interpretation consistent with our nation's underlying values; and it teaches us the important role that morality and values play—or should play—at the intersection of law and politics.

Chapter Five

Little Rock

IN 1957, PRESIDENT Dwight Eisenhower had to answer difficult and historically important questions about how to enforce the Supreme Court ruling in *Brown v. Board of Education* requiring racial integration of the public schools. In the face of fierce public opposition, he had to decide whether (and how) to send troops to Little Rock, Arkansas, in order to enforce lower-court orders designed to provide racial minorities with the protection offered by the equal protection clause of the Constitution's Fourteenth Amendment. The Little Rock cases directly raise the enforcement question—Hotspur's question—that Hamilton had not answered. The Court succeeded in enforcing its decisions, as did the lower courts their orders, but only with key support from the president. This illustrates the often-necessary link between effective enforcement and executive cooperation. The Little Rock cases eventually helped to produce victory for the cause of racial integration, a victory that helped secure the rule of law in America.

BACKGROUND

BEFORE 1954 THE South administered a comprehensive set of rules that legally required racial segregation throughout southern society. These rules forced African-Americans to suffer inferior schooling, inadequate public facilities, and countless other harms and indignities.

In *Brown v. Board of Education of Topeka, Kansas* (and four other cities), the Supreme Court was asked to decide whether "segregation of children in public schools solely on the basis of race," even if the "physical facilities and other 'tangible' factors" were "equal," nonetheless would "deprive[ ] children of the minority group of equal educational opportunities." On May 17, 1954, *Brown* answered this question with the words "We believe that it does." In its most famous sentences, the unanimous Court said: "We conclude that in the field of public education the doctrine of 'separate but equal' has no place. Separate educational facilities are inherently unequal." The Court thus held that the South's legal system of segregation violated the Constitution's guarantee that "no State shall . . . deprive any person of . . . equal protection of the laws."[1]

The legal answer to the question was not difficult. The Court held that the Constitution's words meant what they said. State-imposed racial segregation was directly contrary to the purposes and demands of the Fourteenth Amendment. Racial segregation reflected an effort to wall off African-Americans as an inferior race and produced a segregated society that was unequal.

In deciding *Brown,* the Supreme Court fulfilled its most fundamental role in our democracy, that of guardian of our Constitution. The *Brown* decision was momentous. America at last would try to become the single nation that its Constitution intended. *Brown* led to a large number of subsequent cases and court decisions that sought to implement the constitutional principle that *Brown* reaffirmed.

From the moment it was decided, *Brown* was more than just a legal decision. It validated the moral principle of racial equality that was pressing for recognition in other arenas of American life. It gave new legal legitimacy to the political efforts of the civil rights movement, and thus helped to energize the movement. *Brown* made it possible for Dr. Martin Luther King, Jr., to say, in one of his most memorable phrases as a civil rights leader, "If we are wrong, the Constitution of the United States is wrong." *Brown* became a symbol for the nation—of a new era in race relations in the United States, of what the Supreme Court could contribute to American life, of how law could advance justice. Today, long after it was decided, *Brown* remains one of the most important Supreme Court decisions in our country's history, and one that demonstrates how, at crucial moments, the Supreme Court can summon the country to adhere to its fundamental principles.[2]

Brown did not come out of nowhere. Its groundwork was laid not only by the suffering endured by black people during generations of slavery, inequality, and subordination but also by the efforts of civil rights lawyers to persuade the Supreme Court over many years that its 1896 decision in *Plessy v. Ferguson* (permitting "separate but equal" facilities) was wrong. These lawyers undertook a step-by-step litigation campaign to advance the evolution of constitutional law. The incremental steps taken by the Supreme Court itself, along with measures such as President Truman's desegregation of the armed forces in 1948, helped prepare the country for the ruling in *Brown.* Still, in *Brown* the Supreme Court knew that it was doing something highly significant, and despite its acceptance by much of the American public the Court knew that the decision would meet with resistance in many places.[3]

The Court, understanding the enforcement difficulties, said it would consider "appropriate relief" in a later opinion, and issued a second opinion, *Brown II,* a year later, on May 31, 1955.[4] The National Association for the Advancement of Colored People (NAACP), whose lawyers (including Thurgood Marshall) represented *Brown*'s plaintiffs, had asked the Court to specify that lower courts throughout the South must immediately hold segregation unconstitutional, to require the courts to issue periodic progress reports, and to insist on integration of all public schools no later than September 1956. The attorney general, Herbert Brownell, Jr., one of President Eisenhower's closest associates, echoed the executive branch viewpoint that an integrated education was "a fundamental human right, supported by considerations of morality as well as law." Brownell asked the Court to require school districts to submit desegregation plans to the district courts, tell those courts to supervise the implementation of those plans closely, have the courts submit periodic reports to the Supreme Court itself, and require integration after a one-year transition period (though possibly with reasonable extensions). Brownell's brief concluded that "there can be no justification anywhere for failure to make an immediate and substantial start toward desegregation, in a good-faith effort to end segregation as soon as feasible."[5]

The Court accepted these recommendations, but only in part. It delegated primary enforcement powers to local federal district courts and said that local school authorities must "make a prompt and reasonable start toward full compliance." But it added that "the courts may find that additional time is necessary," because of issues of "administration" related to "physical condition of school plant, the school transportation system, personnel, revision of school district and attendance areas," and "revision of local laws and regulations." It told the lower federal courts that they should consider "whether the action of school authorities constitutes good faith implementation of the governing constitutional principles, [b]ecause of their proximity to local conditions and the possible need for further hearings." The Court summarized its desegregation instructions to the lower courts in the words "with all deliberate speed."[6]

But even with that approach, the Court faced outright opposition to carrying out its order at all. According to NAACP estimates, *no* public schools in the eight southern states were actually desegregated in 1955. At the same time, a large majority of the South's congressional representatives signed the Southern Manifesto declaring their belief that *Brown* was wrongly decided, that it was an "abuse of judicial power," and that it provided an example of the "Federal judiciary undertaking to legislate." The manifesto called for "all lawful" resistance against *Brown* and the Supreme Court.[7]

More ominously, the White Citizens' Council began to organize chapters throughout the South. They claimed that the *Brown* decision itself was unconstitutional. They adopted a form of the "nullification" argument—a constitutional argument used by the South before the Civil War: The state could lawfully ignore *Brown* by *interposing* its own legal authority to prevent integration. In any event, the councils would "never" permit integration. They argued for popular resistance, predicting that there would not be "enough jails to punish all resisters."[8]

Throughout the South these and other integration opponents took punitive actions against those attempting integration. They threatened integration's supporters with loss of jobs or credit. Southern voting registrars increased their efforts to keep black citizens from the polls. The worst forms of racial violence increased. In early 1955, in Mississippi, after several years of relative racial peace, three lynchings took place. These included the lynching of Emmett Till, a fourteen-year-old African-American boy from Chicago who, reportedly, had spoken too informally to a white woman. An all-white jury acquitted those charged with his murder just as all-white juries had recently acquitted thirteen out of fourteen defendants in cases involving serious civil rights violations.[9]

Congress did not help. The Senate refused to enact key provisions of President Eisenhower's Civil Rights Bill, including permission for the attorney general to sue to prevent interference with the constitutional rights of any American. The Senate insisted on jury trials, meaning likely acquittals given local prejudice and exclusion of black citizens from juries. And Congress rejected legislation that would give federal financial aid to local school systems to prevent courts from using that law to advance integration, say by forbidding school districts that received aid from maintaining segregated schools. At the same time, the House passed a bill that stripped civil rights jurisdiction from the federal courts, failing to obtain full consideration in the Senate by only one vote.[10]

Yet there were favorable signs. The District of Columbia, a defendant in the *Brown* case, began to integrate its schools. The other four cities that were defendants in *Brown* prepared to comply. In addition, school officials in a handful of other cities—such as Houston, Texas; Nashville, Tennessee; Greensboro, North Carolina; Charlotte, North Carolina; and Arlington, Virginia—issued statements saying that they too would seek to comply, regardless of how they felt about the merits of *Brown.* In Alabama that same year, 1955, Rosa Parks refused to sit in the back of a public bus. The Montgomery bus boycott had begun. In Little Rock, the school board, pledging to carry out the law, advanced a plan to begin to integrate the public schools.[11]

The President's Role

The events that unfolded in Little Rock in 1957 and 1958 highlight differences between the president's role and that of the Court. In 1954, Little Rock was a segregated city with a segregated school system. Yet the city had a reputation for racial moderation, and in 1952 the school board had considered the possibility of racial integration. In late May 1954, just after *Brown,* the board met, declared that it disagreed with *Brown,* and refused to integrate immediately. But it also recognized its own "responsibility to comply with Federal Constitutional Requirements," and promised to comply after the Supreme Court specified what method to follow. Arkansas filed a brief in *Brown II,* informing the Court that its own remedial policy recognized the Supreme Court's decision and would implement it properly.[12]

In May 1955, just before the Supreme Court issued *Brown II,* the Little Rock School Board announced an integration plan. Its "Phase Program" would begin two years later in September 1957. It would admit a handful of screened black students to Central High School, with a junior high school phase beginning in 1960 and an elementary school phase starting in 1963. A transfer option would assure all white students that they need not attend any high school that was predominantly black.[13]

The NAACP thought the Little Rock Phase Program inadequate and brought a lawsuit, but the federal district court upheld the plan. And in April 1957, the Eighth Circuit rejected the NAACP appeal. However, the NAACP lawsuit was not brought entirely in vain: Even though the district court did not order a speedier integration of Little Rock's schools, it did retain jurisdiction over the case to ensure the school board would follow the integration plan that the board had proposed. Accordingly, during the summer of 1957 the school board picked nine black students for transfer to Central High the coming September. These were the "Little Rock Nine," all of whom had excellent academic records, were intellectually ambitious, and lived near Central High.[14]

During that same summer, however, opposing political forces began to gather. Arkansas voters had approved an amendment to the state constitution requiring the state to oppose "in every constitutional manner the un-constitutional decisions of . . . the United States Supreme Court." The legislature enacted a statute saying that no child need attend a racially mixed school (implicitly threatening to close the public schools). Members of Citizens' Council chapters attended school board meetings where they repeated their claims that the law did not require integration, that the governor could "interpose" the state between the Court and *Brown*'s implementation, and that, no matter what, they would "shed blood if necessary" to stop integration. They gathered support by pointing out that only Central High would be integrated and not Hall High, a school in a higher-income neighborhood.[15]

The Citizens' Council also contacted Arkansas's governor, Orval Faubus, an economic liberal elected as a racially moderate alternative to the segregationists' candidate, Jim Johnson. The council nonetheless tried to convince him to resist integration. They argued that segregation was politically popular, that he was immune from federal court orders, that the board's alternative would bring violence to Little Rock, and that he must stop integration in order to "preserve tranquility." Under this kind of pressure, Faubus began to change his views.[16]

Central High was to open on Tuesday, September 3, 1957, with the nine black students in attendance. As the day approached, political pressure to keep the school segregated increased. In mid-August, Georgia's governor spoke in Arkansas and poured fuel on the flames. Georgia's schools had not yet been forced to integrate. Why, he asked, did Arkansas families have to accept integration when Georgia's families did not? That same night someone threw a stone through the window of the home of the local NAACP president, Daisy Bates. "Stone this time," a note read, "dynamite next."[17]

Governor Faubus sought a state court order to stop Central High's integration. On August 29 that court issued an order complying with the governor's request. The school board immediately asked the federal court to set aside the state court order. The federal court did so the next day, reasoning that the state court injunction would "paralyze the decree of this court entered under Federal law, which is supreme under the provisions of Article 6 of the Constitution of the United States."[18]

On the evening of Monday, September 2, the day before school would begin, Governor Faubus made a televised address to the state. He said he had heard armed caravans were approaching Little Rock, and moreover he, like much of the public, doubted the lawfulness of "forcing integration" on "the people" against their will. For these reasons, at least for "the time being," the schools "must be operated on the same basis as they have before." He announced that he had sent National Guard units to Central High. The audience understood that the guard would prevent integration.[19]

That same night the school board held an emergency meeting. The board asked the black students not to go to Central High until the issue was legally resolved. On Tuesday, September 3, the nine students stayed home, and Central High opened with an all-white student body. Yet that same day the school board returned to federal court to ask for guidance. The judge, finding no evidence of any potential disorder, said that integration should proceed "forthwith."[20]

The board again told the students not to try to attend the school. On Wednesday morning several of the students nevertheless coordinated an attempt to enter Central High, but were turned away by the National Guard. No one, however, could coordinate the entry effort with Elizabeth Eckford, who had no phone, so she arrived at Central High alone.[21]

A large hostile crowd had gathered at the school. Some in the crowd seemingly mistook a black photographer for a student and beat him severely. When Elizabeth Eckford arrived, the National Guard stopped her from entering the school. As she was leaving, a journalist photographed her near a white woman whose face was distorted with rage. The picture quickly became famous around the world.[22]

On Thursday the federal court asked the FBI and the Department of Justice to investigate whether the governor had told the National Guard to prevent enforcement of the court's integration order. The court scheduled a hearing for September 20. The governor agreed to appear. As the world watched, integration at Central High was on hold.[23]

Then, at the request of Brooks Hays, Little Rock's respected member of Congress, President Eisenhower and Governor Faubus agreed to a meeting. On Saturday morning, September 14, Faubus went to Eisenhower's "summer White House" in Newport, Rhode Island, where they first met privately. Eisenhower, Faubus recounted, dressed him down, telling him "like a general tells a lieutenant" that no one would benefit from "a trial of strength between the President and a Governor," and instructing him to have the National Guard protect the black students, not bar their entry into the school.[24]

Although Governor Faubus gave the president the impression that he would permit integration, he did not take that position in front of the press, acting noncommittal instead. Faubus waited for Friday's federal court hearing, where he reported to the judge that he had acted to prevent violence. But when the judge ordered him to stop barring students from entering the school, the governor, along with his lawyers, walked out of the courtroom. Later that day the governor announced that he would withdraw the guard from the school.[25]

On Monday morning, September 23, the Little Rock Nine arrived at Central High. The governor's hostility and the attendant publicity, however, had done their work, and a mob of fifteen hundred waited outside. Some broke through police barricades. Eight of the nine black students managed to slip past the mob and enter the school through a side door. But the chaos was such that by noon police and school officials agreed that the students should go home. The Little Rock mayor blamed the governor, suspecting that his aides and his friends had been present in the crowd urging on the mob. The mayor then sent a telegram to President Eisenhower appealing for help.[26]

Sending the Troops

At this point, Eisenhower, like Andrew Jackson at the time of the Cherokees, had to consider whether to send federal troops into a state to enforce a federal court order. Eisenhower debated the merits of the decision. What would happen to integration plans if the troops met physical resistance and ended up killing, say, women supporting segregation? Suppose other southern cities copied Little Rock? Would sending troops require some form of military occupation, as in the days of Reconstruction?

Moreover, what would happen to the public schools? Jimmy Byrnes, the former governor of South Carolina, a trusted friend of presidents Roosevelt and Truman, and a former Supreme Court justice, had earlier warned Eisenhower that *Brown* would lead the South to abolish those schools. Would precipitating federal action end up depriving both blacks and poor whites of any public education at all?[27]

Furthermore, Eisenhower thought that public education was a local matter for which the states must remain primarily responsible. He had to consider whether the presence of federal troops would play into the hands of segregationists gathered under the popular banner of "state sovereignty" and "no federal interference." An aide wrote privately that the president "is loath to use troops—thinks movement might spread—violence would come."[28]

Yet Eisenhower found the countervailing considerations more compelling. First, the federal court's orders, including an order prohibiting state interference with a local school board's integration plan, made clear that the key issue was whether federal law or state law was supreme. The nation had fought a civil war over the question. By the 1950s the need to maintain federal supremacy was well accepted in both North and South, even among those who hesitated to embrace racial integration.[29]

Second, recent history suggested that without enforcement the court's order would become a dead letter. Governor Allan Shivers of Texas had recently faced a similar order, and his refusal to help with enforcement resulted in no integration.[30]

Finally, there is much indicating that Eisenhower favored racial integration on principle, although historians debate the strength of his commitment. Eisenhower had grown up in a segregated society, but he had witnessed the bravery of World War II's black battalions in action at the Battle of the Bulge. (Indeed, some said, perhaps with only slight overstatement, that the black 332nd Fighter Group had never lost a bomber.) Eisenhower also had begun to understand the injustice of segregation and the need to bring it to a speedy end. In addition, he liked to lead by example. He had already desegregated military bases throughout the South, he had desegregated much federal contracting, and he had desegregated both schools and public accommodations in the District of Columbia.[31]

Herbert Brownell, Eisenhower's friend, ally, counselor, and attorney general, urged the president to take action. On Monday, September 23, Eisenhower made his decision. Unlike President Jackson 120 years earlier, he would use federal troops to support federal law.[32]

In a public statement issued that evening, Eisenhower said, "The Federal law and orders of a United States District Court implementing that law cannot be flouted with impunity by an individual or any mob of extremists." He pledged to use "whatever force may be necessary to prevent any obstruction of the law and to carry out the orders of the Federal Court." He then issued an order: As "President of the United States, under and by virtue of the authority vested in me by the Constitution," I "do command all persons engaged in such obstruction of justice to cease and desist therefrom, and to disperse forthwith."[33]

In 1957, Americans remembered the 101st Airborne Division as the heroes of World War II. They had fought in the Battle of the Bulge and had parachuted into Normandy, many dying when the winds left them dangling from church steeples. Eisenhower told his army chief of staff, General Maxwell Taylor, to send this famous division to Little Rock.[34]

On Tuesday afternoon, September 24, fifty-two aircraft carrying about one thousand troops left Fort Campbell, Kentucky. That evening Eisenhower spoke to the nation about the importance of the orders of the Little Rock federal court being "executed without unlawful interference." By then, the soldiers had deployed around Central High School. That evening Melba Pattillo, one of the Little Rock Nine, wrote in her diary, "I don't know how to go to school with soldiers. . . . Please show me. P.S. Please help the soldiers to keep the mobs away from me."[35]

The next morning a crowd again gathered outside the school, some taunting the soldiers. The soldiers lowered their bayonets, but they injured only a small number. One man was pricked by a bayonet, another hit on the head with a rifle butt. Army jeeps picked up the nine black students. Another black student, Minnijean Brown, said, "For the first time in my life, I feel like an American citizen." At 9:25 a.m., the jeeps delivered the black students to Central High. As reporters and television crews broadcast pictures around the world, soldiers accompanied the students up the steps and into the school. Despite a false bomb scare around noon, the students successfully completed their first day.[36]

The next morning the crowd was gone. The students continued to attend Central High without serious incident. A poll showed that 68.4 percent of Americans approved the president's decision to send the troops (the numbers reflected 77.5 percent who approved in the North and 62.6 percent who disapproved in the South).[37]

Yet the battle was far from over. Governor Faubus announced, "We are now an occupied territory." Senator James Eastland of Mississippi stated at a White Citizens' Council meeting that Eisenhower had "lit the fires of hate between the races." "The use of an army will not win," he added, "because the soldiers cannot stay in Little Rock all the time." Nor can Eisenhower occupy every southern school. After about two months in Arkansas the troops withdrew. The nine black students remained at Central High, finding the atmosphere difficult (many white classmates were silently hostile), though a few white students and many teachers offered comfort and support.[38]

The Supreme Court

Litigation again became the center of attention. Governor Faubus and his allies urged the school board to suspend its integration effort. And in February 1958 the school board returned to federal court.[39]

The board told the court that it was difficult to operate a school system given the hostility from the governor, the state legislators, and the community. They pointed to incidents of segregationist intimidation. Furthermore, the state legislature had recently enacted laws that substituted all-white private academies (operating with state support) for integrated public schools. The board asked the court to suspend integration for thirty months, after which time it expected the courts to have determined whether the private academy scheme was lawful.[40]

On June 21, 1958, the district court granted the board's request for a thirty-month delay, but on August 18 the Eighth Circuit reversed the district court. It then ordered a thirty-day stay, temporarily leaving in effect the district court's order to delay integration. To prevent Little Rock's schools from abandoning integration and instead reopening the school year on a segregated basis, the Supreme Court agreed to hear the case immediately.[41]

The Court held a special oral argument session on August 28 and then again on September 11 in the case of *Cooper v. Aaron.* (William Cooper was a member of the school board, and John Aaron was the parent of a black student.) The NAACP asked the Court to put the

Eighth Circuit's order into effect immediately, that is, to order the lower courts to proceed with integration. The school board registered strong opposition because of the state's efforts to interfere, the "chaotic" educational conditions at Central High, the possibility of the new private academy system, and the need for a thirty-month delay. The executive branch supported the NAACP. With the troops clearly in mind, the solicitor general told the Court that the moment you "bow to force and violence," you "give up law and order." The "country cannot exist without a recognition that the Supreme Court of the United States, when it speaks on a legal matter, is the law." Furthermore, Americans were entitled to a definitive statement from the Court on whether force and violence and opposition to the Court's decision were reasons to delay integration.[42]

Two weeks later the Court issued a brief statement unequivocally denying the school board's request for a thirty-month delay and requiring integration to proceed as originally planned. The Court's unanimous opinion followed on September 29.[43]

In its opinion the Court decided and clarified four important matters. The first concerned the constitutional duty of obedience to the Court's own decisions. The Court highlighted Governor Faubus's claim that "there is no duty on state officials to obey federal court orders resting on this Court's considered interpretation of the United States Constitution." The Court replied with five sentences:

> *Sentence One:* "Article VI of the Constitution makes the Constitution the 'supreme Law of the Land.' "
>
> *Sentence Two:* "In 1803, Chief Justice Marshall, speaking for a unanimous Court, referring to the Constitution as 'the fundamental and paramount law of the nation,' declared in the notable case of *Marbury v. Madison*, . . . that 'It is emphatically the province and duty of the judicial department to say what the law is.' "
>
> *Sentence Three:* "This decision declared the basic principle that the federal judiciary is supreme in the exposition of the law

> of the Constitution, and that principle has ever since been respected by this Court and the Country as a permanent and indispensable feature of our constitutional system."
>
> *Sentence Four:* "It follows that the interpretation of the Fourteenth Amendment enunciated by this Court in the Brown case is the supreme law of the land, and Art. VI of the Constitution makes it of binding effect on the States 'any Thing in the Constitution or Laws of any State to the Contrary notwithstanding.' "
>
> *Sentence Five:* "Every state legislator and executive and judicial officer is solemnly committed by oath taken pursuant to Art. VI, ¶ 3, 'to support this Constitution.' "[44]

Sentences One and Two are unexceptionable. Sentence Three, when closely examined, is particularly interesting, and Sentences Four and Five flow directly from it. Sentence Three does not quote *Marbury*'s actual language; rather, it summarizes *Marbury*'s holding. But in reality *Marbury* did not explicitly say (in the words of Sentence Three) that "the federal judiciary [compared to other branches of government] is supreme in the exposition of the law of the Constitution." Rather, *Marbury* said more ambiguously that "courts, *as well as other departments,* are bound by" the Constitution. Nor, as we have seen, had the cases after *Marbury* clearly demonstrated that either the Court or the country viewed judicial supremacy as "a permanent and indispensable feature of our constitutional system." Thus, the Court in *Cooper* actually decided that the Constitution obligated other governmental institutions to follow the Court's interpretations, not just in the particular case announcing those interpretations, but in similar cases as well—a matter that both Hamilton and Marshall had left open.[45]

Sentence Three reveals that the Court had reached a crossroads. To have used more ambiguous language would have been to hedge or to vacillate, thereby handing a powerful legal and public relations weapon to those who, like Governor Faubus, were trying to convince the South that it need not follow *Brown.* If the Court was to make clear its power to issue highly unpopular constitutional decisions, it had to assume that other officials and the public at large would follow its key interpretations, and not just in the single case before the Court but in similar cases as well. Hamiltonian judicial review demanded Sentence Three.

The second matter concerned the South's claim that the Court's *Brown* decision was legally incorrect. To counter this, the Court emphasized that *Brown* was unanimous and then "unanimously reaffirmed" the decision. It made clear that the three new justices who had joined the Court since *Brown* agreed with the original authors. Furthermore, in a highly unusual step, all nine justices personally signed the opinion (rather than joining an opinion written by one of their number), thereby suggesting that all nine agreed with all of it and stood together in issuing it.[46]

The third matter concerned the board's reasons for requesting postponement, which were the practical obstacles the board faced: the "state government opposed the desegregation of Little Rock schools by enacting laws, calling out troops, making statements vilifying federal law and federal courts, and failing to utilize state law enforcement agencies and judicial processes to maintain public peace." Thus, as the district court's factual findings had revealed, Arkansas had essentially brought the difficulties on itself. The Court refused to accept this as a basis for resisting the desegregation order. As the Court in *Brown II* had held, the Fourteenth Amendment's "equal protection" requirements "cannot be allowed to yield simply because of disagreement with them."[47]

The fourth matter involved the question of remedies, and the Court was divided about the proper approach. Some, such as Justice Hugo Black, believed the South would delay desegregation until the Court set firm, definite, and speedy timetables. Others, such as Justice Felix Frankfurter, thought the Court should continue to follow *Brown II*'s "all deliberate speed" approach, leaving remedial matters primarily up to the district courts, which could shape, or approve, orders reflecting local conditions.[48]

The Court patched together a compromise. On the one hand, it instructed the school boards to "make a prompt and reasonable start toward full compliance." It further specified that "only a prompt start, diligently and earnestly pursued, to eliminate racial segregation from the public schools could constitute good faith compliance." It also addressed the legality of state-supported private segregated academies, remarking and then reiterating that the "Fourteenth Amendment forbids States to use their governmental powers to bar children on racial grounds from attending schools where there is state participation through any arrangement, management, funds or property." On the other hand, the Court repeated *Brown II*'s key language: "all deliberate speed." And it added that courts must consider local conditions, physical plant, transportation, and the other matters that *Brown II* had permitted or required lower courts to take into account. Justice Frankfurter later filed a separate concurring opinion in which he too emphasized both the legal need to follow *Brown* and the practical need to take account of local problems and difficulties.[49]

In its concluding paragraph the unanimous opinion invoked the four words carved above the Supreme Court portico: "Equal Justice Under Law." Those words, it said, set forth an "ideal" to which the Constitution is "dedicated" and which the Fourteenth Amendment "embodie[s]." The amendment, as *Brown* made clear, protects a student's "fundamental and pervasive" right not to be racially segregated. *Brown*'s basic principles, "*and the obedience of the States to them*, . . . are indispensable for the protection of the freedoms" that the Constitution guarantees. *Brown*'s principles, *if obeyed,* make equal justice under law "a living truth."[50]

The last phrase eloquently recognizes the ultimate challenge of the Supreme Court's role in American life. The Court aspires—it must aspire—not only to declare the "truth" about the Constitution's meaning but also to make law "a *living* truth," obeyed by the country and animating its social practices. But its ability to do so is not guaranteed.

Despite the Court's opinion, it seemed that the State of Arkansas and the Little Rock School Board would continue to look for ways to oppose the Court's insistence upon school integration. On September 27, 1958, two days before the Supreme Court released its full opinion, but almost two weeks after it had announced its ruling, Little Rock's citizens voted, by a margin of 19,470 to 7,561, to close Little Rock's public high schools. On September 29, the very day the Supreme Court released its opinion, Governor Faubus closed the schools. And during the next nine months Little Rock's high school students were without public education.[51]

Nonetheless, the Court's opinions, taken together with the determination that the executive branch showed in sending troops, gradually took effect. Matters slowly improved. Federal courts began to hold unlawful many of the state's alternative educational systems, including the leasing of public school buildings to private state-funded academies. With business support, Little Rock elected three moderate members to its school board—thus achieving numerical equality with segregationist members. A local poll of Chamber of Commerce members showed support for reopening the schools. The chamber's board of directors issued a resolution stating that the "decision of the Supreme Court of the United States, however much we dislike it, is the declared law and is binding upon us. . . . [B]ecause the Supreme Court is the Court of last resort in this country, what it has said must stand until there is a correcting constitutional amendment or until the Court corrects its own error." Public opinion was beginning to shift.[52]

Although the board's segregationists continued to press their cause, they were largely unsuccessful. When they sought to deny contract renewal to forty teachers who had tried to help the black students, the moderate members walked out. In the recall election the moderates won a close but clear victory. The newly constituted board then voted to reopen the schools. In 1959, one year after the Court decided *Cooper v. Aaron,* integrated schools returned to Little Rock.[53]

The turmoil and the school closings imposed a high personal cost on many students. Students of both races suffered, some suffering permanent harm. The Little Rock Nine displayed much bravery and dignity in dealing with the hatred around them. Some students (including members of the Little Rock Nine) attended schools in other districts or out of state. Others took correspondence courses from the University of Arkansas. Some followed their teachers' presentations on local television stations. But for many these alternatives did not work. Central High's all-state football team fell apart, and many members never received high school diplomas. And what was true of the team was true of the entire class. Many of Central High's "Lost Class of '59" were unable to qualify for admission to college. Many found their lives changed permanently and for the worse.[54]

In addition to losing their education, their high school activities, perhaps their chance of college, many later came to regret their behavior at the time. They did not know how to explain their refusal to help their new black classmates. Some in later life worked to improve race relations. And in 1999, over forty years after troops appeared at Central High, Hazel Bryan, the woman photographed with her face contorted in rage, appeared publicly with one of the Nine, Elizabeth Eckford, to explain how they had achieved reconciliation.[55]

Others suffered setbacks. Brooks Hays, the congressman who arranged for Governor Faubus to meet with President Eisenhower, became known as a "moderate." He lost the next election, while Governor Faubus remained in office until 1967.[56]

What happened in Little Rock did not produce speedy integration throughout the South. The civil rights movement was just beginning. Judges had not yet tried school busing as a remedy. But the Little Rock case did help prevent further violent community confrontations. It helped begin a process of integration that, in practice, is not complete. But today Central High is integrated. Fifty-two percent of its twenty-five hundred students are black; 42 percent are white. It has become one of the best public high schools in America, with 867 students taking at least one Advanced Placement course.[57]

For present purposes, the Little Rock story represents a hard-earned victory for the rule of law. The Court's determination to enforce *Brown* was not solely responsible. The arrival of 101st Airborne paratroopers made a critical difference, as did the juxtaposition of two photographs, the first showing a white woman's enraged face, the second showing federal troops surrounding and protecting the black children. So did the decision of a district judge ordering a governor to stop his interference, a decision that the president later enforced by sending troops. But the Court's assertion of judicial supremacy—similar to that made earlier by the president, repeated by the Little Rock Chamber of Commerce, and used by others who sought integration (and an end to racial violence) in the South—was a critical ingredient.

Today, only a mile away from Central High, one can find the grave of the wife of the Cherokee chief Ross. That grave marks the spot where she died on the Trail of Tears on her way to Oklahoma—after the government evicted her and her fellow Cherokees from their Georgian lands. The grave and the school together tell a story about acceptance of the rule of law in America. Although the distance between the grave and the school is small, the nation had come a long way in the time between the two decisions that they symbolize. It was moving in the right direction.

Chapter Six

A Present-Day Example

IN RECENT DECADES any number of Court decisions have closely divided the justices and proved highly unpopular with large numbers of Americans. Consider, for example, the decisions protecting a woman's decision to have an abortion in the early months of pregnancy. Or consider the decisions forbidding prayer in public schools. In such cases the constitutional questions are difficult; not surprisingly, the judges, who patrol the Constitution's boundaries, have reached different conclusions. As the issues divide judges, they divide communities. Supporters and opponents have marshaled strong arguments as to why the other side is wrong. Some feel strongly that the life of an embryo must be protected or that young students who attend public schools should be exposed to religion. Others feel strongly to the contrary. Nonetheless, despite the disagreement and related emotions, despite protests, Americans by and large have adhered to the Court's decisions. And most opponents, even, for example, opponents of the abortion decisions, look for lawful methods to change unwanted decisions (for example, through constitutional amendment, the president's appointment power, and consequent erosion of, or change in, current law made by the Court itself).[1]

Focus for a moment on *Bush v. Gore.* The 2000 presidential election was close. The Democratic Party candidate, Albert Gore, won the popular vote nationwide. But the Republican Party candidate, George Bush, after litigation that ultimately reached the Supreme Court, secured Florida's disputed electoral votes, won a majority of the votes in the Electoral College, and became president of the United States.[2]

That result turned on technical but important constitutional matters. The Constitution provides that the "Person having the greatest Number" of (currently 538) electoral votes for president, "shall be the President, if such Number be a Majority of . . . Electors appointed." The Constitution entitles each state to a number of electors equal to the "Number of Senators and Representatives" from that state. Furthermore, it requires each state to select its electors "in such Manner as the Legislature thereof may direct." Florida's legislature, like that in almost every state, directed that the presidential candidate who receives the highest popular vote would receive all the state's electoral votes.[3]

Initially, Bush led Gore in Florida by fewer than two thousand votes out of the roughly six million votes cast. After an automatic recount diminished Bush's margin of victory but still showed him coming out ahead, Gore challenged the results and sought recounts in four congressional districts that traditionally voted Democrat. On December 8, after a series of lower-court decisions, the Florida Supreme Court agreed to order a recount of the entire state. Bush immediately claimed that the Florida court's decision ordering these recounts violated the federal Constitution. On December 9, the Supreme Court agreed to hear the case. And three days later it held in favor of Bush by a vote of 5 to 4.[4]

Three members of the Court majority believed the Florida court's decision strayed so far from what Florida statutes required that it violated the federal constitutional provision empowering the state's legislature (not its courts) to direct how the state should choose its electors. Other members of the Court found a fundamental unfairness in the fact that the Florida court had permitted its statewide recount to proceed with different counties judging the validity of ballots according to different standards, including standards that might favor the candidate of one party over the other. For a combination of these reasons (along with the fact that the Electoral College was soon due to meet) the Court majority ordered Florida to stop its recount—at a point when Bush still held a narrow majority of the popular vote.[5]

Four members of the Court (including me) dissented on the critical point of continuing the vote count. Pointing to statutes that permitted Congress to eventually resolve electoral disputes of this kind, they argued that political institutions and state courts, not the U.S. Supreme

Court, should decide the questions at issue. They concluded that Florida should be allowed to continue to its statewide recount as it wished. I agreed with the dissent. Because I believed that Congress and other political institutions were fully capable of resolving this intensely political dispute, I thought the Court should not have decided to hear the case. I thought the Court, having decided to hear the case, should have decided it differently. I could find no good reason for ordering the Florida Supreme Court to stop its recount, and I would have allowed the recount to continue. Because I believed that the public would consider the Court's decision to be based on political preferences rather than law, I wrote that the decision was a "self-inflicted wound." By stopping the recount, perhaps calling the election, the Court had hurt itself.[6]

Whether the decision was right or wrong is not the point here. If I and three other members of the Court thought the decision was very wrong, so did millions of other Americans. For present purposes, however, what is important is what happened next. Gore, the losing candidate, told his followers not to attack the legitimacy of the Court's decision. And despite the great importance of the decision, the strong disagreement about its merits, and the strong feelings about the Court's intervention, the public, Democrats as well as Republicans, followed the decision. They did so peacefully, with no need for troops as in Little Rock, without rocks hurled in the street, without violent massive protest. The leader of the U.S. Senate, Harry Reid, a Democrat, later said that the public's willingness to follow the law as enunciated by the Court constitutes a little-remarked, but the most remarkable, feature of the case. I agree.[7]

THE CHEROKEE CASE, *Dred Scott*, Little Rock, and *Bush v. Gore* are all different. In the Cherokee case the president sent troops not to enforce the Court's decision but, on the contrary, to evict the Cherokees and send them to Oklahoma. In *Dred Scott* the Court's own faulty decision helped bring about a war that the Court had sought to avoid. In Little Rock a president and the Court together enforced a decision that was highly unpopular in the South and together helped to eventually make the Constitution's protection of racial minorities effective. In *Bush v. Gore* the public simply assumed, as it does today, that it should peacefully follow an important controversial decision.

The cases show that public opposition to a Court decision can take many forms. Like Georgia's governor and his fellow Georgians in the Cherokee case, a public official or the public itself might refuse to follow a Court order. Like Andrew Jackson, opponents might find a way to avoid violating the order in an individual case but still refuse to apply the Court's legal principle to other instances. Like Abraham Lincoln after *Dred Scott,* opponents might express uncertainty about whether the Court has more right to interpret the Constitution than do the states or the people. Or, like much of the South after *Brown,* opponents might simply delay, trying to wait out or outmaneuver attempts at enforcement.

The examples taken together nonetheless make a simple point: America's public officials and the American public have come to accept as legitimate not only the Court's decisions but also its interpretations of the Constitution. The public has developed a habit of following the Court's constitutional interpretations, even those with which it strongly disagrees. Today we find it as normal to respect the Court's decisions as to breathe the air around us.

This public habit has obvious advantages. An effective judiciary, capable of enforcing contracts honestly without corruption, helps, as much as any other institution, to encourage economic investment, and thus growth and prosperity. An increasingly diverse American population has come to realize the importance of resolving serious differences through law, hence following a court's conclusion even when it is unpopular. Furthermore, experience abroad, say in pre–World War II Europe, makes clear that majorities can become tyrants, and it thereby underlines the importance of making effective the Constitution's efforts to protect minorities and to protect individual liberty—even when their enforcement is unpopular.

But that is not the end of the matter. The examples also show that the public's trust cannot be taken for granted. Public trust does not follow automatically from the existence of a written constitution. It must be built, and once built, it must be maintained. To maintain the necessary public confidence in the Court's decisions, each new generation has certain obligations. It must learn how our constitutional government works, become aware of its history, be encouraged to participate in the democratic process, and observe the preceding generation as it builds on those public customs.

This must happen primarily through civic education. But the Court too has responsibilities. Abraham Lincoln, after reading the *Dred Scott* decision, said he doubted that the public was always obligated to follow the Court's "last word." To help maintain the public's confidence, the Court must exercise its power of judicial review in a manner that honors the lessons of the past. Part II will examine some of the ways in which I believe the Court itself can help accomplish this difficult but critical task.

PART II

DECISIONS THAT WORK

THE COURT HAS A SPECIAL RESPONSIBILITY TO ENSURE THAT the Constitution works in practice. While education, including the transmission of our civic values from one generation to the next, must play the major role in maintaining public confidence in the Court's decisions, the Court too must help maintain public acceptance of its own legitimacy. It can do this best by helping ensure that the Constitution remains "workable" in a broad sense of that term. Specifically, it can and should interpret the Constitution in a way that works for the people of America today. Here I explain why and how it can do so.

Part II discusses what the Court must do to deserve and to maintain the public trust it has earned. I argue that the Court can best fulfill this obligation through rulings and interpretations that help the Constitution work in practice. This requires applying constant constitutional principles to changing circumstances. I argue that in making difficult decisions, the Court should recognize and respect the roles of other governmental institutions—Congress, the president, executive branch administrators, the states, other courts—and it should take account of the experience and expertise of each. I describe several distinct approaches, each specific to a particular institution, that I believe will help the Court build productive governmental relationships—but without the Court's abdicating its own role as constitutional guardian.

In addition, I argue that the Court should interpret written words, whether in the Constitution or in a statute, using tools that help make the law effective in practice. Judges should use traditional legal tools, such as text, history, tradition, precedent, and purposes and related consequences, to help find proper legal answers. But courts should emphasize certain of these tools, particularly purposes and consequences. Doing so will make the law work better for those whom it affects.

Taken together, the following chapters describe a set of pragmatic approaches to interpreting the law. I do not argue that judges should decide all legal cases pragmatically. Rather, I suggest that by understanding that its actions have real-world consequences and taking those consequences into account, the Court can help make the law work more effectively and thereby better achieve the Constitution's basic objective of creating a workable democratic government. At the same time, the Court can help maintain the public's confidence in the legitimacy of its interpretive role. This point, which returns full circle to Part I, is critical.

Chapter Seven

The Basic Approach

MAINTAINING PUBLIC ACCEPTANCE requires a Constitution that works well for the people today. The Court can help achieve this objective in two ways. First, the Court should reject approaches to interpreting the Constitution that consider the document's scope and application as fixed at the moment of framing. Rather, the Court should regard the Constitution as containing unwavering values that must be applied flexibly to ever-changing circumstances. The Court must consider not just how eighteenth-century Americans used a particular phrase but also how the values underlying that phrase apply today to circumstances perhaps then inconceivable. Second, when the Court interprets the Constitution, it should take account of the roles of other governmental institutions and the relationships among them.

The Constitution must work in both senses, that is, the Court must interpret the law in ways that help that document work well for Americans, and the public must accept the Court's decisions as legitimate. But this book is essentially about the Court. Thus this part will focus on how the Court might go about producing workable interpretations of the law. (Before continuing to read this part, the reader should now turn to Appendix B and review how the modern Court works.)

Alternative Approaches: Originalism, Politics, Subjective Preference

Some judges believe the best way to interpret the Constitution, while building the public's confidence in the objectivity of the Court's decisions, lies in an approach called originalism. The judges who follow this approach look to history to discover what those who wrote the Constitution most likely thought about the content and scope of a constitutional phrase, and they interpret the phrase accordingly. The Sixth Amendment, for example, says that in "criminal prosecutions, the accused shall enjoy the right . . . to be confronted with the witnesses against him." Does this phrase mean that a child witness, testifying against an accused abuser, must face the accused directly in court—despite the trauma this may cause the child and the potential that he or she will be intimidated by the accused's presence? Does it mean that a prosecutor cannot introduce into evidence the dying statement (obviously made out of court) of a murder victim identifying the accused?[1]

An "originalist" judge looks to history to find not just the basic values that underlie this Sixth Amendment provision but also, say, descriptions of eighteenth-century trial practice that will answer these questions by supporting one view or another of the confrontation clause's present-day requirements.

Originalists hope that judges will find answers to difficult constitutional questions by proceeding objectively, almost mechanically, to examine past historical fact. An objective approach will reassure the public that the Court's interpretation reflects what history shows to have been the framers' detailed intentions, not the judge's own. And the Court will thereby build and maintain continued public support for its decisions.

This historical approach, however, suffers serious problems. For one thing, it is less "objective" than one might think. When courts consider difficult questions of constitutional law, history often fails to provide specific objective directions. The legal question at hand may be narrow. Relevant historical material may be difficult to find. As Justice Robert H. Jackson pointed out, "Just what our forefathers did envision, or would have envisioned had they foreseen modern conditions, must be divined from materials almost as enigmatic as the dreams Joseph was called upon to interpret for Pharaoh."[2]

If there is no historical material directly on point, what should the Court do? Create historical "assumptions" designed to draw answers from a historical void? Or refuse to answer a question of practical importance (for example, involving fair trials for those accused of murder) on the basis of a skimpy, uncertain record of eighteenth-century practice? If the Court is to decide major constitutional questions on the basis of history, then why not ask nine historians, rather than nine judges, to provide those answers?

Moreover, even when faced with major historical questions, historians can disagree. For example, the Second Amendment says that a "well regulated Militia, being necessary to the security of a free State, *the right of the people to keep and bear Arms,* shall not be infringed." Does a local law prohibiting handgun possession violate this amendment? Over the years historians have filed briefs in the Court tracing the amendment's history, but they often disagree about the significance of different pieces of historical evidence. How should the Court treat this kind of disagreement? In 2001 historians awarded the coveted Bancroft Prize to a professor whose book purported to prove that few eighteenth-century Americans possessed firearms. That fact made it unlikely that the Second Amendment was written to protect handgun owners. Yet after investigation cast doubt on the prizewinner's data, the historians, in 2002, took the prize away.[3]

Nor does historical clarity about how the framers believed the provision applied in the eighteenth century always tell us whether or how they thought it should apply in the future. We can be certain that the framers intended the word "two" in the phrase "two Senators from each State" to have a single, fixed reference over time. But we cannot be so certain about the scope of the word "commerce" in the Constitution's grant to Congress of the power to "regulate Commerce . . . among the several States." Indeed, in all likelihood the framers intended the scope of that word to expand, covering more and more items, as commerce itself expands, as technology advances, and as commercial activities in one state increasingly affect those in another.[4]

Consider, too, the Fourteenth Amendment's equal protection

clause—the clause that forbids states to deny any person "equal protection of the laws." Those who wrote this clause in the 1860s knew that segregated schools existed at the time, even in the federal District of Columbia. Suppose they believed that enactment of the clause would *not* require integration of the District's then-segregated schools. Must we then follow those beliefs, say in 1954, when the Court decided, in *Brown,* that the clause forbids segregated schools?

In 1954 the Court did not stick to what the authors of the clause might have thought in this specific respect in the 1860s. By 1954 it had become clear that racial segregation, including school segregation, had denied minority groups the very equality that the clause sought to assure them. And the Court concluded that the authors of the clause would have preferred an interpretation that furthered its vital broad objective (that is, assuring equality) over an interpretation based on a particular factual belief (that school segregation was consistent with equality), which, if respected, would have subverted their more basic egalitarian purposes. Thus, we find an answer to the legal question at issue in *Brown* by applying not particular historical beliefs but the *values* that underlie the equal protection clause. We apply those values to the circumstances of segregation as they existed in 1954. We can reasonably believe that the authors of the clause would have approved our doing so.

Even if originalist answers were easy to uncover and free from historical ambiguity, I doubt that following the originalist approach could help maintain public support for the Court as an institution. After all, the framers could not have been aware of the automobile, television, the computer, or the Internet, but as most originalists themselves will agree, the commerce clause must apply to commerce in those matters. More than that, if we could find a specific historical explanation of the equal protection clause authors' thinking on school segregation, then we should still ask why, given the basic purposes and values underlying the clause, we would place controlling weight on that historical answer. What would the public today think of a Constitution that denied, on the basis of race, the right to attend an integrated school?

Indeed, what would the public think of a Constitution that (through an eighteenth-century-based interpretation of the confrontation clause) prevented a prosecutor from introducing into evidence a murdered wife's pre-death account of her husband's threats of violence—in a case accusing him of her murder? What would the public think of an Eighth Amendment (which forbids "cruel and unusual punishments") that would permit flogging in the navy today on the ground that flogging was common practice on eighteenth-century ships?[5]

Can originalism gain the public's respect? Can it help ensure an affirmative response to practical questions of public acceptance and implementation? Or would it instead instill public doubt because those who interpret the Constitution do so on a basis foreign to their own lives, producing answers that show that the Constitution's protections have become increasingly irrelevant? In a word, why would people want to live under the "dead hand" of an eighteenth-century constitution that preserved not enduring values but specific eighteenth-century thoughts about how those values then applied?

Yet if originalism cannot help (for example, by safeguarding judges from the charge of following subjective preferences), then how are courts to decide difficult questions in ways that maintain the public's respect? Should they simply follow their own political instincts about what the public will accept and shape the law accordingly?

The answer to this question must be no. Indeed, *Dred Scott* demonstrates the debilitating consequences of any other answer. Decisions tailored to the prevailing political winds would weaken—if not eviscerate—the Constitution's protections, particularly as applied to unpopular individuals and groups. Furthermore, the very reason for placing the power of judicial review in the courts is to secure enforcement of the Constitution when it is politically unpopular to do so. If the Court's decisions reflect short-term popularity, then why have the Court conduct judicial review in the first place? Why not place the constitutional review power in a politically responsive body, namely, Congress, particularly because, as *Dred Scott* shows, judges are not accomplished political meteorologists? For that matter, how could a law that reflects public opinion, which can shift quickly, maintain reasonable stability over time?

The best reason for the public in a democracy to support an independent judiciary with the power of judicial review remains Alexander Hamilton's reason: the public will come to understand the need to occasionally tolerate unpopular Court decisions to help ensure a government that stays within the Constitution's boundaries over time. The "political winds" do not offer pragmatic or any other support for a Court's constitutional decision.

But what then? If judges neither follow a deterministic theory such as originalism nor act politically, will they, in difficult cases with important social consequences, simply substitute their own subjective preferences for the law? Are we left with subjective decision making?

To think so is to counsel despair. How could a legal system work if each judge decided even a few important cases on the basis of personal views about what is "good" or "bad"? Given the fact that different cases arising at different times embody different circumstances with different desirable (or undesirable) attributes, it would be difficult for a single judge, let alone nine judges, to remain consistent. Why would a public, aware of that kind of decision making, accept the views of those unelected judges as legitimate? And with different presidents appointing different judges, how could a subjective system remain stable?

A Constitution That Endures—a Pragmatic Approach

Even if "originalism," "politics," and "subjectivity" offer unacceptable answers, they do not exhaustively describe the way judges reach decisions. My earlier book, *Active Liberty,* described a judicial tradition that hesitates to rely on any single theory or grand view of law, of interpretation, or of the Constitution. That tradition can find antecedents in the American judiciary of the eighteenth century, when, as a leading scholar points out, judicial "appeals to reason and the nature of things became increasingly common." The judges took an "unusually instrumental attitude toward law," offering "prudent and pragmatic regulations" and justifying them by what the Connecticut jurist Jesse Root, in 1798, called "the reasonableness and utility of their operation."[6]

Modern American judges working in this tradition, like most

judges, use textual language, history, context, relevant traditions, precedent, purposes, and consequences in their efforts to properly interpret an ambiguous text. But when faced with open-ended language and a difficult interpretive question, they rely heavily on purposes and related consequences. In doing so, judges must avoid interpretations that are either too rigid or too freewheeling. They must remain truthful to the text and "reconstruct" past solutions "imaginatively" as applied to present circumstances, at the same time projecting the purposes (or values) that inspired those past solutions to help resolve the present problem. The judges must seek an interpretation that helps the textual provision work well now to achieve its basic statutory or constitutional objectives.[7]

The Constitution establishes political institutions designed to ensure a workable, democratic form of government that protects basic personal liberties; divides and separates power (among state and federal governments, among three federal branches of government) so that no single group of officeholders can become too powerful; ensures a degree of equality; and guarantees a rule of law. These purposes can guide a judge's efforts to interpret individual constitutional phrases. By taking account as well of the role of other government institutions and the Court's relationships with them, the Court can help maintain these workably democratic constitutional objectives.

The Constitution, by creating several governmental institutions and dividing power among them, stresses the importance of considering those institutions as part of one government, working together. I add that the Court will sometimes find it can better interpret the law by staying aware of the different powers, responsibilities, and capacities with which the Constitution endows these various institutions. In doing so, the Court will reach decisions that take advantage of both its own and other institutions' comparative competences and experience. Those decisions may well garner political support from other branches—the kind of support that flows from an individual's understanding that his or her interests have been addressed even where they have not proved determinative. This is all to the good—simply one more reason why these decisions will likely work well and prove effective in practice.

I do not argue that the Court should simply defer to other institutions. Although the Constitution assigns different roles to different institutions, it subjects all of them to important constraints. Indeed, the very creation of governmental power simultaneously calls for constraints. As Madison wrote in *The Federalist* number 51:

> If angels were to govern men, neither external nor internal controls on government would be necessary. In framing a government which is to be administered by men over men, the great difficulty lies in this: you must first enable the government to control the governed; *and in the next place oblige it to control itself.*

As we have seen, the Court has the duty to ensure that governmental institutions abide by the constitutional constraints on their power. And it must continue to do so.[8]

Thus, the Court can and should take account of purposes and consequences, of institutional competences and relationships, of the values that underlie institutional collaboration, and of the need to assert constitutional limits. The more detailed illustrations in the following chapters make up the substance of my claim that by taking proper account of these matters, the Court can help to maintain the workable democracy that the Constitution foresees.

The approach I have in mind can be described as pragmatic—as that concept is broadly used to encompass efforts that consider and evaluate consequences. Pragmatism in this context requires the Court to focus not just on the immediate consequences of a particular decision but also on individual decisions as part of the law, which is to say as part of a complex system of rules, principles, canons, institutional practices, and understandings.

Although the law is composed of some highly specific rules, such as those about how to deduct charitable contributions from income taxes, it also includes broad understandings, such as methodological understandings about how a judge should apply an earlier decision to a later circumstance, how a lawyer should determine the way in which one decision affects another, or when a court can change an earlier rule of law because the court now thinks it wrong. Pragmatism in respect to law recognizes that individual decisions not only set forth specific legal rules that affect the parties to the case but also interact with other portions of the law's fabric. The resulting fabric affects the world, sometimes more (as in *Brown v. Board of Education*), and sometimes less (as with an interpretation of a technical tax code provision).

Thus, pragmatism does not require a court to *automatically* overrule a decision simply because it produces harmful consequences. Even if all agree that a technical rule of antitrust law embodied in a century-old Supreme Court case produces some harmful antitrust consequences, a court might still preserve it. This is because changing that one legal rule will have implications for overturning others. Furthermore, the act of overruling old cases itself negatively affects the law's stability.

Pragmatic approaches to law are not naive. They can take account of the interactions of a single decision with, for example, other decisions, rules, principles, methods, canons, practices, and the consequential overall effects of modifying the legal fabric. In *Brown v. Board of Education,* for example, the Court fully understood the logical, legal, and practical contradictions between its precedent *Plessy v. Ferguson,* the nineteenth-century case that authorized "separate but equal" facilities, and the basic purposes underlying the Constitution's equal protection clause. Notwithstanding the importance of following precedent, the Court properly overruled *Plessy.*[9]

One might argue that pragmatic criteria, such as workability, just invite the judge to decide cases using political or subjective criteria. But this is not so. For one thing, the simple fact that a judge uses an approach, and eschews a more full-blown detailed theory, does not automatically mean he or she is thereby "freed" to act subjectively or politically. This is because, even without such a theory, many other aspects of the judicial craft constrain the judge's decision making. Judges do not simply announce a legal conclusion. They *reason* their way to that conclusion in an opinion written for all to see. The obligation to provide legally defensible reasoning in a publicly accessible format prevents a judge from escaping accountability. Indeed, a good judicial opinion is transparent and informative. It shows that the decision is principled and reasoned. The strength of this reasoning matters.

Moreover, judges in a constitutional court, like all judges, are constrained by prescriptions of the legal craft that have long guided judges toward better answers, even when a question is difficult and language open. A great judge, Learned Hand, a member of the federal Court of Appeals for the Second Circuit, answered the charge of "subjectivity" by pointing to "those books," the law books, which include a common-law tradition and, in statutory matters, considerations of language, structure, history, precedent, purposes, and consequences.[10]

In constitutional matters, too, language, history, purposes, and consequences all constrain the judge in that they separate better from worse answers even for the most open questions. The Constitution's basic values or purposes—democratic decision making, protection of basic individual rights—constrain the judge by informing an individual case and by setting outer limits. The central values that underlie a particular general phrase set limits—for example, "Commerce . . . among the several States" or "due process of law." Prior Court decisions and the need for stability in the law set limits. So do personal constraints—those that arise out of the judge's own need for consistency. Justice Sandra Day O'Connor has described a judge's initial decisions as creating footprints that his or her later decisions will follow.[11]

Furthermore, to insist that *judges* decide cases by applying an overarching legal theory is to misunderstand the nature of the judicial role. Judges must work quickly, deciding difficult cases in weeks or a few months at most. They inevitably reason through the merits of those cases by appealing to general principles, to the facts at hand, and to more general assumptions about what the facts show.

As the argument proceeds, the judge may modify his view of the facts or of related assumptions. He or she may decide that other basic principles are more directly applicable to the facts at hand. Those involved in the argument may speak at different times at different levels of generality, sometimes referring to specific facts, sometimes to intermediate (more general) facts, sometimes to general principles, and sometimes to consequences (sometimes specific, sometimes more general) evaluated, in turn, by principles, sometimes more, sometimes less specific in nature. Any of these parts of the argument may reshape the judge's views of any of these matters as the argument proceeds.

This may sound complicated, but consider how most practical

arguments proceed: Should we invite your cousin to the wedding? Should we relocate the plant, when and where? As is true of any practical argument, including moral arguments, rarely does a single theory provide a determinative answer. Afterward, legal scholars or philosophers may use a set of determinative theories to evaluate the legal conclusion (as is true of a moral conclusion), but the judge rarely has the time to do so.

Consider how a judge actually decides an open, difficult legal question objectively even when he or she cannot discover a single legal theory that dictates an answer. A particular case will help show how the judge's decision rests upon an evaluation of the purposes underlying a phrase, along with a pragmatic understanding of how the phrase means to help the institution work. At the same time, it shows how different judges might reach different conclusions without "subjective preferences" or "politics" providing the most plausible explanation of the differences.

The case involves Article I, Section 2, Clause 2 of the Constitution, which says,

> No Person shall be a Representative who shall not have attained to the Age of twenty-five Years, and been seven Years a Citizen of the United States, and who shall not, when elected, be an Inhabitant of that State in which he shall be chosen.

Arkansas added a further term-limits requirement. Would-be candidates for Congress in Arkansas could not place their names on the ballot if they had already served three terms. Whether this provision violates the Constitution turns on whether Article I sets forth three requirements (twenty-five years old, seven years a citizen, inhabitant of the state) that are *exclusive* or that constitute a minimum, leaving the states free to add more. The question is difficult. Should the state not be free to exclude, say, those who are mentally ill? But if the state is free to do so, then would the state not also be free to add a property-ownership qualification?[12]

In *U.S. Term Limits v. Thornton,* the case itself, most of the considerations that might help a judge find an answer were almost perfectly balanced. The language favors "minimums" but only slightly. Supreme Court precedent favored "exclusive," but it was not definitive. Hamilton and Madison argued that the requirements were "exclusive." Jefferson and Joseph Story argued that they set "minimums." Many states in 1789 maintained property requirements for public office. But only one state, Virginia, applied those requirements to candidates for federal office. The Tenth Amendment, reserving to the states (or the people) all powers not delegated to the federal government, seems to favor a "minimums" reading; but the federal nature of the legislative body at issue, namely, Congress, argues for uniform (hence "exclusive") federal requirements.

With these and similar arguments counterbalancing each other, the following considerations become critical. To decide against Arkansas would make it virtually impossible for any state to impose term limits on its federal officeholders. But to find in Arkansas's favor could significantly change the way Congress works, either in a democratic direction (by assuring members in closer touch with the state) or in an undemocratic direction (by giving experienced congressional staff members more power). A judge who sees in the Constitution's division of power between federal and state governments an effort to maintain the influence, power, and authority of the individual states would likely place more weight on the first consideration, the need not to restrict state power. A judge who sees the Constitution as creating a tamper-free method for obtaining a democratically elected federal legislature would likely place more weight on the second consideration, the need to prevent a single state from changing the way Congress functions.

The Court by a vote of 5 to 4 held Arkansas's term-limits requirement unconstitutional. Whatever one thinks about the merits of that decision, it is difficult to characterize it as "political," "ideological," or even "subjective." The division between the judges may reflect different points of view—arising from differences in judges' backgrounds and experiences. It may involve different judgments about what interpretation will better help the constitutional provision work effectively. But such differences are inevitable in a judicial body composed of different members selected by different presidents at different times. And, given the diversity present in a nation of 300 million individuals, these kinds of differences among nine Supreme Court justices are healthy and desirable.

Other examples will further illustrate the general pragmatic approach I have in mind. They come from different areas of the law, including statutory interpretation, administrative review, federalism, and individual rights. This diversity is important. Although a pragmatic approach seeks a workable Constitution, not all applications of that approach involve interpretation of the Constitution itself. In fact, most of the Court's work involves interpretations of federal statutes, federal/state relationships, and judicial review of administrative actions, rules, or regulations (see Appendix B). That is because writing statutes and rules makes up much of what government does. A workable Constitution requires judges to remain aware of appropriate institutional roles and relationships in all these areas.

None of the examples I provide in the remainder of this part suggests an all-encompassing theory about how to decide every case in each area. Rather, the examples point to legal tools that are useful for deciding cases in ways that take advantage of the relative competencies of our different government institutions, respect the relationships among these institutions, and make sense in practice. The result is a workable Constitution and continued public faith in the Court's decisions.

Chapter Eight

Congress, Statutes, and Purposes

The Constitution delegates legislative power to Congress. Congress's basic job is to exercise that power by enacting statutes (normally with the president's consent). The Court's basic job is to interpret those statutes, not in the abstract, but by determining how they should be applied in particular cases. And sometimes the Court must also decide whether a statute is constitutional. These tasks make up by far most of the Court's work. How the Court performs those tasks determines whether its interpretations will effectively carry out the statute's objectives and helps determine whether its relationship with Congress will tend more toward the cooperative or the confrontational.

Ordinarily, cases that reach the Supreme Court involve ambiguous statutory language. When judges interpret that language, they look to the words at issue, to surrounding text, to the statute's history, to legal traditions, to precedent, to the statute's purposes, and to its consequences evaluated in light of those purposes. Of these I find the last two—purposes and consequences—most helpful most often. I believe maintaining a strong workable relationship with Congress requires the Court to use these two tools to help unlock the meaning of a statutory text. A strong relationship, in turn, helps the nation's institutions, and the law, function well.

An example will help illustrate this kind of judicial task. In 2008, in France, a train conductor collecting fares found that a passenger had a basket containing two dozen live snails. The passenger, a kindergarten teacher, was bringing them from his home in Normandy to Paris, where he intended to use them for classroom instruction. The conductor's fare booklet said that "purchase of a ticket is required for all animals." The booklet also provided that the fare for an animal should cost half the price of an ordinary ticket, adding that "if the animal weighs less than six kilograms and is carried in a basket, the fare for the animal shall be no more than 5.10." The conductor thus asked the teacher to buy a 5.10 ticket for the snails. The teacher protested that the fare booklet rule surely was not referring to snails. Nonetheless, he paid. The press wrote about the incident, and the train company eventually reimbursed the teacher. But who was right? And why? For that matter, should the conductor have required the teacher to buy two dozen tickets—one for each snail? Here, reduced to its essence, is a problem akin to that of interpreting an ambiguous statute.[1]

Text-Oriented Interpretation

Some judges, lawyers, and law teachers believe that judges, when answering this kind of question, should strongly emphasize the first four tools that I mentioned: text, history, tradition, and precedent. Following this text-oriented approach, they try not to use purpose, consequences, or the legislative debates that compose the history of the statute's enactment in Congress. In my view, however, a primarily text-oriented system cannot work very well. A more realistic example will help me explain why.

A federal statute permits citizens to sue the government and to recover damages for serious harm that federal officials wrongfully caused, including harm to their property. But the act contains a series of exceptions, including an exemption for harm to property caused by "any officer of customs or excise or *any other law enforcement officer.*" Whom exactly does the exempting phrase, "any other law enforcement officer," cover? Does it cover only those law enforcement officers who carry out "customs or excise" duties? Or does it cover (and exempt from liability) other law enforcement officers as well, such as federal prison officials?[2]

Text-oriented judges will carefully examine the statute's language. They may refer to a dictionary or look to surrounding language. They will see if the phrase has some special traditional or historical meaning. They will search the precedent, and, failing to find any strong reason for giving the words a specialized meaning, they will try to give them the meaning they carry in ordinary, non-statutory life. In this case, the key words "any other" are not technical, and dictionaries, history (other than legislative history), tradition, and precedent do not suggest any specialized meaning. So the judge may well conclude that the words "any other" mean what they say, namely, suit is barred against *any* other law enforcement officer, including prison officials.

What is wrong with that? Let us break this question down into two parts: First, what is wrong with the assumption that language in a statute means what it means in ordinary life outside the statute? Unfortunately, such an assumption is rarely helpful. As those who study language have pointed out, we use words, strung together in sentences, uttered on particular occasions orally or in writing, to perform many different functions. We use them to ask questions, to make statements, to agree with others, to write contracts, to perform marriages, to pray, to vow, to inform, to estimate, to recommend. We also use them to write laws—a highly specialized activity. The assumption begs the further question: What part of "ordinary life"?[3]

The statute's language may be vague, and the scope of its coverage may be uncertain. But it does not help us understand a vague statement to pretend that someone else "in ordinary life" made the statement. How often would it help us understand, say, a difficult point in a university lecture to pretend that the lecturer is not a lecturer but a journalist? Similarly, how often does it help us understand a statute's vague or ambiguous language to pretend that its congressional authors were engaged in any activity other than the one they were engaged in, namely, writing a statute?

It is also rarely helpful to rely on dictionaries. Nothing is wrong with turning to the dictionary when a court is trying to interpret a technical word, say the word "percentile" used in a special technical sense in a statute that incorporates the understanding of professional statisticians. In such a case, Congress might well have intended nonstatisticians to look to a dictionary to discover how statisticians use the word.[4]

Far more often, however, statutory uncertainty does not arise because the statute's language has an unclear technical meaning or because ordinary readers fail to understand the general *kinds* of situations to which the statute's language refers. We all know the meaning of the words "any other law enforcement officer." We need not look them up in a dictionary. Rather, here the statute is ambiguous or uncertain in respect to the scope of its coverage. Its general language does not tell us precisely which situations fall outside Congress's demonstrative intent.

Suppose a statute uses the phrase "*any* court." We have no trouble understanding the words, but we may have trouble understanding whether the statute includes foreign courts or limits its scope to American courts. Does a naturalist who tells us "all the beavers are out swimming" mean to include those beavers just born? Does a friend who says "all bicycle shops carry water bottles" mean to include secondhand bicycle shops? Context revealing a speaker's *purposes*, not a dictionary that explains a word's meaning, provides the necessary help here. Sam's mother tells him, "Go to the store and buy some ice cream, flour, fruit, and anything else you want." It is context, not a dictionary, that will help us learn whether Sam's mother has given him permission to buy fifteen comic books.[5]

Now reconsider the phrase in our example, "any officer of customs or excise or any other law enforcement officer." We can be certain that the word "any" here does not refer to any other law enforcement officer in the universe. It does not refer, say, to a German law enforcement officer. Gazing however thoughtfully at the words or consulting a dictionary will not help us discover *which* law enforcement officers Congress intended the phrase to cover. We must look further. Who wrote the words? And we must look to the purpose. Why did they write them?

In this case, it turned out that the statute's drafters drew the language from a similar exemption found in English law. English law limited its exemption to a small subset of all law enforcement officers. Moreover, it was difficult to determine why, in the context of a statute that expanded citizen remedies, Congress would have wanted to limit so severely an injured person's right to recover. For these and other reasons related to Congress's purposes, I would have interpreted the exempting phrase to refer only to those law enforcement officers who performed tasks related to customs and excise duties.[6]

Interpretation Based on Purposes and Consequences

Now let us consider an approach that relies more heavily on purposes and consequences. To determine a provision's purpose, the judge looks for the problem that Congress enacted the statute to resolve and asks how Congress expected the particular statutory words in question to help resolve that problem. The judge also examines the likely consequences of a proposed interpretation, asking whether they are more likely to further than to hinder achievement of the provision's purpose. In doing so, a judge may examine a wide range of relevant legislative materials. Furthermore, the judge can try to determine a particular provision's purpose even if no one in Congress said anything or even thought about the matter. In that case the judge (sometimes describing what he does in terms of the purpose of a hypothetical "reasonable legislator") will determine that hypothetical purpose in order to increase the likelihood that the Court's interpretation will further the more general purposes of the statute that Congress enacted.

An example based on an actual case will show how courts might use purposes and consequences in practice. A federal statute gives disabled children the right to a "free appropriate public education." Pearl and Theodore Murphy have a son, Joseph, who suffers from severe learning disabilities. In September 1997 the Murphys, after receiving a specialist's report that Joseph had a "near total incapacity to process language," decided that the public school district had failed to provide him with the statutorily required "appropriate education." The Murphys thought the school district should not have placed Joseph in classes with nondisabled students.[7]

The statute provides that parents who disagree with a school district's plan for educating their disabled child can contest the plan before state administrative officials. The Murphys did so. The state hearing examiner and an appellate administrator both eventually agreed that the Murphys were right and the school district should pay the cost of placing Joseph in a specialized private school. The school district, however, still hesitated to do so.[8]

The statute also provides that parents such as the Murphys can bring a lawsuit against the school district in a federal court. The Murphys did so and eventually won. The court ordered the district to pay for Joseph's education at a private school.[9]

All these proceedings were expensive. The Murphys had hired an educational expert, who charged them $29,000 for her help. The courts later found that the expert's services were well worth that price. But the Murphys, who were people of modest means, asked the school district to reimburse them for the cost not only of their lawyers but also of their expert. When the district refused, they asked the court to require the school district to pay.[10]

At this point the court had to decide whether it had the power to order the school district to reimburse the Murphys. The federal statute says that the court may "award" a prevailing party like the Murphys "reasonable attorneys' fees *as part of* [*their*] *costs.*" The Murphys argued in court that the word "costs" includes the fees of experts they had to hire to support their case. The district argued that the statutory phrase did not include expert fees. That was the question of statutory interpretation that reached the Supreme Court.[11]

Does the word "costs" include the fees of experts? On the one hand, one can read the statute's language as restricting "costs" to "attorneys' fees" plus a few extra expenses, for example, court filing fees, while excluding the separate fees of experts. Courts have often interpreted the word "costs" when used in other rules and statutes in this way. On the other hand, one might read the word as including the "fees" of experts. Those fees do not differ radically in kind from attorneys' fees. Indeed, attorneys themselves often hire experts and pass an expert's charges on to the client as part of the attorney's bill. Moreover, an expert's fee is a "cost" to the client as the word "cost" is often used in everyday affairs.

It helps to examine the statute's purposes. Overall, the statute seeks to make available to disabled children the kind of education that few parents can afford. The statute more specifically seeks to create procedures (including court procedures) that will allow parents to dispute a school district's claim that it is already doing so. To have any hope of success, parents must often turn to experts, who are expensive. Thus, reading "costs" as *excluding* expert fees, by requiring a winning family to pay those fees, could well place that education beyond the reach of a typical family even if that family shows it is entitled to receive that education. Consider this consequence in light of the statute's basic purpose. Does it not hinder, interfere with, perhaps thwart, the statute's basic purpose, namely, an appropriate education for each handicapped child?[12]

Yet we must go further. After all, Congress might have had a subsidiary money-saving purpose, in respect to legal costs for example. This is why it is important to examine the relevant legislative materials, such as the history of the debates in Congress that led to enactment of the legislation. In this case these materials strongly suggested that Congress intended for the district to pay these expert fees.

A report of a Senate-House conference committee (the joint committee to reconcile House and Senate versions of the bill and produce a final text) said that the statutory language includes reasonable "expenses and *fees of expert witnesses.*" Both houses of Congress unanimously adopted this report. The upshot is that an examination of purposes and consequences would lead the Court to interpret the statute in the way that members of both houses of Congress seemed to intend. It would produce an interpretation that furthered the basic purposes underlying the statute.[13]

Why Emphasize Purpose and Consequence?

As my examples suggest, I believe a purpose-oriented approach is better than a purely text-oriented approach. Three sets of considerations, taken together, explain why I believe the Court is obliged to follow a purpose-oriented approach.[14]

First, judicial consideration of a statute's purposes helps to further the Constitution's democratic goals. In a representative democracy, legislators must ultimately act in ways that voters find acceptable.

But voters are unaware of the detailed language that legislators write. They can do no more than consider whether a legislator's work corresponds roughly to their own views, typically expressed in terms of general objectives, say peace, prosperity, healthy environment, and economizing.

A legislator whose statute furthers a popular objective will seek credit at election time—at least if the statute works reasonably well. But suppose the statute does not work well. Then whom should the voters blame? If courts have interpreted the statute in accordance with the legislator's purposes, there is no one to blame but the legislator. But if courts disregard the statute's purposes, it is much harder for the voter to know who is responsible when results go awry.

Consider the disabled children's education statute. Voters can easily understand what Congress sought to do: It sought to help disabled children, to provide them with a free appropriate education, and to create meaningful procedures enabling a dissatisfied parent to challenge a school board's individualized education plan—all of which will cost the local school districts money. Voters can decide whether they favor these ends and evaluate a legislator accordingly. But what are voters to do when they discover that most parents, because they cannot recover experts' fees, find the statute's challenge procedures useless?

Voters do not know whom to blame. They do not read the texts or readily understand the reasoning of a text-based analysis. Legislators can point out that they thought (as their colleagues unanimously assured them) they supported a statute permitting reimbursement for those fees. By way of contrast, voters can understand purposes; and, where a statute furthers the legislators' purposes, voters more likely know whom to hold responsible.

No single court decision will make a difference. But over time, where vast numbers of statutory provisions are at issue, the following generalizations seem fair. The more the Court relies on text-based methods alone to interpret statutes, the easier it will be for legislators to avoid responsibility for a badly written statute simply by saying that the Court reached results they did not favor. The more the Court seeks realistically to ascertain the purposes of a statute and interprets its provisions in ways that further those purposes, the harder it will be for the legislator to escape responsibility for the statute's objectives, and the easier it will be for voters to hold their legislators responsible for their legislative decisions, including the consequences of the statutes for which they vote.

Second, a purpose-oriented approach helps individual statutes work better for those whom Congress intended to help. The disabled children's education statute offers dissatisfied parents the possibility of challenging a school board decision. An interpretation that denies those parents recovery of expert fees when they successfully challenge a board decision makes the challenge procedures difficult, perhaps impossible, for many parents to use. The result is to deny their children the education that the statute promises. Of course, a denial of expert fee recovery saves the school district money. But Congress did not suggest that it favored that result. Rather, the congressional reports and subsequent legislative votes indicate that Congress expected the contrary. The text-based interpretation undercut the statute's ability to work effectively for parents.

Third, and most important, by emphasizing purpose the Court will help Congress better accomplish its own legislative work. Congress does not, cannot, and need not write statutes that precisely and exhaustively explain where and how each of the statute's provisions will apply. For one thing, doing so would require too many words. Who wants statutory encyclopedias that spell out in excruciating detail all potential applications in all potential circumstances? Who could read them?

For another thing, linguistic imprecision, vagueness, and ambiguity are often useful, even necessary, statutory instruments. Congress may not know just how its statute should apply in future circumstances where it can see that future only dimly, and new situations will always emerge. Congress may want to consider only one aspect of a complex, detailed subject, an aspect that warrants a few general words that simply point a court in the right direction. Congress may want to use a general standard, such as "restraint of trade," while intending courts to develop more specific content on a case-by-case common-law basis. Or, the English language may lack words that succinctly express, say, the necessary quantitative measurement, as, for example, when Congress seeks to punish more severely those who commit "serious" or "violent" crimes.[15]

In these circumstances, congressional drafting staffs may well use general or imprecise words while relying on committee reports, statements of members delivered on the floor of Congress, legislative hearings, and similar materials to convey intended purposes, hence meaning, scope, and reference. Congress can use that drafting system if, and only if, it can count on the courts to consider legislative purposes when interpreting statutes and look at the associated legislative materials to help determine legislative purpose. When courts do so, drafters, legislators, and judges can work together. They act in tandem with Congress, carrying out the legislators' objectives in even the most complex statutes, such as those dealing with bankruptcy, transit system mergers, or pension benefit guarantees.

Without such teamwork, legislators and their staffs would face a drafting task that is daunting and even impractical. The drafters would have to think in advance of every likely combination of circumstances that might arise, perhaps compiling and enacting into law lengthy lists of all possible circumstances. And they would have to learn how courts would interpret each word in the much more lengthy statute, say by looking at past cases where courts have interpreted similar words in related contexts. Were there a single drafting staff for all statutes, were judges able to train the drafters, were we able to develop linguistic codes that legislators and judges would uniformly apply, perhaps we could reach a kind of interpretive consensus that would work. But in the absence of some such linguistic utopia, a text-oriented interpretation of ambiguous statutory language that deliberately avoids a search for purpose too often means an interpretation that, from the perspective of a congressional legislator, does not work properly.

In saying all this, I recognize that the political complexion of Congress can change. By looking at the purposes of those who once enacted a statute as I would do, the Court might produce an interpretation that a more recent Congress would disapprove. But in doing so, the Court emphasizes the need for *legislation,* to depart from an earlier statute, and it thereby also assures the present Congress that their own intentions will be honored later when the Court considers the meaning of a statute that they have passed.

My point, of course, is that the better, simpler way for courts to help

Congress is by looking for purposes. Drafting staffs can then, and more easily, indicate clearly (although not necessarily in the statute itself) the statute's relevant purposes and objectives. They, like Congress, can then assume that the courts, partners in the enterprise, will interpret a statute's open language accordingly.

A Qualification

To be sure, the dichotomy drawn between text-oriented and purpose-oriented approaches is oversimplified here. Many good judges might consider themselves text oriented even though they sometimes take account of statutory purposes and consequences. Furthermore, purposes and consequences do not unlock the meaning of every ambiguous statutory phrase. Purposes are sometimes hard to determine. And, regardless, purpose cannot produce an interpretation that the statute's language rules out of bounds. A statute that forbids importing "rocks" does not forbid importing trees irrespective of whether including trees would further the statute's purposes. Still, the dichotomy exists. Text-oriented judges emphasize the use of language, history, tradition, and precedent while minimizing their use of purpose and consequence as statutory tools. By contrast, purpose-oriented judges view purpose and consequence as particularly useful tools.

Objections to the Purpose-Oriented Approach

What can be said against a purpose-oriented approach? Some argue that it is linguistically inappropriate to attribute a purpose to an institution such as Congress, rather than to the individuals who make up that institution. In any event, individual legislators have purposes that can differ wildly from the purpose that a judge would attribute to a statute. Suppose a legislator's purpose in voting for a bill was to help a party leader. Suppose a legislator voted for an amendment in order to defeat the bill by attaching a "poison pill" that he hoped would sabotage the bill. Suppose he did not read the bill. Suppose no member of Congress read the bill, or even thought about the particular matter before the Court.[16]

It is not conceptually difficult, however, to attribute a purpose to a corporate body such as Congress. Corporations, companies, partnerships, municipalities, states, nations, armies, bar associations, and legislatures engage in intentional activities, such as buying, selling, promising, endorsing, questioning, undertaking, repudiating, and legislating. These corporate bodies may have purposes different and separate from those of the individuals who comprise them. A basketball team's movements can reveal the *team's* defensive purpose even if each individual player's thoughts are a mile away. A municipality can promise to build a new baseball stadium with the purpose of attracting a major-league team even if no elected official really wants the team but rather hopes the stadium will never be built and privately intends never to provide the necessary funding. Linguistic and social conventions (complicated but well understood) tell us when and how to attribute purposes to these bodies. Lawyers learn how to ascribe purposes and intentions to Congress. There is no rule of language that forbids our doing so.

Moreover, even if Congress did not consider a matter at all, judges can still ascertain a purpose. Here judges can use an artificial construct that disregards the unhelpful silence of congressional reality in order to produce an interpretation that will help the statute work well (in light of the more general purposes that the judge can find). They can ask what a *reasonable member of Congress would have intended.* This hypothetical question helps judges see the statute as a coherent whole and avoid interpretations that are inconsistent with that more general view. For instance, in the previous example, if the conference report had not confirmed that "costs" meant to include expert fees, the Court could still have looked to the overarching purpose of the statute (to provide a free, appropriate education to disabled children), and the absence of any money-saving purpose, to answer the question.

What if Congress deliberately chooses a vague or ambiguous word to avoid deciding an issue? Members of Congress sometimes disagree on specific terminology, even if they agree on the general need for a statute. If the disagreement is strong, they may deliberately write vague or ambiguous language to secure the necessary votes to enact the legislation. When a court later interprets the language, it can examine the general need for, and purpose of, the statute. Under these circumstances, is the court not open to the criticism that it is just "taking sides" on the open or contested issue? The answer is no. The court is doing its best to make the statute work in the best way possible, by interpreting the provision in light of the statute's purposes.

A further criticism is that purposes are sometimes difficult to ascertain. Moreover, purposes can be described at different levels of generality. How should a judge describe the purpose of the education act's cost reimbursement provision? Is it to help disabled children at any cost? Is it to try to help children while keeping costs within certain bounds? Is it just generally to do a good thing for children?

But what is the special problem about finding the "right" level of generality? Normally, we look to context to decide what purposes the speaker has in mind and which of those purposes is relevant. We do the same with statutes. Three men sailing in a balloon over a Maine potato field are lost. One shouts to a farmer down below, "Where are we?" The farmer replies, "In a balloon." The joke lies in the farmer's failure to take account of the balloonist's purpose as made clear by context. When my wife says, "There isn't any butter," I have no problem understanding that she is referring to the refrigerator, not to the corner store.

Why is it *especially* difficult to determine a statute's purpose? Every time we hear another speak, every time we read a book, we could and often do look for the speaker's or writer's purpose. We normally and automatically derive the purposes from the context in which the relevant statement appears. Normally, it is easy to find purpose; sometimes it is not. How does a statute, in this respect, differ from any other writing? The fact that it is *sometimes* difficult to determine a relevant purpose should not lead courts to abandon that effort across the board. Like Pascal's wager, the effort, where successful, will end up helping the judge. At worst little is lost.

Moreover, we can look at congressional reports, floor statements, and related legislative material, all part of the relevant context, to help determine the relevant purposes. The conference report on the disabilities education bill and the accompanying votes help make clear that the cost recovery provision was not intended to save money.

The use of legislative history is also criticized. If courts examine congressional documents, reports, floor statements, and the like, in an effort to ascertain purpose, will they give too much power not to the elected legislators but rather to the unelected congressional staffs who write such history? Will those staffs write their own views into law?

If the staff system is working properly, this material will not substitute the views of unelected staff for those of elected representatives. A legislative committee staff circulates drafts of reports to all members of the committee. Elected senators and representatives (directly or through staff) can, and do, object to particular statements in the reports. If a committee member disagrees strongly, he or she can write a different view. Like heads of corporations, trade unions, and the president of the United States, members of Congress must rely on staffs and take responsibility for the staff's work. In a word, when the staff system works properly, the courts need not fear paying attention to staff work. When the system does not work properly, the cure must lie with Congress, not the courts.

Finally, the most strongly held criticism of purpose-oriented interpretation is that this method allows judges to interpret statutes subjectively. Will the purpose-oriented judge resolve linguistic uncertainty by substituting his or her own subjective policy views—that is, the judge's own purposes—for those of Congress? This criticism, however, applies to the *mis*use of a purpose-oriented method, not to its proper use. All methods of statutory interpretation are open to misuse. A judge who relies on text alone could misinterpret an ambiguity in order to substitute his own subjective policy views for those of Congress. A judge, when examining precedent, might misread precedent to do the same. The judge's need to write an opinion explaining his or her reasons for reaching a conclusion helps guard against misinterpretation. And that safeguard works particularly well when the judge uses a purpose-oriented method. In this instance, the judge cannot simply state how he interprets an ambiguity. Rather, he must spell out in detail how he derives relevant purposes, what those purposes are, and how and why he finds that they illuminate the statute's text.

Why, then, should judges look to purposes and consequences when they interpret statutes? Because they will help ensure democratic accountability. They will tie statutes more closely to the human needs that called them into being. And they will help Congress carry out its own constitutional responsibilities. A court that looks to purposes is a court that works as a partner with Congress. It is a court that helps make the Constitution work better in practice. And it is a court that achieves results that the general public should find easier to accept—even if the court's conclusions are, as is inevitable, sometimes wrong.

Avoiding Constitutional Questions

Sometimes the purpose-based approach must yield to another principle—the need to interpret statutes in a way that will save them from potential invalidation as unconstitutional. This interpretive principle is an established part of the Court's practice. The case of *Zadvydas v. Davis,* in 2001, illustrates how this interpretive principle works.[17]

The case involved two aliens. The first, Kestutis Zadvydas, was born of Lithuanian parents in 1948, lived in a German displaced-persons camp, came to the United States at the age of eight, and unfortunately entered into a long career of criminal activity. After he served his prison sentences, the government sought to deport him. But no country would take him, not Germany, which said he was not its citizen, not Lithuania, which had denied him citizenship, and not the Dominican Republic, his wife's country, which denied that he had any relevant tie. So the government simply kept Zadvydas in custody under the authority of a statute that permits it to keep deportable aliens in custody for ninety days plus some unspecified additional time.[18]

The case also involved Kim Ho Ma, a native of Cambodia who came to the United States in the early 1980s at age seven. He too was convicted of a serious crime, participation in a gang-related shooting. He served his sentence, after which the government sought to deport him. But the United States has no repatriation treaty with Cambodia, so it seemed unlikely that Cambodia would take him. While searching for a country that might take Kim Ho Ma, the government kept him in custody—well beyond the ninety-day removal period.[19]

Both Zadvydas and Kim Ho Ma filed petitions in federal court attacking the constitutionality of the statute that, in the government's view, authorized their continuing custody. That statute makes clear that the government can hold in custody an "alien ordered removed" for certain reasons (for example, violation of entry conditions, the commission of crimes, and reasons related to foreign policy and security) at least for ninety days while it looks for a country that will take the alien. The statute adds that the alien "*may be detained beyond* the [ninety-day] removal period" *if* the attorney general determines that the alien *is a* "*risk to the community* or unlikely to comply with the order of removal." Both detainees argued that the statute, if read literally, would permit the attorney general to hold them in custody forever. The government did not deny that the statute could be read that way. But it said that Congress intended to give the government the authority to hold aliens in custody for as long as the attorney general thought necessary.[20]

As interpreted by the government, the statute raises a serious constitutional question. The Constitution forbids the government to "deprive[]" any "person . . . of . . . liberty . . . without due process of law." Freedom from imprisonment lies at the heart of the "liberty" that the Constitution protects. Imprisonment here is not for a crime (the aliens had served their sentences) but for other reasons, namely, to avoid the risk that the alien will run away or commit more crimes in the future. Reasons of this sort may sometimes justify imprisonment, say, temporarily before a criminal trial or longer if the detained person is mentally ill and a danger to others. But the imprisonment was not necessarily temporary. Furthermore, it involved administrative proceedings that lacked the strong judicial protections that accompany a criminal trial, and the individuals were not unusually dangerous or mentally ill. The Court divided 5 to 4. The majority wrote (in a decision that I authored) that the "serious constitutional problem arising out of a statute that, in these circumstances, permits an indefinite, perhaps permanent, deprivation of human liberty without any [ordinary judicial] protection is obvious."[21]

Rather than subject the statute to even a risk of invalidation, the Court interpreted it as authorizing detention only for "a period *reasonably necessary* to secure the alien's removal." It said that the statute (which was silent on the matter) did *not* authorize permanent detention. The Court added that a federal court, reviewing an administrative decision to detain an alien beyond ninety days, should look with suspicion at a period of detention greater than six months. If there is no significant likelihood that a country will take the alien in the reasonably foreseeable future, the judge should order the alien released from detention. The judge could impose other conditions that would help the government keep track of his whereabouts. It might, for example, require the alien to report regularly to immigration officials.[22]

This interpretation of the statute may *not* be faithful to congressional purpose. After all, the statute's basic purpose is to ensure confinement while the government looks for a country that will accept the alien. Neither the statute nor its history tells us what should happen if no such country can be found. Perhaps Congress would have wanted to keep the alien in confinement.

Nonetheless, as the Court pointed out, when there is a "serious doubt" about a statute's "constitutionality," the Court "will first ascertain whether a construction of the statute is fairly possible by which the question may be avoided." And that is what the Court did. It pointed out that the statute's specific purpose was not "clear." But it then went on to produce an interpretation of the statute that might not have been Congress's first choice.[23]

The Court chose the risk of ignoring Congress's purpose over the risk of setting the statute entirely aside. It chose to interpret the statute in a way that was consistent with the Constitution. It thereby stopped unconstitutionality in its tracks. And it seems reasonable to assume that Congress would have preferred this trade-off if given the option. That is, Congress would likely favor an interpretation of the statute that ensured its continued validity to an interpretation that made it vulnerable to invalidation.

Although this interpretive principle may depart from an ordinary purpose-based approach, it serves the same practical function. Like the purposive approach, it seeks to minimize friction between the Court and Congress. The interpretive principle recognizes that the Court can, and where possible should, avoid friction by not interpreting a statute in a manner that requires invalidation (or seriously threatens that result). If a court finds a statute unconstitutional, it cannot avoid friction. It has to strike the statute down. Thus, the interpretive principle helps the two governmental institutions, Congress and the Court, work together in carrying out the Constitution's practical objectives. It helps maintain a constitutional system of government, and forms part of an overall approach that promises a workable Constitution and helps to secure continued public acceptance of the Court's decisions.

Chapter Nine

The Executive Branch, Administrative Action, and Comparative Expertise

How much deference should the Court give to an executive branch agency's own formulation of a policy or to an agency's determination of what a statute means? How willing should the Court be to overturn or to sustain an agency's decision about these matters? The answers to these technical-sounding questions are more important than one might think. Administrative decision making constitutes the bulk of executive branch work; and the bulk of its administrative decisions are subject to judicial review. Hence, the questions' answers help to define much of the Court-executive relationship. Moreover, agencies act within the confines of statutes. Hence, in answering the questions, the Court must keep Congress in mind.

Most important, the answers affect the lives of ordinary Americans. While it is easy to see the effect of executive branch decisions on basic rights, such as the presidential order to send troops to Little Rock to enforce *Brown*, it is harder to remember that routine agency decisions can also affect our daily existence, often in profound ways.

The answers matter, for they affect the way government works, the ability of modern government to solve the problems of ordinary Americans, and consequently the broader question this book considers: how the Court can earn the public's confidence by developing relationships with other institutions that will help government work well.

Executive Branch Administration

Whether we like it or not, government administration is everywhere. The Constitution vests the "executive Power" of the United States in the president. The executive branch exercises that power by administering the laws that Congress enacts, and those laws are numerous. Government administrators implement laws that regulate the conduct of private businesses or individuals, that obtain money from citizens and businesses, that disburse funds, and that provide some goods and services directly. Federal statutes, for example, require or permit government officials to obtain, provide, or regulate taxes, welfare, Social Security, medicine, pharmaceutical drugs, education, highways, railroads, electricity, natural gas, stocks and bonds, banking, medical care, public health, safety, the environment, fair employment practices, consumer protection, and much else besides (including the armed forces, which for present purposes I put to the side).[1]

Statutes delegate the authority to administer these programs sometimes to the president himself but more often to a (typically presidentially appointed) head of a cabinet department or bureau or perhaps an independent agency, such as the Federal Reserve Board, the Federal Communications Commission, or the Securities and Exchange Commission. "Independent agencies" are labeled as such because, unlike executive branch agencies, their members serve fixed terms and are removable by the president only for good cause, rather than on the basis of policy disagreements. Because of their relative autonomy from the president, some have called the independent agencies a "headless fourth branch" of government. But I believe them best considered as part of the executive branch.[2]

Agencies (and here I include virtually all civil executive branch agencies, bureaus, and departments) typically possess great power. They write regulations that, like congressional statutes, take effect as law. They resolve disputes, often in much the same way that courts adjudicate controversies. They investigate private behavior. They impose sanctions, such as heavy fines, on those who violate their rules, and they license businesses or individuals to perform services. They regularly consider and grant requests by individual private citizens for goods or services, ranging from books of the president's speeches to local weather forecasts.

In a word, federal government programs are many, they come in different shapes and sizes, and they employ millions of government officials and ordinary workers (two million civilian employees in 2009). It is important to keep their size, complexity, and diversity in mind even though here I use the singular term "agency" to refer generically to the units that administer most government programs. I shall also overlook the fact that some agencies enjoy special independence from presidential control.[3]

Administrative Law and Court Review

Despite the size and complexity of government administration, the Court often applies principles drawn from one branch of law, administrative law, when it reviews the lawfulness of an agency's actions. Our legal system asks courts to review agency work because the technical nature of modern society, along with the public's desire for Social Security, medical care, and the like, has brought laws that delegate enormous decision-making power and responsibility to administrators who are not themselves elected. The federal government has regulated railroads since the 1880s (through the Interstate Commerce Commission), pharmaceutical drugs since the beginning of the twentieth century (through the Food and Drug Administration), and unfair or deceptive business practices since World War I (through the Federal Trade Commission).

Technological change and changing political attitudes during the 1930s led to President Roosevelt's New Deal, which significantly expanded the scope of federal regulation. The New Deal created and augmented the power of many independent regulatory commissions, such as the Securities and Exchange Commission, the Federal Power

Commission, the National Labor Relations Board, the Civil Aeronautics Board, and the Federal Communications Commission.

Government again expanded the scope of regulation significantly in the 1970s with the creation of powerful but not necessarily organizationally "independent" regulatory authorities, such as the Environmental Protection Agency, the Occupational Safety and Health Administration, and the National Highway Traffic Safety Administration. The deregulation movement of the late twentieth and early twenty-first centuries changed somewhat the manner and extent to which the government regulated. A few regulatory programs and agencies were abolished (such as the Civil Aeronautics Board and the Interstate Commerce Commission). More commonly, Congress changed the name and government location of an agency, for example, changing the name of the Federal Power Commission to the Federal Energy Regulatory Commission and moving it to the Department of Energy—all without major change in function or performance.

The Roosevelt administration and later administrations saw the expansion of government authority as a practical necessity. Just after the New Deal, James Landis, a strong advocate of activist government, wrote that the "administrative process is, in essence, our generation's answer to the inadequacy of the judicial and legislative processes." But the resulting growth and concentration of power also led the public to return to Madison's basic observation: "if angels were to govern," there would be no need for "controls," but in a world where government is "administered by men," how do we make government "control itself"? How can we ensure that related administrative decisions are fair and reasonable? Or, as the ancient Romans put it, *quis custodiet ipsos custodes?* Who will regulate the regulators?[4]

At the time of the early New Deal, some thought the "science" of administration itself would check administrative behavior, rather in the way that medical science and canons of ethics limit doctors' behavior. But few today believe in a "science" of regulation or administration "canons" that, if followed, would bring about fair, reasonable decisions. Rather, we have relied on Congress, the president, and the courts to oversee administrative decision making.[5]

Congress oversees agency decision making through hearings, budget decisions, and ultimately legislation. But congressional oversight is limited by the same lack of time, knowledge, and expertise that led Congress to delegate power to the agency in the first place.

The executive branch relies on a number of sources to check agency action. For example, it uses ombudsmen and inspectors general to detect improper behavior. Perhaps most significant, it conducts policy oversight through the Office of Management and Budget (OMB). A small OMB bureau, now called the Office of Information and Regulatory Affairs (OIRA), seeks to coordinate the regulatory work of the sprawling executive branch and improve its efficiency. But OIRA can review only a few agency policy decisions made each year. Furthermore, it may seek to influence an agency's policy decision but lack the legal authority to change that decision. Outside OIRA, the president may not have the time or willingness to review decisions, even those of his own political appointees.

Thus, courts too must have an important role in reviewing executive branch agency decisions. A member of the general public who will likely suffer concrete harm as a result of an agency action may typically seek judicial review. Applying basic principles of administrative law, a court may consider whether the agency properly found the facts, followed proper procedures, and followed its own rules and regulations. A court may also consider whether the agency's determinations, including those of policy, are reasonable; not "arbitrary, capricious, [or] an abuse of discretion"; conform to certain basic principles of fairness; are consistent with relevant statutory requirements; and are consistent with the Constitution.[6]

COMPARATIVE EXPERTISE AND JUDICIAL DEFERENCE

COURTS FIND THE notion of comparative expertise useful, indeed necessary, when reviewing administrative decisions. Courts ask which institution, court, or agency is comparatively more likely to understand the critical matters that underlie a particular kind of legal question, broadly phrased. Courts are more likely to have experience with procedures, basic fairness to individuals, and interpreting the Constitution.

Thus, where questions of this kind are at issue, courts are less likely to give much deference to agency decisions. Agencies, however, are more likely to have experience with facts and policy matters related to their administrative missions. Thus courts will likely give agencies considerably more deference when decisions are about these matters.

This notion helps courts answer a key question of administrative law: What *attitude* should a reviewing court take toward the administrative agency's decision? What do I mean by "attitude"? That word refers to the standards that judges use when reviewing the lawfulness of a decision made by other judges, by juries, or by administrators. For example, an appellate court will set aside a lower-court judge's finding of a fact only if the finding is *clearly erroneous.* A judge reviewing a jury's decision that a criminal defendant is guilty will overturn the jury's verdict only if *no reasonable person* could have reached that decision. And a judge reviewing administrative agency findings of fact will set them aside only if they are not *supported by substantial evidence.* Each standard gives slightly more leeway to the fact finder than the preceding one.[7]

Some argue that applying these different standards is a psychological impossibility. A distinguished circuit judge, Harold Leventhal, for example, once facetiously wrote that he "thought" he had found the case "dreamed of by law school professors," a case where he could "conscientiously" distinguish among the standards, upholding an agency's finding of fact because it was supported by "substantial evidence," even though, had that finding been made by a district judge, he would have struck it down as "clearly erroneous." But he decided on second thought that the finding was not supported by "substantial evidence" either.[8]

Judge Leventhal's reaction is an overstatement. Judges are able to apply different standards—at least to some degree. When they review a lower-court judge's decision about what the law means, they can simply ask themselves, "Is it right?" When they review a jury decision, they can ask, "Am I completely certain the jury is wrong, to the point where no one could sensibly come to that conclusion?" A reviewing judge can also think, "I wouldn't have come to that conclusion, but I can see how someone else might."

The matter of different standards for review is often better expressed in terms of degree, not kind. To what extent does the reviewing judge give the other decision maker leeway to come to a decision that the judge, on his own, would likely think wrong? A judge who grants that other decision maker at least some leeway in respect to a decision has adopted an *attitude of deference.*

Many administrative law questions—particularly those that define the relation between judges and administrators—can be put in terms of deference: How much deference should the reviewing court grant? For example, should it give the agency the benefit of *any* doubt, thereby coming close to presuming the correctness of the agency's decision? Should it instead review the agency's decision from scratch, giving the agency little or no benefit of any doubt? Administrative lawyers would describe the first attitude as one of strong *deference* to the agency, the second as one of no deference at all. Should a court give an agency deference? When should it do so? How much deference should it give?[9] These are key questions defining relationships between the courts and much of the executive branch.

During the New Deal many administrative law experts supported greater deference. They believed that agency administrators used expertise to determine "scientifically" such matters as the proper level of railroad rates or when an agency should suppress competition on the ground it was "destructive." At the same time, they believed that courts, often hostile to regulation, would prove too willing to substitute their own views for those of the administrators. Today, however, the public has less confidence in agency expertise. Political appointees, often not experts, are normally responsible for managing agencies and determining policy. And policy often reflects political, not simply "scientific," considerations. Agency decisions will also occasionally reflect "tunnel vision," an agency's supreme confidence in the importance of its own mission to the point where it leaves common sense aside. At the same time, courts no longer seem particularly hostile to regulation as a matter of principle. Hence, the public now relies more heavily on courts to ensure the fairness and rationality of agency decisions.

Expertise is still relevant, however, to the question of how much deference to give—although "comparative expertise" is a better term. Courts will exercise relatively more control over issues within *their* expertise while according agencies relatively more leeway (but not unqualified deference) as to issues within theirs. How the Court has applied these principles to two types of agency decisions—those relating to policy and to the interpretation of statutes—is the question to which I now turn.

Reviewing Agency Decisions of Policy

Consider more specifically how comparative expertise helps determine deference in respect to agency policy decisions. In reviewing such a decision—for instance, about what standards to impose on tire manufacturers in order to ensure automobile tire safety—a court often must answer a legal question: Is the agency's tire safety decision "arbitrary, capricious, an abuse of discretion"? A realistic appraisal of comparative expertise would start with an understanding of the kinds of problems facing the agency and how agencies would typically go about solving such problems.[10]

An agency staff formulating rules for automobile tire safety might begin with little expert knowledge. Nonetheless, it has time to learn and will likely research the subject matter for months, perhaps longer. The staff can consult with outside experts, learning from those experts even where they have competing interests. It can ask for public comments on its initial efforts and revise those efforts accordingly. It can seek information and reactions from colleagues at other agencies. In a word, it can develop subject-matter expertise.

At the same time, the agency staff must make technical decisions and write technical standards based on what they have learned. To do so, they must decide such technical issues as whether to employ cost-benefit analyses or whether to base standards on product design or product performance. And to be effective, they may also have to take account of the views of those who favor or oppose their work, perhaps writing standards that reflect political compromise.

By way of contrast, consider the judge's expertise in such matters.

Judges have little time to spend on any one case, such as a case in which a party contests the reasonableness of the agency's tire safety regulations. They deal with a record that rarely reflects all that the agency or its staff had to consider. They cannot look for information beyond that record. They must respond to the arguments of the lawyers. They do not necessarily have much political experience.

It is not surprising, then, that courts, recognizing the institutional differences, find agency policy decisions "arbitrary, capricious, an abuse of discretion" only in rare and clear cases. Courts have struck down, for example, a National Labor Relations Board election rule that allowed officials to buy drinks for the voters on Election Day—a policy that reflected considerations beyond the area of the labor board's special expertise. But ordinarily, courts, while insisting on proper procedures, will allow agencies considerable leeway. Courts very much defer to agencies when they review agency determinations of policy.[11]

Reviewing Agency Interpretation of Statutes

A difficult and important problem involving judicial attitude arises when a court reviews an agency decision interpreting a statute. Should a court ever defer to an agency's decision about the meaning or scope of statutory language? Or should a court always decide what a statute means uninfluenced by the agency's interpretation? It may seem surprising that courts sometimes take the former approach.

Why would courts ever defer to an agency's interpretation of a statute? Statutory interpretation is a basic judicial job that courts perform day in and day out using a well-developed set of tools. If ever courts have comparatively more expertise, isn't this the place? But let's imagine that Congress writes a statute that specifically grants to an agency leeway to fill in the blank. Suppose, for example, Congress writes a labor statute that uses the term "employee" and adds "the labor board shall have the power to determine in accordance with the objectives of this statute what kinds of employees fall within this term." In that case, Congress has given to the agency the power to write a regulation that takes effect as a law. If a court is to maintain a workable relationship with Congress, it must respect *that* decision. Now suppose that Congress does the same thing implicitly. That is, it delegates to the agency the power to define "employee," but not by *explicitly* delegating this power in the statute. A court should similarly respect Congress's implicit decision.[12]

Consider the vast number of statutory provisions that Congress writes to handle the business of government. Many of these provisions concern matters of detail, some quite technical, that are important for the operation of the program. Agency officials are likely to understand these details, but courts may not. Indeed, Congress may have delegated power to the agency in the first place because it, too, lacks this expertise. If so, the court will likely defer to a reasonable agency interpretation of the statutory provision.[13]

But how does a court know whether Congress intended the court to defer to a reasonable agency interpretation of a statute? Congress is normally silent on the subject, delegating interpretive power to the agency implicitly if at all. Furthermore, Congress could not have taken from the courts all their ordinary power to interpret statutes. Nor would Congress likely have intended to give the agencies free rein to interpret statutes in ways that, for example, diminish the limits on their delegated powers. Hence the problem: When should courts, recognizing an agency's comparative expertise, defer, or not defer, to the agency's interpretation of the statute?

The question is important. It embodies a modern democratic dilemma. No one doubts that the conditions of modern life require Congress to grant agency officials broad authority to decide many questions that affect our daily lives—for example, whether gasoline can contain lead, whether power plants must eliminate sulfur dioxide, whether garbage must be recycled, whether telemarketers can interrupt families during dinner, whether shippers must pay higher charges to railroads, or whether interest rate costs must be fully disclosed. But *how much* authority should a legislature delegate?

In determining how much authority Congress did delegate in a particular statute, a court must balance two countervailing concerns. On the one hand, the court must not recognize more agency authority than Congress intended, because doing so would unnecessarily limit the citizens' ballot box control over government actions that importantly affect their lives. On the other hand, the court must not recognize less authority than Congress intended, because doing so would prevent citizens from securing basic objectives that they cast their votes to achieve, say a cleaner environment or greater consumer protection. The public cannot achieve its military objectives if Congress is required to enact a statute that tells the army in detail how to take a particular hill—nor is Congress likely to write such a statute. Statutes that tell administrators precisely which pollutants to regulate, and where and how to regulate them, can prove similarly counterproductive. The legislator who tries to become a super-detailed air pollution regulator can easily end up with dirtier air.

The Court considered the deference question in a well-known case, *Chevron v. National Resources Defense Council.* The case involved an environmental statute that said the Environmental Protection Agency (EPA) must regulate "new or modified stationary *sources*" of pollution in regions of the country that had not yet met the statute's clean air goals. The EPA had developed a system of regulation that in effect treated each machine that emitted a pollutant as a separate "source" that must meet a specified standard. The EPA then changed its system so that it no longer treated each machine as a separate source. Instead, hoping to achieve greater efficiency, the EPA placed an imaginary "bubble" over a factory and treated all the emissions within the bubble as if they came from a single source. This meant a company could keep some dirty machines in operation as long as it offset the resulting emissions by using cleaner machines elsewhere. The question was whether the EPA could apply the statutory word "source" to include all the machines within the bubble taken together, and the Court held that it could do so.[14]

In this case the Court set forth a general rule describing when courts should defer to an agency's interpretation of a statute. It said that if the answer to the statutory question is "clear," a court should not defer to the agency's interpretation of the statute; rather, it should provide the answer irrespective of what the agency says. But if the answer is not clear—where, for example, the statute itself is "silent or ambiguous"—then courts should assume that Congress intended to *delegate to the agency* the power to interpret the statute, and they should defer to (and uphold) a "reasonable interpretation made by the administrator of an agency."[15]

The deference rule has not completely resolved the problem, however. Taken literally, it would give agencies authority to resolve virtually all statutory ambiguities. The Court has not permitted this result, because the deference question arises in respect to so many different programs involving so many different statutory provisions, potentially applicable to so many different kinds of circumstance, raising so many different administrative problems, that a single formula about deference cannot work every time a statute is ambiguous. Thus, the Court has treated *Chevron*'s rule not as a universally applicable formula but as a guiding rule of thumb. When there are good reasons to think Congress would not have wanted the Court to defer to an agency interpretation, the Court has not done so.

In 2007, for example, the Court considered a critically important environmental question. Does the Clean Air Act give the EPA the authority to regulate greenhouse gases, such as carbon dioxide? The statute said that the EPA should regulate "any air pollutant" that "endanger[s] public health or welfare." The statute defines "air pollutant" as including "any air pollution agent . . . including any physical, chemical . . . substance . . . emitted into . . . the ambient air." The EPA had interpreted the statutory words "air pollutant" as excluding greenhouse gases, but the Court by a narrow majority reversed that determination. In holding that the statute did cover greenhouse gases, the Court did not defer to the agency's own interpretation of the statute. Even though the statutory word "any" (in the phrase "any air pollution agent") created potential ambiguity, the Court thought that Congress would not have intended to delegate to the agency the legal power to interpret the statute to exclude gases that were major contributors to global warming. The decision is also consistent with the view that Congress would not have wanted to grant the agency the power to decide by itself such an important general policy question.[16]

In another, less important case the Court made clear that *Chevron* does not set forth an absolute deference rule. A statute authorizes the U.S. Customs Service to "fix" according to Treasury Department regulations the "final classification and rate of duty applicable" to imported merchandise. A customs service officer, applying a Treasury Department regulation, classified three-ring binder "day planners" among "diaries," placing them in a high-duty category rather than among "other" items in a low-duty category. In deciding this case, the Court held that the reviewing court, the U.S. Court of International Trade, should *not* defer to a customs officer's interpretation of the relevant regulations. The Court was convinced that Congress would not have intended that deference because of the large number of customs officers, the large number of such rulings, the speed and informality with which they were made, and the presence of a specialized reviewing court.[17]

What explains these decisions? Why does the Court sometimes defer to an agency's interpretation of a statute and sometimes not? Why does *Chevron* not always work as an explanation? The answer begins with the democratic dilemma mentioned earlier. To defer to an agency's view is to give the agency power to say what the law means. In principle, Congress, elected by the people, should decide how much power the agency should have. But what are courts to do when Congress does not say? As in all statutory matters, the answer will depend on the statute's purposes and context, and particularly on matters of comparative expertise.

It is more reasonable to believe that Congress (had it considered the matter) would have wanted the reviewing court to defer to the agency's views if an agency has special expertise regarding the legal question, if the question concerns detailed matters of the agency's program or its administration, if the legal question has little general importance, if the agency has considered the matter with greater care, and if the statute's language is ambiguous.

Congress (had it considered the matter) is more likely to have thought that the reviewing court possessed the relevant expertise (at least comparatively speaking) and did not intend deference to agency views, however, when the agency does not fully consider the question, the question involves important general matters of policy, or an answer is likely to clarify, illuminate, or stabilize a broad area of law. In both sets of circumstances, looking at the statutory purposes and context and the comparative expertise of the agency and the Court produces a decision that facilitates, rather than impedes, the working of the statute in the real world.

In the EPA case the breadth and importance of the legal question at issue seemed more significant than the fact of greater EPA technical expertise in respect to carbon dioxide. The Court could reasonably think that the relevant expertise needed to answer the question was primarily legal, not administrative, and that the agency ruling misinterpreted Congress's intent. The Court was (relatively) better positioned to consider the purposes of the statute and the related consequences of excluding or including greenhouse gases.

In the U.S. Customs Service case, the Court noted that the service's expertise argued in favor of deference. But the officers' informal ruling letters were "churned out at a rate of 10,000 a year at [the] agency's 46 scattered offices," which suggests those letters were done quickly without too much concern for their consistency with statutes, regulations, or one another. Moreover, the reviewing court, the U.S. Court of International Trade, not just the customs officers, had expertise in these matters. Hence, the Court concluded that Congress could not have intended deference.[18]

THE COURT, INTERPRETING congressional silence, has worked out a practical system of deference. Using comparative expertise as a touchstone, courts by and large defer where, comparatively speaking, agencies are likely better able to solve the problem. They do not defer where, comparatively speaking, courts are likely better able to solve the problem. This approach is consistent with the Constitution's democratic aims. It recognizes that decisions about how much authority to delegate to an agency, like other statutory matters, rest ultimately in the hands of Congress. And Congress is responsible to voters. But importantly, those voters may be unaware of the details and may well only know whether Congress's statutes are "working out well."

The approach, complex though it is, therefore creates a workable partnership between the courts and Congress. Furthermore, it respects the role of agencies in performing the functions of government. By taking account of comparative expertise, the Court allows agencies to handle matters within their competence while subjecting them to appropriate constraints. Congress likely intends this arrangement for the simple reason that it can make statutes work better. It helps the tripartite system work well in practice. And that in turn helps to maintain public acceptance of the Court's decisions.

Chapter Ten

The States and Federalism: Decentralization and Subsidiarity

THIS CHAPTER CONCERNS ways of maintaining a strong working relationship between the Court and the states. This relationship embodies the constitutional idea of federalism, an idea that concerns the *level* of government at which Americans should try to solve common problems. The question of "proper level" often turns on empirical matters. And Justice Brandeis, dissenting in *New State Ice Co. v. Liebmann,* invoked four famous propositions about the relations of courts and legislatures in respect to empirical matters. First, when government seeks a solution to an economic or social problem, empirical matters are often highly relevant. Second, comparatively speaking, judges are not well equipped to find remedies for economic or social problems. Third, legislatures, comparatively speaking, are far better suited to investigating, to uncovering facts, to understanding their relevance, and to finding solutions to related economic and social problems. Fourth, the Constitution embodies a democratic preference for solutions legislated by those whom the people elect. These propositions are often relevant when federalism is at issue.[1]

With these "truths" in mind, the Court has tried to apply principles of federalism while relying on those with greater factual knowledge or experience to help it determine where the law assigns responsibility for a particular problem.

Underlying Ideas

Constitutional federalism embodies a historical idea about the legitimacy of federal governmental power. Madison expressed this idea when he described the Constitution as a "charter[] . . . of power . . . granted by liberty," not a "charter[] of liberty . . . granted by power." His point is that in America, "We the People" are the source of the legitimate exercise of federal power. We the people delegate to the central government the power that it has. This means that any power that the Constitution does not delegate must be reserved for a free people, who Madison thought would not delegate to a central government the power to deprive them of their freedom.[2] In contrast, Madison suggests, Europeans have often located the source of legitimate power in a king. In such a system, power flows from the center. And power not delegated elsewhere, say to the people, remains at the center. Thus, even if a liberal king grants liberties to the people, those liberties constitute a *grant* of freedom by someone with power, namely, the king, to those otherwise without it.[3]

The difference between these two approaches is stark. In the one case, the legitimate power of government originates at the periphery, and in the other case, at the center. As the framers recognized, the former, "local" approach has several advantages. For one thing, constitutional federalism helps democracy itself work better. By assuring state and local officials broader decision-making power, it simultaneously places greater power in the hands of those who elect those officials. That smaller number of people can better understand the nature of local problems. They can more easily communicate with those who stand for office and can more accurately evaluate the work of their elected officials. Moreover, by placing power in local communities, federalism reflects the democratic ideal and encourages citizens to participate in government, particularly in local government, where they can more easily make a difference.

In addition, constitutional federalism is practical. Those whom a problem affects more directly are more often likely to understand it and find ways to resolve it. Local firefighters, police departments, health officials, and those whom they serve are more likely to understand local conditions, including community needs and resources. In essence, they possess comparative expertise. At the same time, a national bureaucracy, subject to the control of national officials and a national electorate, is needed to deal with issues that are national in scope such as those associated with foreign affairs, war, interstate commerce, and much of the environment. Ideally, constitutional federalism matches the issues with government units that will best handle them.

Constitutional federalism reflects a further practical idea—the benefits of experimentation. In the mid-1930s depression, Justice Brandeis, in his *New State Ice* dissent, succinctly expressed this idea: "It is one of the happy incidents of the federal system that a single courageous state may, if its citizens choose, serve as a laboratory; and try novel social and economic experiments without risk to the rest of the country." The value of not adopting a solution, even to a national problem, too quickly; of trying different approaches; and of trying out different ideas before committing the nation to one approach—all of these reasons call for ensuring that states have constitutional leeway to experiment.[4]

Subsidiarity

These several different ideas underlie a concept that modern European courts have found useful in a roughly comparable context, namely, the concept of *subsidiarity.* This concept originated in late-medieval religious thought, yet it provides one general method for applying federalism in this more democratic age. Subsidiarity insists that governmental power to deal with a particular kind of problem should rest in the hands of the smallest unit of government capable of dealing successfully with that kind of problem. One begins by assuming that power to solve a problem should remain at the local level. One then asks whether it is necessary to abandon this assumption in order to resolve the problem. One can continue to ask this question, level by level. And one should answer it by climbing no higher up the governmental unit ladder than necessary to deal effectively with the problem.[5]

The European Union (EU) has written this principle into its treaties. The treaties leave in the hands of the member states the authority to deal with issues that can be handled better at that more decentralized level. These issues include consumer protection, education, labor relations, taxation, and public health, as well as numerous matters of local government. At the same time, the treaties create binding legal rules at the central EU level for managing multination matters, particularly those that affect trade among the member states. The treaties also permit the EU to write laws concerning, for example, common currency, finance, worker migration, the environment, and other matters better handled at the EU inter-nation level.[6]

The European Court of Justice sometimes resolves legal questions about the meaning of the European treaties. And it may apply the concept of subsidiarity when it does so. For example, the court considered whether Italy, a member state, could ban the sale of dry pasta not made exclusively from *grano duro*, a type of wheat grown in southern Italy. The court held that the treaties forbid Italy's restrictions on the kinds of pasta that could be sold on the ground that they unreasonably inhibited the sale in Italy of imported pasta. The court nonetheless permitted Italy to protect its own consumers by insisting that all pasta indicate on the package whether the product is made from *grano duro*.[7]

As used today and considered in general terms, the principle of subsidiarity incorporates an approach that can help guide American, as well as European, policy makers. The approach sees power as flowing from "below," it finds democratic advantages in localism, and it sees practical value in local control and local experimentation. So viewed, the concept incorporates the historical, democratic, and practical ideas that underlie American constitutional federalism. The underlying thought, like that of the Constitution itself, is that the national government should resolve national problems while state and local governments should retain the power to deal with more local problems, with which they are more likely to deal effectively.

Recognition of the importance of these ideas, which make up federalism, and the empirical nature of the determinations needed to apply them can help the Court maintain an effective working relationship with the states as well as with the federal government. Discussion of several related areas of law will illustrate the interplay between basic federalism principles and empirical judgments.

Limiting Federal Legislative Authority

My first federalism subject concerns Congress's power to legislate. The Constitution sets forth a specific list of legislative powers that it delegates to Congress. It uses broad language to describe the items on that list, for example, by granting Congress the power to "regulate Commerce with foreign Nations, and among the several States." It adds further that Congress may "make all Laws which shall be necessary and proper for carrying into Execution" those powers. The Court must sometimes try to interpret these provisions—to determine their limits and their reach. In doing so, the Court must apply principles of federalism. But, as Brandeis noted, the Court cannot easily make or evaluate the relevant facts. The result is that in this set of cases, practical principles of federalism counsel the Court to turn over the lion's share of interpretive responsibility to Congress itself.[8]

A 1995 case, for example, required the Court to decide whether the Constitution gave Congress the authority to enact a statute forbidding the possession of a gun near a local school. The Court held that statute did not fall within the scope of the legislative authority that the commerce clause delegated to Congress. Rather, it represented a congressional effort to usurp the legislative powers that the Constitution reserved for the states. The case was difficult to decide largely because of the factual interconnections that underlay the Court's judgment, as they often do where legal questions involving federalism are at issue.[9]

For one thing, today's world requires governments to enact laws affecting matters that often have strong local connections as well as potential multistate connections. Chemical substances spewed into the air in one city can, through wind and rain, affect air and water in cities thousands of miles away. One state's efforts to control auto exhaust can, by affecting the technological makeup of automobiles, affect the price, quality, production, and ultimately the use of cars throughout the nation. Growing wheat, or growing marijuana, at home for personal use can, if the practice is widespread, affect the price and the consumption of the product in other states.[10]

For another thing, there is rarely an easy answer to the question of what level of government should be primarily responsible for helping to resolve the problems that potentially call for legislation. Which unit of government should be responsible for providing the education that will enable the future workers, mobile Americans, who may live in many states during their lifetimes, to compete effectively in a world where commerce is international? Where should responsibility lie for a worker's health care? When should we separate out for local resolution one aspect, for example, robberies, of a broader problem, in this case crime?

These questions show that often it is reasonable to subdivide problems, treating some aspects of a problem as local and others as national. But whether, when, and how governments should do so depends on policy makers' views about the nature of the particular problem. It is one thing in general to favor decision making at a more local level. It is quite another to estimate the comparative effectiveness of local versus national authority in a factually interconnected world. Facts help determine the answers. Legislators are better able than courts to gather empirical information, to make fact-based predictions, and to exercise informed policy judgment. Hence the Court should often hesitate before substituting its own judgment for that of Congress.

At the same time, if the Court should so hesitate, this does *not* leave the states without protection. Members of Congress themselves, while federal officeholders, are nonetheless state officials. State and local voters elect them all. Thus members of Congress must, and they do, try to further the interests of those state and local voters. They must, and they do, remain aware of state and local issues. They must, and they do, frequently consult governors, state legislators, mayors, city council members, school board officials, chambers of commerce, union locals, and, of course, the voters themselves. The fact that federal legislators must maintain such strong local ties means that, insofar as the public favors local control and insofar as it is suspicious of authority exercised from a distant city (whether America's capital, Washington, or the EU's capital, Brussels), locally elected legislators will take local views into account.

Moreover, the vast bulk of American law—including all family law, most criminal law, almost all tort law, almost all property law, most business law, most education law, most health law, most welfare law, even much environmental law—is state law, not federal law. When Congress does legislate nationally, imposing burdens or obligations on the states, it often does so by granting federal money to states or localities, perhaps simultaneously imposing federal standards. Congress also has created joint state-federal cooperative regulatory systems, such as the Clean Water Act. Thus, the elected members of Congress, in making judgments about where problems are better resolved, have left the vast bulk of American law for the states to create, to apply, and to develop. They have created federal legal regimes foreseeing state-federal cooperation. And they have thereby helped to protect the states from federal efforts to accrue power at their expense.

Now let us return to our 1995 guns-in-schools case. The question was whether the Constitution's commerce clause grants Congress the authority to enact a statute forbidding the possession of a gun near a local school. In deciding the case, the Court took as given certain long-held underlying legal principles. The commerce clause, for example, grants Congress the power to regulate items that *move in* interstate commerce and activities that *affect* interstate commerce. Moreover, when the Court determines whether an activity, say growing wheat for home consumption, has the required interstate *effect,* it must assume that Congress has the power to act in light of the total effect by *aggregating* instances of similar activity. Even though one farmer's home-grown wheat supply would not affect the interstate price, an aggregation of *all* wheat that *all* farmers grow at home might well do so. Between 1938 and 1990, the Court, applying these and similar legal principles, consistently upheld federal statutes on the ground that the underlying activities significantly affected interstate commerce.[11]

The Court, however, struck down the federal statute making criminal the possession of a gun near a school. The Court said that education and crime were primarily local matters, that gun-related violence would primarily affect local communities, and that the criminal laws of the states could adequately deal with the gun-possession problem.[12]

Although there is a certain logic to that position, it is not difficult to find potential interstate effects that could justify making possession of a gun near a school a federal crime. Possession of guns in schools means violence, and violence means poor education. Poor education means an unproductive, noncompetitive workforce. And that kind of workforce negatively affects not just one state but all states. School violence, of which guns are a part, arguably presents a national problem warranting a national solution.[13]

Thus, we have two sets of logical links, pointing in opposite legal directions. Which should control the outcome of the Court decision? The answer requires the judge to make a decision about the importance of each of the underlying connections. That judgment must be informed by fact, and legislators are more likely to find those facts and better able to determine their policy relevance. That is why courts, aware of Brandeis's four "truths," should defer strongly to Congress's judgment about such matters. And it is why a workable relation between state and federal governments depends in large part on courts granting Congress that deference.

In short, application of the subsidiarity principle to the legal problem of interpreting the Constitution's list of federal legislative powers requires the Court to consider matters that are primarily empirical and are often matters of degree. And the Court is not well suited institutionally to make those kinds of determinations. Consequently, and not surprisingly, the Court's decision in the gun case did not stop Congress from reenacting a virtually identical statute. This time the statute applied its strictures only to guns that had *moved in,* not just *affected,* interstate commerce. And virtually every gun satisfies that condition.[14]

The Court, then, has found it difficult to discover a principled way to interpret the Constitution's list of legislative powers, including the commerce clause, so as to be able to use principles of federalism or subsidiarity to limit those powers. This does not reflect any failing on the part of the principles or of the Court. Rather, given the underlying fact-based nature of the problem, it reflects today's world as it is.

Protecting the National Market

My second federalism subject concerns legislative action that threatens to violate federalism principles. Here the Court can, and does, take a more active role in resolving the resulting federalism issue.

The issue arises from the following circumstances: The Constitution seeks to grant the federal government the authority to handle national issues. High on the list of such issues is maintaining a national market. The commerce clause specifically grants Congress the power to regulate interstate and international markets.[15]

Furthermore, the Court has long interpreted the commerce clause as furthering that basic purpose by forbidding states to interfere with the maintenance of a national market, even in the absence of a specific congressional law. Applying what it calls the "dormant commerce clause," the Court strikes down as unconstitutional any state law that significantly interferes with the operation of national or international markets.[16]

This principle is clear. But, again, the need for factual information and technical judgment makes it difficult for courts to implement the principle in practice. Examples illustrate the difficulty. Suppose a state enacts a law that prohibits bringing into the state peaches grown with the use of certain pesticides. Or, a state law insists upon the use of special steel for elevator cables. Or, a state law prevents interstate trucks from transporting dynamite during daylight hours. Are these state laws designed expressly to protect local producers from out-of-state competition? If so, they violate the dormant commerce clause. They interfere with the national market in order to protect local business, which is the very evil the clause seeks to prohibit. But suppose these state laws are designed primarily to protect citizens from dangerous pesticides, from faulty elevators, or from the risks of an explosion. If so, their objectives might well justify the negative impact on interstate trade.[17]

How are courts to determine whether these laws protect consumers from serious harm or have a more sinister intent? Like the earlier questions asking whether a congressional law falls outside the Constitution's delegation to Congress, this question calls for investigation of the factual circumstances. The answer likely turns on general facts and an understanding of how the relevant markets work. It likely turns on the exercise of judgment in light of that technical knowledge.

Unlike the first federalism subject (that of Congress's power to legislate), the answer to this commerce clause question cannot be found by permitting courts to accept virtually any reasonable solution that a legislature adopts. This is because a *state* legislature is more likely influenced by the very interests the national commerce clause seeks protection against, namely, the parochial state interests that threaten a national marketplace. When discussing the first subject, we saw how the fact that a state's voters elect that state's national senators means that their elected senators will pay attention to state interests when they vote for federal legislation. But here, the converse fact that a state's governor, say California's governor, is *not* elected by another state's voters, say Florida's voters, means that California's governor has little reason to pay attention to Florida's interests when deciding whether to sign a law that effectively bans the sale of Florida avocados in California.

Thus, when the Court has faced a problem of a state law that threatens the national market, it has not simply deferred to state legislatures. Rather, it has applied disinterested judicial decision making while trying to overcome its major institutional disadvantage, that of finding general legislative facts. And it has done so not by deferring to a legislature's judgment but by making clear that whatever the Court's own decision, the *federal* legislative body, Congress, remains free to overturn that decision. If, for example, the Court finds that a state law prohibiting daylight transportation of dynamite violates the dormant commerce clause by interfering with interstate commerce, Congress, pursuant to its own power to regulate interstate commerce, can authorize the state to reenact that very law.

Furthermore, Congress can delegate its own power to have the last word to an administrative agency. Thus it can give the federal Department of Transportation the power to decide whether a state's prohibition of daytime dynamite transport significantly interferes with the national market. The Department of Transportation can authorize the state to maintain its law. And, if a court were to review that Transportation Department decision, it would do so only in the way it would review any other agency decision, giving deference to the agency and setting aside the agency's determination only if unreasonable.

The upshot is a tripartite institutional arrangement—Court, Congress, and agency working together in an empirically based area of law to determine whether and when a state has violated a basic constitutional principle. The arrangement permits the Court to work cooperatively with both legislative and executive branches of government, taking advantage of their expertise in giving concrete meaning to federalism's subsidiarity principles.

Protecting State and Local Authority

The third federalism subject returns to the problem of the national legislature, namely, Congress, seeking to invade state authority. It focuses this time on the basic unlisted powers that the Tenth Amendment "reserve[s] to the States respectively, or to the people," and not on the list of legislative powers that the Constitution grants to Congress. Here the Court can often best protect the federalism principles, not by striking down federal laws as contrary to the Tenth Amendment or by trying to define the specific nature of the reserved powers to which it refers, but by keeping the basic federalism (or subsidiarity) principles in mind, using them as *factors* that help guide the Court to a better result in specific cases involving statutes and other parts of the Constitution.

Consider a widespread legal problem, preemption. When Congress enacts a federal statute, say regulating interstate trucking equipment, it has the legal power to invalidate related state laws. It might invalidate all the state laws that cover the same general subject matter, for example, all those regulating interstate trucking equipment. It might invalidate state laws that directly conflict with the federal statute, for example, those that create an opposite headlight rule for interstate trucks. It might invalidate state laws that stand as significant obstacles to the federal statute's accomplishing its basic objectives, for example, those that set rules requiring truckers to put various kinds of opaque rain screens just above the headlights. In any actual statute, however,

Congress may not say precisely what it has done, so courts may have to decide whether the federal statute implicitly preempts, hence invalidates, a particular state law.

For example, Congress enacts a statute delegating to a federal agency, the Food and Drug Administration (FDA), the authority to require specific forms of labeling to ensure drug safety. The FDA then determines that drug manufacturers should list five different risks on a drug label. Can a state require the firm to add a sixth risk? Can it authorize a jury in a state court tort suit to find a manufacturer liable for failing to warn about that sixth risk and to assess large damages?[18]

The federal statute itself does not say whether it means the agency's requirements to act only as a floor, thus permitting the state to add further requirements, or also as a ceiling, such that the state cannot add further requirements. Nor does the purpose of the statute—increased safety—tell a court very much. Adding words on the label to avoid tort liability will sometimes mean a safer product (when the words properly identify a further risk) and sometimes a riskier product (when the requirement leads drugmakers to modify an otherwise adequate drug label, confusing consumers and thereby making all labels less effective).

Can the basic federalism or subsidiarity principles help? They tell us to leave matters at the local level unless federal regulation is needed. But once again we need considerable factual and technical knowledge about how drug regulation works before we can know whether, on balance, state tort suits will help or harm the federal statute's efforts to put pharmaceutical drugs in the hands of those who need them without undue risk.

At this point we might refer back to the discussion of the dormant commerce clause to consider again the cooperative institutional effort that works well in that context. Will it work well here? The issue before the Court involves Congress's delegation of authority to a federal agency. In this example the statute is silent about preemption. There are strong arguments both for and against permitting local decision making (that is, state tort suits) to supplement federal decision making (that is, the FDA's labeling requirements). And the application of a federalism principle (such as subsidiarity) helps us only if we can obtain considerable factual information and experience (about how the drug and related federal regulation work in practice).

Who has that factual information and experience? An agency, not a court. Thus, as in the dormant commerce clause area, the Court might turn to the agency for help. The agency has or can obtain and evaluate the information; the agency understands the statutory scheme; and the agency, when deciding policy matters, must normally solicit and consider the views of all interested parties, including the states. Why not, then, let the agency make the relevant preemption decision? If the agency decides that its rules preempt state tort suits, then the Court would defer to that agency decision. If the agency says nothing, the Court could assume that the FDA's rules are not intended to, and do not, preempt state law.

This example shows how the Court might interpret ordinary statutes in light of basic federalism principles. The Court will ascertain Congress's basic statutory purpose. In doing so, it might look particularly hard to find ways, consistent with that basic purpose, for states to play a role, particularly in areas where states have special experience. The Court might also turn to, and rely upon, a specialized agency for obtaining and evaluating relevant empirical information while deferring to agency decisions that rest on that agency's expertise. In a word, the Court can search for partnerships among government institutions, including Congress, agency, and Court, in an effort to make more informed, more effective decisions, where each can make use of the competences of the others.

THE COURT CAN also help protect the states in several ways when it interprets seemingly unrelated provisions of the Constitution. *New State Ice,* mentioned earlier, provides a good example. In 1925, Oklahoma enacted a law that regulated the business of selling ice, which was used to cool refrigerators. At that time Supreme Court precedent said that the Constitution's prohibition against taking "property" without "due process of law" only permitted this kind of regulation if the business was special in some way—in particular if it was "affected with a public interest." The Liebmanns, who wanted to enter the ice business, argued that it was not special and ice was just like meat, potatoes, or other commodities, only colder. The Liebmanns were likely right about the relation of ice to other commodities. But even so, Justice Brandeis (joined by just one other dissenter) voted to uphold the law. He interpreted and applied a constitutional provision, namely, the due process clause, which on its face says nothing of federalism, in light of one of federalism's basic objectives, namely, allowing the states to act as laboratories engaged in economic experiment.[19]

A more recent example shows how the Court can implement federalism by keeping that objective in mind when it considers other constitutional provisions. The Court in 2007 faced the question whether the Constitution's equal protection clause forbade two cities, Seattle and Louisville, to consider their students' racial heritage in developing plans that further racial diversity in primary and secondary public schools.[20]

Until the *Brown* decision, Louisville had had a totally segregated school system, after which it desegregated under the supervision of a federal court. When the federal court finally ended its direct supervision of the Louisville schools (many years later), the overall school population was about 30 percent black and 70 percent white. The school district then drew boundaries, arranged student transfers, and administered other parts of a complex plan all designed to make certain that every school had a racially diverse student body. No school was to have fewer than 15 percent or more than 50 percent black students.[21]

In Seattle, the school board had tried voluntarily to integrate its racially divided school system, only to discover that many white families were moving to the suburbs, leaving many city schools without racially diverse populations. Seattle developed a complex plan designed to attract white suburban students back to city schools. The plan ensured each student the freedom to choose a high school. But when that freedom meant a particular school was oversubscribed, the plan provided a race-based tiebreaker. If the school's minority or majority race enrollment fell outside a 30 percent range centered on the overall minority/majority population ratio within the district, then a student might have to delay entering for a year. This was also the case if a student's immediate entry would make the school less diverse than the range permitted.[22]

Four members of the Court found both the Seattle and the

Louisville plans unconstitutional, reasoning that the use of virtually any race-based criteria violated the equal protection clause. A fifth member joined them on somewhat less restrictive grounds. The remaining four members of the Court (I was one of them) disagreed strongly. We argued that the Fourteenth Amendment applies more strictly when a race-based distinction thwarts its basic purpose—when it puts racial minorities at a disadvantage—than when a race-based distinction seeks to further that basic purpose by, for example, seeking increased racial diversity. We pointed to precedent that we believed strongly supported the minimal use of racial criteria where needed to achieve integration. We added that a history of segregation, followed by efforts to achieve integration in the two cities, supported use of the race-based criteria before the Court. And we said that use of those criteria furthered *Brown*'s practical antisegregation objectives.[23]

The results were hotly disputed, for each side felt strongly that the other side had misunderstood or misapplied precedent, had misunderstood or misapplied the Constitution's basic objective, or had miscalculated the likely effects of their positions on the nation's ability to end racial discrimination. I shall not repeat the major arguments, for only one of them is directly relevant to the subject matter here, namely, federalism.

This particular argument looked in part to principles of federalism as supporting the dissenters' views. The dissenters pointed out that the Court has long based its "public school decisions" on the view that "the Constitution grants local school districts a significant degree of leeway where the inclusive use of race-conscious criteria is at issue." It thereby takes account of the importance of local communities, understanding their own needs, resources, histories, and conditions, to find their own locally oriented solutions to a lack of diversity. In fact, *Brown II* had said that judges should take account of such factors, even though doing so might hinder integration. To the dissenters it was clear that the Court should address these factors—reflecting principles of federalism—when local communities seek to *achieve Brown*'s basic goals.[24]

The dissenters' federalism point was the following. No one can be certain how best to achieve the Constitution's goal: "how best to stop harmful discrimination; how best to create a society that includes all Americans; how best to overcome our serious problems of increasing *de facto* segregation, troubled inner city schooling, and poverty correlated with race." The "Constitution creates a democratic political system through which the people themselves must together find answers." And respect for local institutions is one part of that system. The Court should be aware of that fact (as it was in *Brown*) even when it interprets a part of the Constitution that does not explicitly refer to federalism, here the equal protection clause. In this way principles of federalism, by informing an interpretation of many separate provisions of the Constitution, added weight to the dissenters' interpretation of the equal protection clause.[25]

This chapter illustrates how the Court (aware of Brandeis's four "truths") has applied principles of federalism or subsidiarity in different ways in different circumstances. When the Court seeks to determine whether Congress has reached beyond its delegated legislative powers, these principles may well lead the Court to defer more willingly to Congress. When the Court seeks to protect the national marketplace, the principles may lead the Court to count on Congress or an agency for continued dialogue. When the Court seeks to protect state authority, the principles may lead the Court to interpret statutes and seemingly unrelated constitutional provisions in ways that reflect federalism principles. Through these kinds of nuanced applications of subsidiarity, the Court's decisions can promote workable relationships with government officials, whether federal or state, while simultaneously drawing government solutions closer to the people. Thus the Court's decisions can have pragmatic as well as democratic value, which is a powerful combination for securing continued public acceptance.

Chapter Eleven

Other Federal Courts: Specialization

So far, I have explored ways in which the Supreme Court makes its decisions workable (and therefore acceptable) by respecting the roles of, and relationships with, other governmental institutions. Now, can it accomplish the same thing with other federal courts? Obviously, courts at different levels within the judicial system perform different tasks. By throwing this fact into its decision-making balance and giving it considerable weight, the Court can help maintain a judicial system that works well taken as a whole, a judicial system that resolves disputes fairly and expeditiously overall. To elaborate on this, I provide illustrations in which the Court's members disagreed about the importance of specialization, that is, about how much weight to give to a lower court's comparative advantages.

Specialization

By "specialization," I refer to the different judicial tasks that ordinary federal courts perform at different levels of the judicial system. Of those ordinary courts, trial courts are at the bottom, appeals courts in the middle, and the Supreme Court on top. This hierarchical organization reflects the fact that the "higher courts" have the last word in respect to the meaning of a text. But to consider hierarchy alone is to fail to consider the specialized roles of these different courts.

Numbers may be helpful. Federal trial courts are organized nationally into ninety-four geographic districts. The annual number of cases filed in all federal trial courts (not including bankruptcies) amounts to about 340,000 per year (less than 2 percent of the number filed in state courts) and constitutes the vast bulk of the work of the federal court system. Federal courts of appeals are organized into twelve geographic circuits throughout the nation plus the Court of Appeals for the Federal Circuit. Litigants who lose in a trial court normally have the right to file an appeal, and each year they file about sixty thousand appeals, which appellate courts consider on the merits. The Supreme Court receives about eight thousand requests for full consideration each year. The Court grants about 1 percent of the requests filed and thus decides about eighty cases annually.[1]

The courts at each of three different levels carry out different tasks. Trial courts—the front line—perform the great majority of all judicial work. They respond to a universal need present in every society, that for some method for resolving disputes among individuals. Trial judges consequently specialize by focusing on individual disputes. When the parties bring a dispute to court, the trial judge encourages the parties to settle it. If settlement fails, the trial judge manages the resulting litigation, including discovery procedures, thereby permitting each party to obtain information from the other. The judge supervises the presentation of evidence at trial and instructs the jury about the law. The jury (or, if there is no jury, the judge) will find the facts. In doing so, the judge or jury may have to make credibility judgments, that is, decide whom to believe when witnesses give conflicting testimony. And the judge ultimately determines whether a verdict for one or the other party is consistent with the law. In carrying out these tasks, the judge may well meet the parties face-to-face and will likely learn how the law will affect the parties and perhaps other interested individuals as well. At a minimum, the trial judge comes to understand the underlying circumstances of a particular dispute.

Then comes the job of the appellate judge. The losing party in the trial court can appeal, claiming that the trial judge made a mistake of law or found facts contrary to the evidence. When considering appeals, appellate judges have two different roles. First, they engage in "error correction." The appellant may argue that the trial judge mistakenly applied well-established law, say when the trial judge admitted or refused to admit certain testimony or allowed the jury to reach a factual conclusion that, in the appellant's view, the evidence did not support. To decide whether the appellant is right, appellate judges may have to review the record, examining the circumstances of an individual trial. They may have to look at the evidence presented to decide whether it warranted the instructions the trial judge gave or whether it provided adequate support for the factual conclusions the jury reached.

Second, appellate judges engage in textual interpretation. They examine a phrase in a statute or in the Constitution in order to decide what it means or how it applies.

A party who loses an appeal may ask the Supreme Court to conduct further review. As Appendix B explains, the Supreme Court engages almost exclusively in textual interpretation. The Court's role differs from that of federal appeals courts in that *constitutional* interpretation makes up a considerably larger portion of its interpretive diet.

Numerous legal rules (often originating in customary practice and now more often embodied in specific written rules or case law precedent) help to make the court system function more effectively by recognizing the specialized nature of the tasks in which different courts engage. Rules governing appellate court review, for example, recognize the trial court's fact-finding role by severely limiting an appellate court's consideration of factual matters. The trial jury or, if there is not a jury, the judge makes most factual determinations. Normally, a court of appeals may reverse a trial court's finding of fact only if the appellate court concludes that the jury made a finding no reasonable person could make or if the trial judge made a finding that is not simply wrong but *clearly* wrong. Appellate courts also recognize the trial judge's specialized role by granting broad leeway when reviewing a trial court decision related to case or trial management, such as a discovery ruling or a decision about what witnesses to allow and what they may be asked.[2]

The Supreme Court, working at an even greater distance from the legal front line, also follows rules and practices that increase its effectiveness by recognizing functional specialization. Those rules and practices tend to prevent the Court from engaging in case management or second-guessing related trial court decisions. They also leave to appellate courts the work for which those courts are better suited.

For example, the Court follows a special rule in respect to matters of fact. If two lower courts—say, both the trial court and the reviewing appellate court—reach the same factual conclusion, the Supreme Court will take that fact as established and refuse to examine the extent to which the evidence in the record supports the fact. The Court also will not normally review a factual determination made by an administrative agency, recognizing that appellate courts (which review most agency decision making) are better suited to undertake this task.[3]

These rules and practices reflect a practical need. The Supreme Court justices rarely delegate work to each other. Each listens to the others but also makes up his or her own mind after separately reviewing the underlying law and relevant facts. This practice often results in a better decision by bringing different points of view to bear on the same problem. In the context of fact-finding, however, this practice would be counterproductive. Nine members cannot easily comb lengthy records in order to make factual determinations. Hence fact-finding and record-based review of fact-finding are better delegated to lower courts.

The Supreme Court's practice of taking most cases primarily for the purpose of resolving conflicts among the lower courts also serves practical ends related to specialization. Lower-court judges are not more likely to commit errors than are Supreme Court justices. Rather, as Justice Robert H. Jackson pointed out years ago, the Supreme Court is not "final" because it is "infallible"; rather, it is "infallible" only because it is "final," that is, it has the last word. The Court is right by definition. Even if the Court does not provide a "better" decision, a single Supreme Court provides a single interpretation of the law. And national uniformity has obvious advantages.[4]

Moreover, Court review brings to bear the different perspectives of different justices. These differences are likely helpful when the Court decides a difficult case where lower courts have reached different conclusions. But they are not always helpful when the Court reviews law that is already uniform. Thus, the Court tends to reserve its time and effort for those cases where existing divisions among the lower courts make a single final Supreme Court decision necessary.

Examples

The following two examples illustrate the need for the Court to place considerable weight on specialization when it reviews lower-court fact-based or case-management decision making.

Horne: *Why Take the Case?*

Horne v. Flores helps illustrate the difficulties facing the Supreme Court when it undertakes a task more easily performed in a court of appeals, namely, reviewing a lengthy fact-specific record to determine whether the lower courts properly applied a set of complicated legal standards. *Horne* involved the application of a federal statute requiring states to take "appropriate action" to ensure that their school systems do not discriminate against students who do not speak English. As interpreted, the statute requires the state to have some system for teaching English to non-English-speaking students, to see that the program has reasonably adequate resources, and to see that program and resources together produce at least minimally sufficient results. In a word, the statute sets a minimal floor with respect to the existence and effectiveness of a state program.[5]

In 1992, a group of parents whose children spoke only Spanish brought a lawsuit in federal court in Arizona. The parents claimed that Arizona's English-teaching programs were not "appropriate" because they fell below the federally required floor. After months of proceedings and a lengthy trial, the trial judge held that the parents were right. Arizona did have a plan for programs to help non-English-speaking students, which cost approximately $600 per student. But Arizona provided only $150 per student in funding. Consequently, the court ordered the state to reconsider its programs and come up with funding appropriations that had at least a "reasonable relation" to its programs' needs.[6]

During the next several years, Arizona took steps to improve its system. The legislature provided additional funding, and the state enacted a new statute that it hoped would satisfy the court. In light of these efforts, the state asked the district court to cancel its order. New district court proceedings followed, then an appeal, a full evidentiary hearing in the district court, and another appeal. Eventually, the district court wrote an opinion that set forth numerous factual findings and held that the new state law and new programs reflected progress but remained inadequate. The court found the state had not yet complied with the original order and funding was still well below what the programs themselves considered necessary. State officials appealed. The court of appeals reviewed the evidentiary record, thousands of pages, and wrote a detailed, nearly forty-page opinion affirming the district court's decision. The state then successfully petitioned the Supreme Court to hear the case.[7]

Horne v. Flores raised questions about the application of agreed-upon statutory standards to a large number of circumstance-specific findings of fact. To what extent would the state's new approach to teaching English, called English immersion, likely produce better results at lower cost? To what extent would increased state budget funds likely reach those students who needed to learn English? To what extent had reorganization of the local school district helped? To what extent would a new federal law, the No Child Left Behind Act, which required states to set English-language-learning goals and report results, make a difference? To what extent should the district court, in all such matters, give leeway to the state's own efforts to answer these questions? To what extent should the need for a new budget appropriation—necessitating state legislative action—require the district court to set aside its earlier order so that it would avoid conflict between a federal court and an elected state legislature?

The difficulty the case posed for the Court lay in the fact that no one doubted the relevance of all these questions. The case did not raise a straightforward question about how to interpret a statute. Rather, it raised questions of degree, which were best determined in light of local facts and circumstances. The question before the Court was whether the district court had paid the right *degree* of attention to the state and to the legislature when it considered the matters I have just described.

To resolve these questions, the Court had to read the lengthy fact-based record and then make judgments on the basis of that record, rather as a court of appeals might do.

Ultimately, five members of the Court concluded that the district court had not given sufficient weight to the new federal No Child Left Behind Act. Nor had it given sufficient negative weight to the undesirable institutional aspects of a court's requiring a state legislature to appropriate new funds. The Court sent the case back to the district court so that it could consider the matter again, in light of the Court's concerns. Four dissenting members of the Court (of which I was one) concluded that the court of appeals was right in finding that the district court had treated all these matters appropriately.[8]

The case required the Court to do what an appeals court does best—review a lengthy record in order to decide whether a district court has properly applied the relevant legal standards. And what did the Supreme Court accomplish by conducting this review? The circumstance-specific nature of the decision sapped its power to use the case to guide other courts. The Court's review might not even have changed the result in the case before it, for the Court's decision permitted the district court, after further review, to reach the same conclusion. In any event, the district court itself had written that the state's new programs were helpful. It expected the state to take further steps that would permit it to set aside the court order in the near future regardless.[9]

How did Supreme Court review hurt? Further proceedings, of course, cost the parties considerable money. Further proceedings also consumed state and local officials' time, leading to further delay in fulfilling the statutory objective, namely, teaching Spanish-speaking children to work in English. The majority believed the decision would lead courts in the direction of greater respect for a state's management of its own educational programs. Yet circumstance-specific opinions, including this one, may fail to guide lower courts even in this respect, especially when the Court is closely divided as to the extent to which the record supports particular circumstance-specific findings.

The division is not surprising. Nine different judges reading a record may well reach different conclusions about the relevant circumstances when the record is unclear, particularly when some judges tend to read the law as emphasizing state autonomy while others read it as emphasizing the importance of the particular language-learning federal educational goal. More important, few, if any, members of the public will ever know who is right. The Court's competing opinions each set forth lengthy detailed accounts of the record. A reader can choose between them only by reading the record—a heroic undertaking, which will illuminate little of the law.

The upshot is that the Court spent a considerable amount of time to decide a close legal question producing opinions that the public cannot evaluate and that may have little effect beyond (and perhaps not even in respect to) the individual case. The principle of specialization warns the Court against undertaking this kind of task.

Amchem: *Let the District Court Manage the Case*

The second example concerns the Court's efforts to review district court case-management proceedings. It, too, shows why I believe the Court should give great weight to the court system's specialization of functions.

Background: General Underlying Circumstances. The example involves asbestos cases. Workers and their families sued an employer, claiming that the employer's negligence led to the workers' exposure to asbestos, perhaps many years earlier. And that workplace exposure brought about the workers' later sickness or death. Because over several decades so many workers were exposed to asbestos, the cases against even a single employer sometimes numbered in the hundreds of thousands. Many employers and the companies that insured them were willing to settle the cases without going to trial. The employer and its insurer would make a large contribution to a special fund. An administrator would manage the fund and would pay compensation to exposed workers and their families according to a schedule that correlated the amount of payment to the degree of harm. They would pay those workers who had brought suit and others who might bring suit in the future.[10]

However, a condition of the defendant companies' willingness to settle was the court's assurance that the amount they would put into a fund was the maximum amount they would have to pay. In other words, employers wanted to be certain that once they contributed, say, $1 billion into a fund, workers would later address their claims to the fund administrator and not bring further lawsuits. Many of the workers who had already brought suit, as well as lawyers who specialize in asbestos litigation, thought this condition was reasonable. They wanted the court to accept the condition so that they could settle the cases and get on with the business of obtaining compensation from the fund.[11]

Class Actions. A procedural technique—called the class action—seemed to provide a method for accomplishing the settlement. In a class action a small number of lawyers representing a few typical plaintiffs can speak for an entire class of plaintiffs. Moreover, these typical plaintiffs have the power to enter into a settlement on behalf of the entire class, thereby binding all class members—even those who have not yet brought cases. Thus, lawyers for a class of those workers employed at company A between 1950 and 1960 could enter into a settlement that would bind all the members of that class to accept the administrative fund as a remedy. All class members would have to turn to the fund to compensate them for any harm caused them by an asbestos-related disease, whether that harm had or had not yet become apparent.

To protect all members of the class from unfair treatment, however, the law requires the trial judge to find that *all* the workers (including those not present) are adequately represented and that the settlement is *fair* in respect to all of them. Trial judges apply an intricate set of legal rules to determine whether a class action meets these criteria. As relevant here, a trial judge may only allow a class action in certain specific situations. For example, a trial judge may certify a class when (1) *common questions* of law and fact predominate over separate questions, (2) the use of a class action provides a *superior* method for resolving the dispute compared with other methods, and (3) all potential members of the class receive notice and a chance to *opt out* of the class and pursue a separate legal action should they wish to do so. The overarching goal of these legal rules is to ensure that the identified plaintiffs and their lawyers fairly and adequately protect the interests of the entire class.[12]

These legal rules leave much to the district court. They use words such as "fair," "adequate," "typical," and "predominate," the application of which depends on the detailed factual circumstances of the individual cases. Application of these detailed rules often lies at the heart of a district court's management of a particular case. And district court judges, familiar with the cases before them, are in a substantially better position than appellate judges or Supreme Court justices to interpret the rules and apply them to particular circumstances.

The Case. In *Amchem* the trial judge, applying the class action rules, certified a class made up of all workers who had worked at certain times for certain specified employers, thereby bringing into the case workers who had not yet filed suit against the defendants. The judge then approved a settlement that required the employers and their insurers to pay many millions of dollars into a fund that would remain in existence for many years. The fund set minimum criteria for compensation. The settlement provided that the administrator would pay injured workers who met those criteria several thousand to several hundred thousand dollars each, depending on how much harm the worker had suffered.[13]

The trial judge found that a class action was appropriate because *common* questions of law or fact *predominated* over *separate* questions. He decided that the class action method was *superior* because otherwise too many workers would have to wait too long to receive too little compensation. And he concluded that given the alternatives, the settlement was a good one—even for those exposed workers who had not yet shown any sign of disease.[14]

The Supreme Court eventually heard the case and disagreed. The Court conceded that the entire set of cases presented some "common questions of law or fact." Each case involved exposure to asbestos. Each plaintiff would benefit from a quicker settlement involving fewer costs of administration. But the individual cases also differed in many important respects—for example, in the kind of exposure, length of time exposed, and kind of disease that the exposure produced. The Supreme Court thought the district court should have created subclasses of plaintiffs. Each subclass would represent a subgroup with members who had more in common. Different lawyers representing different subclasses would help the judge better ensure fair representation of the different groups, particularly those made up of individuals whose disease had not yet appeared. Given the possibility of subclasses, the Court held, the common interests among the plaintiffs in the single big class did not *predominate,* and the single big class therefore did not "fairly and adequately protect the interests of the class."[15]

All the members of the Court recognized that the district court was more familiar with the case than were they. And they all were willing to give weight to the district court's analysis and conclusions. Nonetheless, the majority thought that the district court had gone beyond a fair application of the class action rules, whereas in my (dissenting) view the law gave the district court adequate authority to decide as it did. The district court had considered the matter at length; it had weighed (1) the *common fact* of asbestos exposure and the plaintiffs' *common interest* in receiving compensation quickly without paying large legal fees (2) *against the differences;* and it had made more than three hundred factual findings that explained why the former predominated. The district court had concluded that the settlement was fair to all, in particular because the fund would contain enough money to pay those who were not yet ill and not yet represented.[16]

The difference between the majority and the dissent is one of degree, not of legal principle. Yet practical considerations support more, rather than less, deference, and they thereby underline the need to take full account of specialization. The district court found that, had the *Amchem* settlement taken effect, it would have paid "an estimated $1.3 billion and compensate[d] perhaps 100,000 class members in the first 10 years." The alternatives to settlement included long delays, high administrative costs, potential bankruptcies, and smaller eventual payment to victims, or perhaps no payment. Indeed, empirical studies show that the difficulty of handling the hundreds of thousands of asbestos cases that crowd court dockets means that, without settlement, administrative costs exceed amounts paid victims by a ratio of nearly two to one. Delays were often so long that in one 3,000-member asbestos class action, 448 class members died during the course of litigation.[17]

Moreover, a basic mission of the court system as a whole is to bring about the fair and speedy resolution of disputes. The circumstances of asbestos litigation offer a vivid illustration of the Court's need to grant trial courts considerable leeway in their effort to bring about a fair resolution of the underlying disputes. That leeway finds its justification in the principle of specialization. Adherence to that principle helps courts work more effectively, which in turn helps maintain public acceptance.

Chapter Twelve

Past Court Decisions: Stability

When the Supreme Court considers issues that it has previously decided, how much weight should it give to precedent? When should the Court overrule that precedent? The relevant legal doctrine, stare decisis, emphasizes the need to "maintain what has been decided." Judges do not find it difficult to follow that doctrine when they believe an earlier decision is right. But suppose a judge believes an earlier decision is wrong. And suppose the judge belongs to a Supreme Court with the power to overrule an earlier decision. What then? Under such circumstances, the judge must make a pragmatic decision, weighing the harms and benefits of stability against change. Furthermore, the judge must emphasize stability. Stability makes the judicial system and the law itself workable. Without stability the Court's decisions seem ad hoc and unpredictable—not part of a system at all. This is contrary to the Constitution's objectives and tends to undermine public acceptance of the Court's decisions.

Brown—When Stability Must Give Way

Sometimes a court must overrule an earlier decision. The passage of time may make clear that the legal rule set forth in the case was wrongly decided to begin with. It may also show that the earlier case is harmful or that it has become outdated as, in light of changing circumstances, the law in related areas has passed it by. Consider *Brown v. Board of Education.* An earlier case, *Plessy v. Ferguson,* decided by a Court fifty-eight years before, examined whether a state could require a railroad's black customers to sit in a separate railroad car, segregated from its white customers. The Court answered that question yes, and in doing so, it established the legal doctrine of "separate but equal." The case held that the Fourteenth Amendment's equal protection clause permitted a state to segregate the races by law as long as it provided members of each race with equal facilities.[1]

In *Brown* the Court overruled *Plessy* and substituted for "separate but equal" the doctrine that segregated facilities are inherently unequal. The Court had to weigh the benefits of stability against those of change. On the one hand, the South had relied on the *Plessy* decision. Indeed, southern states had built not only schools but an entire society on racially segregated foundations. Their citizens had woven racial segregation into the fabric of their daily lives.[2]

On the other hand, the Court, the legal community, and much of American society had begun to see the *Plessy* decision as legally wrong and the segregated society it helped build as morally wrong. It is difficult if not impossible to reconcile racial segregation with the language and purpose of a Fourteenth Amendment that forbids "any State" to "deprive any person of . . . the equal protection of the laws." *Plessy*'s rule was no longer in step with constitutional case law that had required the South to integrate its schools of law and of education. Nor was it in step with a society that, in its armed forces and elsewhere, had begun to embrace integration.[3]

Most important, it was clear by 1954 that *Plessy*'s rule had worked incalculable harm. That rule could not achieve its own stated goal. Instead, schools, parks, and public (and private) facilities were separate but hopelessly unequal. If *Plessy* had hoped that "separate but equal" would create a way station on the path to equality, that way station had become a terminal destination. It was impossible to see how a racially segregated nation could become a nation that equally respected all its citizens.

Thus, in *Brown* a unanimous Court overturned an earlier decision that the justices considered legally wrong, out of step with society and the law, and unusually harmful. Subsequently, the Court modified or overturned law set forth in a host of other cases, destroying rules that permitted racial segregation, and modifying the law of remedies, in order to make its *Brown* decision effective.[4]

Directly overruling an earlier decision, as the Court did in *Brown,* is exceptional. Ordinarily, stare decisis is the rule. Lower-court judges, lawyers, clients, and ordinary Americans all need stable law so that judges can decide their cases, lawyers can advise their clients, clients can make decisions, and ordinary Americans can buy homes, enter into contracts, and go about their daily lives without fear that changes in the law will turn their lives topsy-turvy.[5]

A printed, circulated Supreme Court decision helps the judge, lawyer, client, and ordinary American know what the law is. By overturning a case, the Court can create uncertainty and undermine the reliance that bench, bar, and public have invested in the earlier decision. Moreover, the more the Court overrules earlier cases, the more it will gain a reputation for being willing to do so. And that reputation itself creates uncertainty. Is the legal material circulated authoritative? Will it remain so? Will legal changes undermine business, family, or social decisions? Will a new case that resolves uncertainty long remain the law, or will a new Court overturn it, thereby denying the public the advantages of the newer, "better" second decision for which the Court had hoped? At the same time, a Court that overturns too many earlier decisions encourages the public to believe that personalities or politics, not law, determine the outcome of Court cases. And that belief undermines the public's confidence in the Court.

General Principles

If the Court should normally apply the principle of stare decisis but can sometimes overturn an earlier case, how does it know when to do which? The Court has referred to several factors that help answer the question. First, the Court has said that the principle of stare decisis applies more rigorously when a statute, rather than a constitutional provision, is at issue. That is because Congress can easily change a statutory decision, but neither Congress nor anyone else can easily amend the Constitution. Normally, the only practical way to change a constitutional decision is for the Court to reconsider it.[6]

Second, the public's reliance on a decision argues strongly (but, as *Brown* shows, not determinatively) against overruling an earlier case. The public may well rely, for example, on a decision that affects property or contracts. Individuals and firms may have invested time, effort, and money based on that decision. The more the Court undermines this kind of reliance, the riskier investment becomes. The more the Court engages in a practice that appears to ignore that reliance, the more the practice threatens economic prosperity.[7]

Third, the more recently the earlier case was decided, the less forcefully the stare decisis anti-overruling principle should be applied. When only a short time has elapsed, we may not yet know that a decision will have harmful effects; it is also unlikely that either the bar or the public will yet have relied significantly upon the earlier case.[8]

Fourth, the Court can, and often should, overrule an earlier decision that has created a set of unworkable legal rules. Such a decision may have proved confusing or created legal conflict or otherwise caused serious harm. Confusion may mean no one reasonably relied on the case. In any event, overruling is more likely, on balance, to prove beneficial.[9]

Fifth, if case B has overruled case A, it is more reasonable for the Court to overrule B, thereby restoring A. That is because case B has already upset expectations and a restoration may not, on balance, cause further difficulty.[10]

Sixth, the Court should exercise particular caution before overturning a case that has become well embedded in national culture. In the 1960s, for example, the Court decided *Miranda v. Arizona,* which held that the police must warn a suspect of his constitutional rights to remain silent and to have a lawyer. Over the next few decades most Americans, through television or otherwise, became aware of this basic legal rule—that the police must warn suspects before questioning them. Then, in 2000, when the Court considered whether to overrule *Miranda,* it took account of the fact that the general public understood

Miranda and had come to expect the police to follow its holding. And for that reason even members of the Court who thought *Miranda* wrongly decided have refused to overrule it.[11] On the other hand, the law has long strictly regulated (and often forbade) expenditures made by corporations and trade unions to help elect candidates for public office. Yet, in January 2010 the Court (by a vote of 5 to 4) held that a congressional statute of this kind violated the First Amendment's free speech guarantees. In doing so, the Court overturned two recent cases, and in the view of the dissenters (of which I was one), the Court disregarded a traditional legal view that stretched back as far as 1907.[12]

Resisting the Temptation to Overrule

The above six principles emphasize harm, confusion, change, and lack of reasonable reliance as justifications for overruling an earlier case. But (as the examples just given, of *Miranda*-warnings and campaign expenditures suggest) they often do not dictate any particular result, they can conflict, they are highly general, and their application calls for the use of pragmatic judgment. That is, these principles can do no more than guide judges who might well disagree about how they apply in any particular case. Nonetheless, several special features of the Supreme Court offer a temptation to overrule earlier cases. In order to resist that temptation, when we apply our principles, we should ordinarily place a thumb on the scale in the direction of stability.

First, an earlier decision that the Court's members now think wrong is not likely to change without their intervention. That fact is obvious when the earlier decision interprets the Constitution, for it is difficult to amend the Constitution. Doing so normally requires a favorable vote of two-thirds of each house of Congress and ratification by three-fourths of the states. And the nation has amended the Constitution only twenty-seven times. The difficulty of obtaining change is less obvious when the Court interprets a statute, but it is nonetheless true. In theory, Congress can write a new statute. In practice, Congress will do so only if it can find the legislative time and the necessary political will. It will probably find that political will only when change is politically popular or when well-organized groups make that change a major issue. Thus judges sometimes think that they themselves should overturn a case that they believe is wrong or when change will probably never take place.[13]

Second, the Court does not have many opportunities to overturn earlier cases. The Court fully hears only about eighty cases per year, very few of which require or permit the Court to reconsider a previously decided case the Court believes is wrong. Those that do involve such a case may fail to meet other criteria, such as a division of opinion among the lower courts, that determine whether the Court should hear a case. Thus justices who have before them a case that provides an opportunity to overturn an earlier decision that a number of them think is wrong know that the opportunity will not likely arise again. It is "now or never."

Third, because life tenure for the justices means a Court membership that changes only slowly over time, it also means that different members appointed after long intervals by different presidents may well have different philosophical views. A president cannot control the votes of the Court during his limited time in office or even of the judges that he has appointed. President Theodore Roosevelt appointed the great justice Oliver Wendell Holmes, who almost immediately took an antitrust-law position totally contrary to Roosevelt's views on the subject. And Roosevelt reportedly responded, "I could carve out of a banana a judge with more backbone."[14]

Presidents and their judicial appointees are more likely, however, to share a basic philosophical approach to the country and to the law, and how they relate to each other. Thus without any Court judge compromising his or her total independence, different judges will have different philosophical approaches about how best to apply highly general constitutional terms such as "liberty," "equal protection," and "due process of law." And judges on one Court may have different basic views on such subjects from their predecessors. It is consequently not surprising if a later Court considering an earlier case believes that the earlier Court decision was absolutely wrong.

Members of the Court might reasonably think (1) "that earlier case is completely wrong, even untrue to the Constitution," (2) "if we do not change it, no one will," and (3) "it's now or never." I would add one further consideration, namely, that a case does not always unambiguously stand for a clear proposition of law. Consider a mother who tells a child not to bring up medical matters when Grandma comes because it will make Grandma think of her own recent illness. The mother has taught the child a rule of behavior, but she cannot describe its precise boundaries. Consider a case that holds that when a policeman properly arrests a driver, he can search the car without getting a warrant. What shapes the boundaries? Police safety, the need for a clear, simple rule, both? How does the case apply to a search after the arrested driver is handcuffed and put in the back of a squad car? My point is that stare decisis is not mechanical and fidelity to an earlier Court decision is often a matter of degree or interpretation.[15]

As a result, a judge will find it psychologically difficult to remain faithful to a decision with which he or she disagrees. A judge will almost inevitably resist adherence, for example, to an earlier interpretation that gives the Constitution a meaning that the judge is convinced the Constitution does not have. At the same time, overruling inevitably reflects a pragmatic decision-making process in which different judges give different weights to the individual factors that the Court has found relevant. Thus in one recent term, the members of the Court debated (dividing 5 to 4) whether they should overrule or depart from prior decisions in numerous areas of law, such as abortion, campaign finance, and antitrust. In all of these decisions I was in the minority in part because I thought the Court had overruled prior decisions and was wrong to do so.[16]

The strength of the forces pushing the judge toward overruling earlier cases makes it particularly important for a pragmatic judge, before deciding to overrule an earlier case, to take careful account of the opposite considerations, those that favor stability and stare decisis. Those considerations do not always convincingly militate against overruling an earlier case. To the contrary, the Court was surely right to overrule *Plessy v. Ferguson.* And by unanimously overruling that decision, it helped overcome the claim of *Brown*'s opponents that the *Brown* decision was not legally sound.

Still, the psychological factors I have mentioned indicate that the

Court in each instance should check any impulse to overrule against the need to overrule. The Court should remain aware of the nature of its own temptations to "straighten out" the law as well as the practical advantages of unanimity and uniformity. Although these practical considerations do not dictate outcomes, they require a judge to think long and hard before overruling. Doing so helps to maintain the Court's institutional strength and a system of Court decision making that works well in practice. Both, in turn, help to maintain public acceptance of the Court's decisions.

PART III

Protecting Individuals

The Constitution imposes limits on government in an effort to protect the rights and liberties of individuals. Part III continues the discussion of pragmatic approaches while considering, through examples, how the Court applies the permanent principles underlying that protection to changing circumstances. It focuses on the Second Amendment, with its protection of the right "to keep and bear Arms," to illustrate how the Court locates the appropriate permanent value as well as how it applies that value in the presence of critically important competing interests. And it describes the Japanese internment and Guantánamo Bay cases to illustrate the practical problems involved when the Court seeks to protect basic individual liberties during wartime or when special national security needs increase the difficulty of the Court's holding a president accountable.

Chapter Thirteen

Individual Liberty: Permanent Values and Proportionality

THE CONSTITUTION EXPRESSLY protects the liberty of individuals through the Bill of Rights. The First Amendment, for example, says that "Congress shall make no law respecting an establishment of religion, or prohibiting the free exercise thereof." Nor can Congress enact any law "abridging the freedom of speech, or of the press; or the right of the people peaceably to assemble, and to petition the Government for a redress of grievances." The Fourth Amendment protects individuals against "unreasonable searches and seizures." The Fifth and Sixth amendments guarantee certain rights, including fair trial rights, to those accused of crimes. The Fourteenth Amendment makes these, and other, constitutional protections applicable where state governments, not just the federal government, are involved.

Virtually every Court case that involves the protection of individual liberty also involves the Court's relation with some other government institution. For this reason, individual liberty cases may call for the application of the approaches already described. When the Court considers a constitutional "free speech" challenge to a statute regulating campaign finance, for example, the Court may have to look to the statutory approaches discussed earlier, such as purpose-based interpretation or constitutional avoidance, before it decides a free speech issue.

Individual rights warrant special attention when we consider how to make the Constitution work in practice. This is partly because of the importance of individual rights. Whether the Court can protect them adequately tests Hamilton's thesis that the Court is the best repository of the power to interpret the Constitution. In addition, we should address individual rights separately because their enforcement can demand special interpretive tools, among them the use of *values* and of *proportionality* in determining where and how a rights-safeguarding provision applies.

These two approaches might not be necessary if the constitutional provisions setting forth individual rights were absolute. Justice Black believed that the First Amendment's protection of free speech was absolute. If asked about the First Amendment, he would pull out his pocket Constitution, point to the words "no law," and say "no law" means *no law.* Yet even Justice Black had a difficult time deciding how the amendment applied to speech-related activity, such as union picketing. This is because the First Amendment's next few words, "abridging the freedom of speech," are less definite. What precisely constitutes "freedom of speech"? And just when does a law abridge that freedom?[1]

Moreover, a rigid, absolutist approach would deprive others of equally important rights. As Justice Holmes pointed out long ago, the Court would not permit a prankster to shout "fire" in a crowded theater, risking the lives of others in the audience. Nor can individuals incite riots where the direct, known, and intended consequences include the deaths of innocents. A totally rigid approach is not always workable, and in the many instances where it is not, proportionality helps reconcile competing rights and interests in a workable way.[2]

Indeed, an absolute test only occasionally resolves a case that comes before the Court. As I said, the Constitution's language—"freedom of speech" in the First Amendment, "unreasonable searches" in the Fourth, "liberty" in the Fourteenth—does not itself describe its scope. And the Court has often had to struggle with difficult questions as to the language's application. How does the First Amendment apply to the Internet? How does the Fourth Amendment apply to the police department's use of barriers created to stop all cars and search for drugs? What are the bounds of the protection that the Constitution's word "liberty" gives to those who wish to school their children at home?

Furthermore, important rights and interests can conflict. How should we reconcile the press's interest in uncovering secret jury deliberations with the defendant's interest in a fair trial? How should we reconcile "freedom of speech" with the "fair election" interest furthered by imposing limits on the amounts that individuals can contribute to a political campaign? To what extent can the government prevent a newspaper from publishing a story in order to protect national security, sometimes a matter of life and death?

Finally, a host of practical problems can arise, which stand in the way of any single simple solution to a difficult constitutional problem. Consider electoral gerrymandering. The Fourteenth Amendment guarantees equal treatment of each person's vote. But gerrymandering sometimes makes it futile for some voters to exercise their rights, say certain Republicans in a state that heavily gerrymanders districts to favor Democrats or vice versa. The Court has recognized the problem, but it has thought it so difficult to create a remedy that it has abandoned its efforts to help.

In a 2004 case, *Veith v. Jubelirer,*[3] for example, the Court (overturning an earlier case)[4] held by a vote of 5 to 4 that courts should not hear a gerrymandering claim. That claim accused the Pennsylvania legislature of creating new congressional districts with "meandering and irregular" boundaries, and, in doing so, ignoring "all traditional redistricting criteria . . . solely for the sake of partisan advantage." In dissent I argued that sometimes gerrymandering, without advancing any plausible democratic goal, can threaten serious democratic harm. It will sometimes stop voters from "throw[ing] the rascals out." It will sometimes entrench a minority party in power. I also argued that courts can identify at least extreme instances; and they can create workable remedies in those instances. States wishing to avoid court involvement could create fair redistricting commissions—a procedural remedy sufficient to the problem.

Today, were I to have three wishes to turn dissents into majority opinions, I would place this case on the list. My reason is that the practice of gerrymandering has not abated; and gerrymandering, by isolating legislators from credible electoral challenge by the opposition, has often forced legislators to take more extreme views, thereby making it more difficult to govern the nation as a whole. For present purposes the case illustrates some of the complexities and difficulties that defy easy answers. It also helps show why simple reference to language or history or tradition or precedent, or a simple absolute test, is often insufficient.

The upshot is that a Constitution that protects individual rights in practice needs tools that translate its written provisions into workable reality. Those tools must help the Court provide adequate protection for individual rights. And they should also help the public accept as legitimate the Court's unpopular decisions. Two basic tools are values and proportionality.

VALUES

VALUES ARE THE constitutional analogue of statutory purposes. When faced with a difficult question of constitutional law, judges initially examine the constitutional provision as they would other texts using the tools of language, history, tradition, precedent, purposes, and consequences. The last two tools, purposes and consequences, may be particularly important when the Constitution is at issue. But when referring to the Constitution's protection of individual rights, I would substitute the term "values," for it better describes the deep, enduring, and value-laden nature of the Constitution's protections. Courts must consider how these values, which themselves change little over time, apply to circumstances that today may differ dramatically from those of two hundred years ago.

Consider examples of constitutional questions that arise today. Does the Fourth Amendment protect the homeowner from the government's use *outside* the home of a device that registers invisible heat emissions and thereby detects growing marijuana *inside* the home? We know that protection of privacy—particularly that of the homeowner—is a basic value underlying the Fourth Amendment. Hence we have confidence that the Fourth Amendment will protect the homeowner against use of this machine insofar as it invades the homeowner's privacy. That is so even if no one in the eighteenth century dreamed of this kind of invasion.[5]

Similarly, the expressive values underlying the First Amendment's speech protection tell us that the amendment strongly protects political speech over the Internet while offering little if any protection to Internet fraud schemes. Similarly, the values underlying the Eighth Amendment's prohibition of "cruel and unusual punishments" suggest that today the amendment would prohibit flogging even if many eighteenth-century Americans thought flogging was neither cruel nor unusual.

Judges, of course, can disagree about just which values underlie a particular constitutional provision or how they apply. The Fourteenth Amendment's equal protection clause forbids any state to "deny to any person . . . the equal protection of the laws." Most judges believe that the clause insists that the government treat all persons with equal respect. But some believe that the clause thereby denies the government the power to take account of race, even for the purpose of increasing racial diversity, say in a law school class. Others deny that the clause requires that admissions be color-blind. Rather, it gives the government a degree of leeway when it adopts race-conscious policies that seek to include within mainstream American society members of "groups long denied full citizenship stature."[6]

The disagreement is not easy to resolve. The Court took the latter view in a case involving law school admissions. It held that in light of the purpose of the clause, the Court should treat differently (1) race-conscious rules that include and (2) those that exclude. But the point here is that the debate was only partly about the values that underlie the clause; it was also about how those values should apply in our modern society.

Proportionality

The second tool or approach, *proportionality,* is useful when a statute restricts one constitutionally protected interest in order to further some other comparably important interest. It is specially designed for a context where important constitutional rights and interests conflict. Suppose, for example, the state forbids electioneering within a hundred feet of a polling place on Election Day. The prohibition restricts speech, and it also delineates an area where the election's mechanics, and the voting itself, can proceed calmly without campaigning. Judges who use proportionality ask whether the restriction on speech is proportionate to, or properly balances, the need. They pose a similar question when considering whether campaign finance laws violate the First Amendment, whether a workplace-related speech restriction that the government imposes on its own employees is constitutional, and whether and how the Constitution permits the government to regulate commercial speech such as advertising.

Proportionality involves balancing, which the Court has sometimes tried to minimize. For example, the Court has said it will apply tests that are highly protective of political speech and try to avoid balancing in that area. But in other areas, the Court more directly weighs harms, justifications, and potentially less restrictive alternatives. How serious is the harm to free speech that a certain statute may cause? How important are the statute's countervailing objectives? To what extent will the statute achieve those objectives? Are there other, less restrictive ways of accomplishing as much? The Court sometimes uses different words to describe what it is doing when it asks these or similar questions. But ultimately the Court must determine whether the statute threatens a constitutionally protected interest with harm that is disproportionately severe when considered in light of the statute's justification.[7]

Heller

A recent decision illustrates how the two tools—values and proportionality—work in practice. The Second Amendment says, "A well regulated Militia, being necessary to the security of a free State, the right of the people to keep and bear Arms, shall not be infringed." Meanwhile, the District of Columbia forbids possession of handguns, loaded rifles, and loaded shotguns within the District. In 2008 the

Court had to decide whether the District's law violated the Second Amendment and held 5 to 4 that it did. The Court majority and the dissent disagreed both about the values that underlie the Second Amendment and about how they apply in today's world.[8]

Second Amendment Values

What values underlie the Second Amendment? What is the amendment's basic purpose? The majority found those values and purposes in the words "right . . . to keep and bear Arms." To determine what our eighteenth-century founders might have thought about the nature of the right and its specific content, the majority examined early legal sources, including writings of the eighteenth-century legal scholar William Blackstone and books and pamphlets reporting fear among seventeenth-century English Protestants that an English Catholic king would disarm them. This historical examination led the majority to conclude that in the eighteenth century an individual's right to possess guns was important both for purposes of defending that individual and for purposes of a community's collective self-defense. It then determined that the framers intended the Second Amendment to protect an individual's right to keep and bear arms not only to effectuate the more general right to maintain a "well regulated Militia" but also independently as an end. For the majority, history, not militia-related purposes, would define the right's scope.[9]

The dissenters (of which I was one) focused on the words a "well regulated Militia, being necessary to the security of a free State." In their view, that language identifies the amendment's major underlying value. Its purpose is to ensure the maintenance of the "well regulated Militia" that it mentions. The dissenters' own examination of eighteenth-century American history convinced them that the framers wrote the amendment because Article I of the Constitution granted Congress extensive power to regulate state militias and to "employ[]" militia members in federal service. Some people feared at the time that Congress would use these regulatory powers to weaken or destroy state militias. The Second Amendment sought to assure the public that Congress would not be able to do so. That is to say, the amendment's language granting a "right . . . to keep and bear Arms" sought simply to assure the people that Congress could not use its Article I authority to do away with "well regulated" state military entities.[10]

The majority and the dissent disagreed not only about the relevant values but also about the way in which judges should use values and purposes to help resolve a constitutional question. The majority, for example, conceded that at least one of the reasons the founders included in the Constitution an amendment protecting a "right . . . to keep and bear Arms" was to help ensure well-regulated state militias. But even so, they looked primarily to history, not to that purpose, to define the scope of that right, that is, to determine to what, and just how, that right now applies.[11]

The dissenters, however, even had they believed that the amendment sought in part to protect an individual's right of self-defense, would not have looked to history alone to determine the scope of that right. They would have asked: What are the basic values—values related to personal security—that the amendment seeks to protect? And how do today's laws promote or interfere with those basic values? Thus the dissenters, after identifying the relevant values, would have gone on to consider relevant differences between an eighteenth-century, primarily rural America, where frontier life demanded guns, and the present, primarily urban America, where gun possession presents a greater risk of taking innocent lives. While seeking to maintain the basic values underlying a constitutional provision, they would place greater weight than did the majority on changing circumstances.[12]

Second Amendment Proportionality

Despite their differences, both majority and dissent agreed that they must ask a final question: In light of the values and purposes that underlie the amendment, was the District's handgun prohibition constitutional? For the dissent, the question was not difficult. The amendment's basic purpose concerned the maintenance of a well-regulated state militia. The District's civilian handgun ban did not significantly interfere with that objective. Hence the ban was constitutional.[13]

Neither did the majority find the question difficult. In its view, the amendment's central "value" concerned "the inherent right of self-defense." Handgun possession is important, perhaps necessary, to secure that value. Handguns are easy to "store in a location that is readily accessible in an emergency." They are easy to "use for those without the upper-body strength to lift and aim a long gun." They are capable of being "pointed at a burglar with one hand while the other hand dials the police." They are not "easily . . . redirected or wrestled away by an attacker." They are "the quintessential self-defense weapon," particularly in the home. Yet the D.C. law bans that "entire class of 'arms.' " Few gun laws in the nation's history have been so restrictive. Hence the law "fail[s] constitutional muster."[14]

Although the result in this case turned primarily upon the identification and application of values, the case also illustrates how the Court might use proportionality—a tool that the majority did not use but that the dissenters considered.

Put in terms of constitutionality, the proportionality question is the following: Does the handgun restriction *disproportionately* interfere with the values that underlie the Second Amendment? This question encompasses several subsidiary questions: To what extent does the restriction interfere with the protected interest? To what extent does it further a compelling interest? Are there superior, less restrictive ways to accomplish the statute's important competing objective? The answers to the subsidiary questions help answer the ultimate question: Does the statute disproportionately restrict the value or interest that the Constitution protects? The Court has frequently asked these kinds of balancing questions, sometimes using different language, where similar constitutional conflicts—say between free speech and privacy—are present.[15]

The District's law, while restricting possession of handguns, does so in order to advance a *compelling* interest, namely, an interest in life itself. The Court has held that this interest can justify interference even with very important competing constitutional interests. Consider, for example, laws that forbid speech where speech would reveal important military secrets. Consider also laws that would forbid religious practices that threaten individuals with physical harm.[16]

It is less clear whether the District's handgun law *significantly furthers* a lifesaving interest. On the one hand, in 1975, when the District enacted its ban, there were in the United States about 25,000 gun-related deaths annually and about 200,000 injuries. In the District, 155 of 285 murders, 60 percent of all robberies, and 26 percent of all assaults involved handguns. But twenty years *after* the District enacted its law, the nation's gun-related death figure had risen to 36,000. More than 80 percent of all firearm homicides were committed with handguns. And the District's violent-crime rate had increased, not diminished. Moreover, some social scientists had found that strict gun laws are generally associated with more, not less, violent crime. Others found a positive empirical relationship between gun ownership and legitimate self-defense. Still others found that there are so many illegal guns in the United States the D.C. law could not have any significant positive effect.[17]

On the other hand, without a handgun ban, D.C. crime rates and crime-related deaths might have been still worse. Handgun laws cannot promise to take guns from criminals, but they might help. And D.C.'s laws might lead other communities to adopt gun restrictions of some kind. One cannot be certain whether D.C.'s gun law worked. To answer the overall question—to what extent did the D.C. law achieve its objective?—requires facts and fact-related judgments. Legislatures are better equipped than courts to try to find the answer. Thus the Court should accept the legislature's judgment about gun possession and saving lives—as long as that judgment is reasonable. (I thought it was.)[18]

What about the other side of the coin? To what extent does the District's handgun ban *burden* the gun-related interest that the amendment seeks to protect? To answer this question, we must return to the values that underlie the amendment. Because the justices disagree about that matter, we can examine all plausible values in turn. If the value is that of preserving a "well regulated Militia" or protecting sportsmen or hunters, the handgun ban imposes little or no burden. Those who seek training in the use of guns, target practice, or hunting can join gun clubs in nearby Virginia or Maryland and, for the price of a subway ride, join their fellows for training, recreation, and sport. But if the value is that of using handguns for self-defense, we must recognize that the statute imposes a burden. The handgun ban interferes significantly with the homeowner's possession and use of a handgun kept in the home for the purpose of self-defense.[19]

The Court then must try to balance the statute's efficacy, in terms of community safety, with the obstacle it imposes to self-defense. We might try to avoid the need to balance by looking for a superior, less restrictive way to achieve the District's lifesaving objective. But probably there is none. The very characteristics that make a handgun a particularly good choice for self-defense include the fact that it is small, light, and easy to hold and control and leaves one hand free for maneuvering. Those very same characteristics make handguns susceptible to misuse, by children for example, easy to steal and to hide, and a good choice for a criminal intent on committing, say, a robbery.[20]

So far, proportionality has helped frame the question. The handgun ban burdens (what the majority found was) an important Second Amendment objective. At the same time, it does so in order to further (and the legislature could reasonably find it tends to further) a competing and compelling interest, namely, saving innocent lives. There is no obvious, less burdensome, similarly effective way to further that objective. We therefore cannot escape the need to decide the balancing question, namely, whether the District's handgun law, in its efforts to save innocent lives (a compelling interest), *disproportionately* burdens the interest the amendment seeks to protect, namely, "self-defense."[21]

In my view the burden is proportionate, not disproportionate, and the statute is constitutional. The District's law was properly tailored to the urban life-threatening problems that it sought to address. It involved only one class of weapons, leaving District residents free to possess shotguns and rifles along with separately kept ammunition. The amendment's first clause, the "Militia" clause, indicates that even if self-defense is one protected interest, it was not the exclusive or primary interest that the framers had in mind. Perhaps most important, changes in the nature of society, the development of the urban police force, the nature of modern urban crime, the movement of population away from the frontier, with frontier life's particular dangers and risks, all have made gun possession less important in terms of the amendment's objectives—even if those objectives include the value of personal safety.[22]

Whether one agrees or disagrees with the proportionality analysis just presented, the underlying approach focuses the Court's attention on the practical underlying constitutional considerations, namely, harm (to protected interests) compared with need. The Second Amendment example shows that proportionality is complex and difficult to apply in practice. But what is the alternative? Today's Court should not base an answer to a question about an issue such as gun control on the facts and circumstances of eighteenth-century society. Nor should a judge base an answer to that question on the judge's own intuitive balancing of harm versus need—without saying how that balancing works. Why should the Court simply announce that handguns are important and imply that the answer is consequently obvious? Why should the public find acceptable such complete reliance on either an eighteenth-century alternative or an unexplained judicial intuition?

Those who disfavor the use of a proportionality approach, or similar approaches, criticize them as "judge empowering." But a judge who uses such an approach must examine and explain all the factors that go into a decision. The need for that examination and explanation serves as a constraint. It means that the decision must be transparent and subject to criticism. Because the approach just illustrated can require the judge to accept reasonable legislative determinations of empirical matters, it is "legislator empowering," not "judge empowering." In the democratic society that the Constitution creates, legislative empowerment is a virtue.

In sum, the Second Amendment example shows how the use of values and proportionality can help produce constitutional interpretation that allows the Constitution to adapt its permanent values to fit society's changing needs. The use of values and proportionality introduces its own complexities. But those complexities often arise out of the underlying problem itself—a problem that requires a court to determine how much protection a right warrants when it conflicts with another right or critically important interest. Other, simpler approaches come with costs attached, such as the difficulty of explaining to the public why it should accept a decision that embodies eighteenth-century factual assumptions or pure judicial intuition. To use values and proportionality is to promote transparent opinions, to rely heavily on rational explanation, and to protect the individual rights that underlie constitutional provisions.

Chapter Fourteen

The President, National Security, and Accountability: Korematsu

The Court's relationship with the president is complicated by the fact that it is often forged in times of war or national emergency. In such times the Constitution remains applicable. The nation has long abandoned Cicero's view that "in time of war the law is silent." Furthermore, the Court retains the power of judicial review. In principle, it can invalidate presidential actions that violate the Constitution. But in practice, to what extent can—or should—the Court hold the president accountable to the Constitution in the face of war or national emergency? How can the Court maintain a workable relationship with the president and enable him to discharge his constitutional duties without abdicating its responsibility to safeguard constitutional liberties and enforce constitutional limits? As elsewhere, the Court must find the right constitutional approach, thereby helping to ensure public acceptance of its decisions, if not always as correct, then always as legitimate.

The Constitution delegates to the president broad powers to conduct foreign affairs, wage a war, and safeguard national security. But sometimes a president can go too far. During the Civil War, President Abraham Lincoln suspended the writ of habeas corpus, thereby allowing the army to arrest and detain American citizens without judicial review. Subsequently, Chief Justice Taney issued a writ of habeas corpus ordering the army to release a Confederate sympathizer, John Merryman, a citizen of Maryland, whom Union soldiers had arrested. Taney thought that the suspension of the writ violated the Constitution because Article I gives *Congress,* not the president, the authority to suspend the writ of habeas corpus.[1]

President Lincoln then ordered his generals to ignore the writ. "Are all the laws, *but one,* to go unexecuted," Lincoln asked, "and the government itself go to pieces, lest that one be violated?" Congress righted matters by enacting legislation that suspended the writ. Yet the fact remains that President Lincoln ignored a judicial effort to set aside a wartime action he thought necessary.[2]

In 1950 the Court reviewed another presidential action taken in time of war. During the Korean conflict, President Truman had seized steel mills belonging to private companies. He thought the seizure necessary to avert a strike that could seriously interfere with the war effort. The Court held that without congressional authorization President Truman lacked the legal authority to seize privately owned steel mills. Hence, the seizure was unconstitutional. Justice Jackson, concurring, emphasized the fact that Congress had not authorized the seizure. He wrote that actions taken by the president fall into three categories: (1) those taken pursuant to congressional legislation; (2) those taken without congressional legislation; and (3) those taken in conflict with congressional legislation. He added that as one travels from the first category to the third, the scope of the president's authority to act, even in wartime, diminishes. Truman accepted the Court's decision and returned the mills to their owners.[3]

When the Court faces a wartime president who has curtailed ordinary civil liberties, and when it faces a claim he has gone too far, it will also face a president whose constitutional authority is likely at maximum strength. The president will have acted pursuant to his war, foreign affairs, and national security powers. Congress will likely have enacted broad statutes delegating to the president the authority to act as he did. At the same time, the president will have determined that the factual circumstances warrant curtailment of an individual's liberty. This last consideration is important both because the president is more expert than is the Court in wartime matters and because the precise protection that the Constitution offers individuals often varies with the circumstances. The Fourth Amendment's insistence on search warrants, for example, does not apply where police see a robber with a hostage run into an apartment house.

Given the strength of the considerations that favor deference to the president—considerations of expertise, of constitutional role, of congressional delegation, of factual circumstance—can the Court say no to the president? If not, will the relationship between Court and president almost inevitably become a one-way street? Put simply, how can the Court protect civil liberties in time of war?

At least one Court case provides grounds for pessimism. During World War II the Court upheld as constitutional a decision by President Franklin D. Roosevelt to forcibly remove seventy thousand American citizens of Japanese ancestry from their homes on the West Coast and require them to live in "relocation camps" in eastern California and the Rocky Mountain states. Scholars have had great difficulty finding any reasonable justification for the president's decision in this case, *Korematsu v. United States.* Most describe the Court's decision as mistaken, and they include it among the Court's worst. Yet the Court majority included even Justices Hugo Black and William O. Douglas, who ordinarily found in the Constitution strong protection for individual liberties. It is important to understand why and how the Court reached its conclusions. The case illuminates the difficulties for the Court of maintaining that protection where a president, with his powers at full strength, acts to the contrary. It also shows the importance of holding the president constitutionally accountable in those circumstances.[4]

The Relocation

In February 1942, President Roosevelt signed an executive order (number 9066) that delegated to military commanders the power to relocate persons of Japanese ancestry living in the United States. Why did he do this?[5]

Only a few weeks earlier, Japan had bombed Pearl Harbor, and West Coast civilians and many in the military feared a Japanese invasion of the West Coast. Although public opinion in California had initially followed the advice of the *Los Angeles Times,* "Let's not get rattled," that opinion soon turned against California's Japanese residents. Some Californians panicked, refusing to buy vegetables from Japanese truck farmers and firing Japanese servants for fear of being poisoned.[6]

Soon radio commentators, editorial writers, influential agricultural groups, and political figures began to argue, in the words of one congressman, that "all Japanese, whether citizens or not, be placed in inland concentration camps." The *Los Angeles Times* reversed field. California's governor asked for removal of all Japanese from California, and the entire congressional delegation supported removal as well. Although he subsequently apologized, even Earl Warren, then California's attorney general, supported removal. Later, as chief justice, Warren strongly supported civil liberties—writing the Court's opinion in *Brown v. Board of Education*—but in early 1942 he told a group of state sheriffs that the fact that "we have had no fifth column activities" or "sabotage" shows "a studied effort" by Japanese living in California "not to have any until the zero hour arrives." He argued essentially that the *absence* of "sabotage" itself showed that many resident Japanese were disloyal.[7]

Significantly, the army general in charge of the Sixth Military District, which included the West Coast, strongly supported removal. Stationed in the Presidio of San Francisco, General John L. DeWitt told the War Department that he feared invasion; that Japanese had frequently signaled valuable targeting information to Japanese submarines offshore; and that Japanese residents had helped commit acts of sabotage and espionage. Because DeWitt believed that many Japanese residents were disloyal and that no one could distinguish between those who were loyal and those who were not, he concluded that the only safe thing to do was to remove them all. Further support came from the report of a commission headed by the Supreme Court justice Owen Roberts, which quickly investigated the Pearl Harbor attack. The commission stated that "persons having no open relation with the Japanese foreign service" had provided help to an espionage ring. To the public those words spelled "fifth column"—or, in today's vernacular, terrorist cells in our midst.[8]

Removal did have its opponents—including the FBI and its leader, J. Edgar Hoover. Hoover said the FBI could distinguish the loyal from the disloyal. They had rounded up about two thousand Japanese aliens immediately after Pearl Harbor and saw no need to remove all citizens of Japanese ancestry.[9]

Some army generals, such as Mark Clark, thought the logistical problems associated with relocating and housing 112,000 Japanese civilians would prove overwhelming. And Justice Department officials, concerned with the threat to civil liberties, found the removal of 70,000 American citizens horrifying. How, they asked, can we relocate American citizens of Japanese origin but not those of German or Italian origin? Furthermore, if the government permitted citizens of Japanese origin to remain at home in Hawaii, why remove citizens of Japanese origin from California?[10]

At first the attorney general, Francis Biddle, and the secretary of war, Henry L. Stimson, leaned against removal. But the War Department's assistant secretary, John McCloy, argued strongly for removal. Ultimately, the War Department and the Justice Department cleared DeWitt's removal recommendation and sent it on to the president, who approved it.[11]

The president's executive order gave military commanders the authority to designate "military areas" and to impose restrictions on those present in the areas. Congress subsequently ratified the order with a statute that imposed criminal penalties on anyone who knowingly "shall enter, remain in, leave, or commit any act in any . . . military zone . . . contrary to" applicable "restrictions." On March 2, 1942, General DeWitt designated the western portions of California, Oregon, and Washington as a special "military area." And within the next few weeks DeWitt issued several orders that applied to all persons of Japanese ancestry.[12]

The first order imposed a curfew. A second required all persons of Japanese ancestry to remain within the West Coast "military area," and then a third simultaneously told them to leave every part of that area but certain specified "assembly centers," including Tanforan and Santa Anita racetracks near San Francisco and Los Angeles, respectively. The orders thereby required all persons of Japanese ancestry to gather together at those racetracks and similar designated areas. The government transported them to internment camps in the eastern parts of California and in the intermountain states. By early June 1942, 100,000 and by October 112,000 "persons of Japanese ancestry," including 70,000 American citizens, were living in those camps, behind barbed wire and under guard.[13]

Camp facilities have been described as "spartan in the extreme." Those interned lived in barracks built of tar paper and pine. The internal walls were made of thin plywood. Inside, sheets and blankets divided the bunks. The residents used common bathing and toilet facilities. In some camps daily winds would blow dust and sand everywhere. The Japanese internees lived in the camps for two to three years. Within a few months of their arrival, however, any realistic threat of a California invasion had disappeared. The American armed forces began to win victories in Europe and the Pacific. Indeed, thousands of Japanese-Americans joined the U.S. Army. The Nisei 442nd Regimental Combat Team emerged as the "most decorated unit" in Europe, having received more than eighteen thousand decorations for valor.[14]

The government authority that ran the camps, the War Relocation Authority (WRA), itself began to recognize that it lacked any justification for continuing to confine the residents. By October 1942 the WRA had developed a screening program to identify internees whose loyalty was in doubt and whom it sent to a camp at Tule Lake, California. The WRA offered to release the rest, provided they agreed not to return to California, where anti-Japanese sentiment was strong. By 1943 the WRA had begun to abandon this requirement, and by late 1944 the government had announced it would close all the camps the following year, eventually permitting the residents to return to California.[15]

Before that happened, a few of the affected Japanese-Americans tried to contest the legality of the relocation orders, and four cases eventually reached the Supreme Court. Two of the cases, those of Gordon Hirabayashi and Fred Korematsu, were critically important. The

Court held against both Hirabayashi and Korematsu. Nearly forty years later, in 1988, Congress enacted a resolution of apology for what one of the camp residents, Fred Korematsu, properly described as "a great wrong." But what about 1944? Why did the Court not reach the same conclusion then?[16]

Hirabayashi

GORDON HIRABAYASHI WAS an American citizen born of Japanese parents in Auburn, Washington. A pacifist, he deliberately violated the curfew and the exclusion orders in May 1942. Immediately thereafter, he went to the FBI, bringing with him a briefcase containing papers that documented his violations, and explained that he wanted to test the orders' lawfulness.[17]

The government charged Hirabayashi with two criminal misdemeanors, the first for refusing to report to an assembly center, the second for not keeping the curfew. He was convicted of both. The federal judge, after holding the curfew orders constitutional, sentenced him to consecutive sentences of thirty days of imprisonment for each violation—a total of sixty days. When Hirabayashi discovered that he would serve his thirty-day sentences in the local jail, he asked to serve instead in an outdoor work camp. The judge, making a decision that had surprisingly important later consequences, accommodated him, changing Hirabayashi's sentence to ninety days for each violation to run *concurrently,* that is, ninety days in total.[18]

Hirabayashi appealed his convictions to the Ninth Circuit Court of Appeals. That court held the case on its docket for several months without reaching a decision. On February 19, 1943, the appeals court heard oral argument. Then, at the Justice Department's request, it asked the Supreme Court to consider the constitutional questions. The Court announced on April 5 that it would decide the case.[19]

Both sides saw the case as a test of the government's internment authority. The American Civil Liberties Union (ACLU) guided the preparation of Hirabayashi's brief, which focused on detention. How could the Constitution permit detention of American citizens without any procedural safeguards? How could it permit detention of a group whose members were mostly indisputably loyal? How could it select that group on the basis of race? Why, at the very least, did the government not begin a loyalty screening program immediately after internment began?[20]

The government did not find these questions easy to answer. How could the War Department argue against loyalty screening? It recognized that many citizens of Japanese ancestry were undoubtedly loyal. In early 1943 it had created that highly decorated Nisei fighting unit, the 442nd Regimental Combat Team. And as I've mentioned, the War Relocation Authority began a screening program that would allow loyal citizens to return to the West Coast, but with a catch. A screening question asked if the internee was willing to "serve in the armed forces of the United States on combat duty." The WRA counted a negative answer, even from women and children, as suggesting uncertain loyalty. It then decided there were too many negatives to warrant allowing any internees to return to California. Regardless, why not screen and return?[21]

The War Department began to lose confidence in General DeWitt. The general filed a long report in which he justified the original relocation on grounds of military necessity (invasion, sabotage, espionage). He justified the lack of screening *not* on grounds that "there was insufficient time" but for reasons resting on racial stereotype: "the realities" are, he said, "that an exact separation of the 'sheep from the goats' was unfeasible." DeWitt also opposed introduction of a new screening program because doing so now would lead judges to ask why it could not have been done earlier. After reading the report, John McCloy concluded that it sounded racist and would hurt the government's cause, and therefore refused at first to make the report public.[22]

At the same time, the Justice Department began to lose confidence in the War Department. Edward Ennis, a Justice Department lawyer, read an October 1942 *Harper's Magazine* article whose author appeared to be a high-ranking Naval Intelligence officer. The author revealed that within six weeks of Pearl Harbor the Office of Naval Intelligence (in charge of the armed forces' Japan-related intelligence) had estimated the number of potential "saboteurs or agents" within the United

States at approximately thirty-five hundred. He wrote that "the entire 'Japanese Problem' has been magnified out of its true proportion, largely because of the physical characteristics of the people," and he recommended that the problem "be handled on the basis of the *individual*, regardless of citizenship, and *not* on a racial basis." He concluded that it would be necessary to evacuate, at the very most, ten thousand individuals whom the Office of Naval Intelligence could identify by name. After reading this, Ennis asked the solicitor general how the department could tell the Court that individual screening prior to relocation would have been impractical, when it seemed that General DeWitt was told the contrary. Moreover, the British had provided individual hearings within a few months to more than a hundred thousand German and Italian "enemy aliens."[23]

When it argued in the Supreme Court, however, the government followed DeWitt's line of thinking. The solicitor general told the Court that in January 1942 the army thought invasion possible. Fears of espionage and sabotage by Japanese-Americans were "realistic and not a figment of the imagination." Furthermore, the "task of promptly segregating the potentially disloyal from the loyal," though "comparatively simple," would have taken "many months, perhaps years," because Japanese-Americans "had never become assimilated" and some "may lack to some extent a feeling of loyalty toward the United States" as a result of discriminatory treatment. The solicitor general spoke of the fear that among the Japanese-Americans there were "a number of persons who might assist the enemy." He said this fear was "not based on race but on these other factors," that is, aiding the enemy. Lawyers representing California, Washington, and Oregon had obtained copies of DeWitt's report and used it to provide support for similar race-based arguments.[24]

On June 21, 1943, the Court released its opinion. It did not decide the most important question presented—that of relocation. Instead, it stated that it needed only to decide the curfew question. If the curfew order was valid, then what was in effect a single ninety-day sentence was valid, and all the other issues in respect to Hirabayashi's punishment were purely hypothetical. And, in the Court's view, the curfew order was legally valid.[25]

The Court thought the congressional legislation and the executive order clearly delegated to a military commander the power to issue a curfew order. The basic question was whether the Constitution permitted that commander to do so, given that the order restricted the freedom of American citizens to leave their homes and that it was race based. The Court answered this question by holding the curfew constitutional, on the basis of the wartime emergency, the constitutional grants of the war powers to the president and to Congress, and the consequent need for judges to defer to military decision making.[26]

The Court, it said, cannot "sit in review of the wisdom" of the warmaking activities of the executive and legislative branches; nor can it "substitute its judgment for theirs." Rather, a court should simply ask whether "in the light of all the relevant circumstances" as seen at the time there was a "reasonable basis for . . . imposing the curfew." The Court then explained why it believed there was a reasonable basis here.[27]

As to wartime need: the military authorities feared invasion, arguing that the risk of sabotage and espionage in the relevant geographic area seemed obvious. In any event, the military authorities made "findings of danger from espionage and sabotage, and of the necessity of the curfew order to protect against them."[28]

As to race: the "danger of espionage and sabotage, in time of war and of threatened invasion," warrants an exception to the general rule that "discrimination based on race alone" amounts to a "denial of equal protection." The "solidarity" of those of Japanese origin, their comparative lack of assimilation, and their resentment provoked by restrictions all taken together may have "encouraged the continued attachment of members of this group to Japan"—or at least the relevant military authorities may have so found. And "we cannot reject as unfounded the judgment of the military authorities and of Congress that there were disloyal members of that population, whose number and strength could not be precisely and quickly ascertained."[29]

The conclusion: because the "circumstances within the knowledge of those charged with the responsibility for maintaining the national defense afforded a rational basis for the decision," the "curfew order as applied, and at the time it was applied, was within the boundaries of the war power."[30]

Although the decision was unanimous, three justices wrote separate opinions as well. Justice Douglas underlined the Court's inability to second-guess the military. Given that "the orders . . . have some relation to 'protection against espionage . . . ,' our task is at an end" (although some reclassification system might eventually be necessary). Justice Frank Murphy deplored the racial distinctions but thought they were necessary here because of the "great emergency," the "critical military situation," and the "urgent necessity of taking prompt and effective action to secure defense installations and military operations against the risk of sabotage and espionage." Justice Wiley Blount Rutledge wrote that General DeWitt had "wide discretion" to take action "necessary to the region's . . . safety," but there may still have been judicially enforceable "bounds beyond which he cannot go."[31]

The government thus won the comparatively easy curfew case. But what of the harder, more central cases challenging the relocation program itself? Fred Korematsu had been convicted for refusing to report to Tanforan for relocation. His case, too, was before the Court. Although the lower courts thought a technicality (related to the sentence imposed) might block Supreme Court review, the Court held that it did not. Still, it did not decide the relocation issue. Instead, it sent Korematsu's case (along with another "curfew" case, that of Min Yasui) back to the lower courts for further consideration.

Korematsu

Fred Korematsu, an American citizen, was born of Japanese parents in Oakland, California. He studied briefly at Los Angeles City College and then became a welder. He tried to join the navy, which rejected him for medical reasons.[32]

Korematsu refused to report for relocation, and on May 30 local police arrested him. Although some of the internees he knew advised him against contesting relocation, he decided to mount a legal fight. He explained why:

> Assembly Camps were for: Dangerous Enemy Aliens and Citizens; These camps have been definitely an imprisonment under

> armed guard with orders shoot to kill. In order to be imprisoned, these people should have been given a fair trial in order that they may defend their loyalty at court in a democratic way, but they were placed in imprisonment without any fair trial! Many Disloyal Germans and Italians were caught, but they were not all corralled under armed guard like the Japanese—is this a racial issue? If not, the Loyal Citizens want fair trial to prove their loyalty! Also their [*sic*] are many loyal aliens who can prove their loyalty to America, and they must be given fair trial and treatment! Fred Korematsu's Test Case may help.[33]

In mid-1942, Korematsu was convicted of violating the statute enforcing the exclusion (that is, the "report for internment") orders. As I mentioned, the Court did not resolve the relocation issue the first time it heard his case but instead returned the case to the court of appeals for further consideration. The Supreme Court might have heard the case in the spring of 1944, but further delay, in part because of disagreements among the lawyers, meant that it did not hear the case until October 1944.[34]

In the meantime, the factual foundation underlying the government's arguments began to crumble. General DeWitt had written a new, more complete final report in which he repeated his claims of espionage, sabotage, and dual loyalty. He claimed, for example, that before the relocation he had received "hundreds of reports nightly of signal lights visible from the coast, and of intercepts of unidentified radio transmissions" from the mainland to offshore submarines. The report became public. Newspapers across the country wrote about it. One press article said that in 1942 the "Japs attacked all ships leaving coast" (*Washington Post*). Others said that "signals from the shore aided the Japanese in attacks on the West Coast" (*San Francisco Examiner*) and that there were "plenty of reasons for removing Japs" (*Los Angeles Times*). The press criticized the "reluctance of the Justice Department" to accept and enforce all DeWitt's recommendations.[35]

But DeWitt had gone too far. The publicity led two Justice Department lawyers working on the *Korematsu* case to ask the Federal Communications Commission (FCC) and the FBI to look into the report's claims. The FCC returned with documents showing that, at DeWitt's request, soon after Pearl Harbor the FCC had set up a communications detection system with roving patrol boats. But they had found no clandestine transmissions; any reports of those transmissions had come from untrained army privates who did not know how to use the electronic detection equipment. And they had told DeWitt this at the time. The FCC had investigated 760 reports of suspicious signals in the first half of 1942, and none came from Japanese-American sources. (Of the 760 instances, 641 involved no signal, the remaining 119 emanated from ordinary sources, such as army and navy transmitters and licensed commercial broadcasting stations.) The upshot, said the FCC, was that at the time of relocation "there wasn't a single illicit station and DeWitt knew it."[36]

The FBI report said the bureau had no information linking attacks on ships or the shoreline immediately after Pearl Harbor to espionage activity onshore or to illicit radio or light signaling. The report traced DeWitt's sabotage charges to three instances in which offshore Japanese vessels had shelled or bombed West Coast targets, two of which took place *after* the relocation and the third (ineffective shelling near Santa Barbara) was based on information collected long before Pearl Harbor. The FBI reiterated that J. Edgar Hoover had opposed the relocation as unnecessary at the time.[37]

Faced with the FCC and FBI reports, the Office of Naval Intelligence recommendation against evacuation, and Hoover's initial opposition, the Justice Department could not easily claim military necessity to justify the relocation. The two Justice Department lawyers wrote a draft brief referring to *Hirabayashi*'s upholding the curfew while specifically claiming only that in 1942 army officials had "ample ground" to fear that Japan would attack the West Coast. The lawyers added a draft footnote that asked the Court *not* to take "judicial notice" of facts stated in DeWitt's final report. The draft footnote said that the report's "recital of the circumstances justifying the evacuation as a matter of military necessity" is "in several respects, particularly with reference to the use of illegal radio transmitters and to shore-to-ship signaling by persons of Japanese ancestry, in conflict with information in the possession of the Department of Justice."[38]

The War Department and others in the Justice Department strongly objected to the draft footnote. Eventually, the assistant attorney general for war, Herbert Wechsler, drafted a compromise, which appeared in the final brief. It said: "We have specifically recited in this brief the facts relating to the justification for the evacuation, of which we ask the Court to take judicial notice; and we rely upon the Final Report [of DeWitt] only to the extent that it relates to such facts." The lawyers reluctantly agreed to the compromise and signed the brief.[39]

While the department was preparing to defend the relocation in the Supreme Court, internment itself was drawing to a close. The War Department had recognized DeWitt's hostility to Japanese-Americans (he had once told officials there "isn't such a thing as a loyal Japanese") and had replaced him with successors who thought that camp internment should end. The threat of invasion had long since passed. Whatever screening could be done had been done. The War Relocation Authority saw no reason to prolong internment, and the Justice Department, too, wished to end it. California's political officials, however, recognizing the unpopularity of the Japanese-Americans' return, favored continued internment. The president seemed to agree, reportedly stating in May 1944 that he thought it would be a mistake to do anything "drastic or sudden," at least until after the 1944 election.[40]

Regardless, the Court had set *Korematsu* for argument. Along with *Korematsu,* the Court had agreed to hear the case of Mitsuye Endo. Endo, an American citizen who had worked for the State of California, had been taken into custody and sent to a relocation camp. In July 1942 she filed a habeas corpus petition in the federal district court in San Francisco arguing directly that her continued confinement in a camp was unconstitutional and requesting release. The War Relocation Authority considered her loyal and offered to release her if she would promise not to return to California. She refused to promise and pursued her request for judicial relief, but the lower courts denied her request.[41]

WHAT COULD THE government argue in the Supreme Court? Its claim that military necessity justified the original internment had been weakened if not destroyed. Internment itself was on its last legs, perhaps over. The government's *Korematsu* brief therefore relied heavily on the fact that Korematsu's conviction rested on his violation not of an *internment* order but of an *exclusion* order that required him to stay on the West Coast while leaving all parts of the West Coast except Tanforan Racetrack, a relocation assembly area. The government added that Korematsu, like Hirabayashi (who had violated the curfew order), had been convicted simply of being in a place where he had no right to be at the time. The government still defended the internment program but emphasized what had previously been a subsidiary point, namely, that the program was lawful as a measure to "alleviate tension and prevent incidents involving violence between Japanese migrants and others."[42]

In Endo's case, the government virtually conceded that the War Relocation Authority could not detain loyal American citizens of Japanese ancestry beyond a period necessary to screen them for loyalty. But it added that Endo had to comply with the authority's leave policy—that is, promise not to return to California—before she could be released.[43]

On Korematsu's side of the case, the ACLU, represented by Charles Horsky, pointed to the government's footnote, which Horsky called "extraordinary." He said the footnote effectively disavowed DeWitt's security-based claims of military necessity. The Japanese American Citizens League supported Korematsu by filing a two-hundred-page brief referring to numerous scholarly studies that undermined claims of Japanese-American race-based or culture-based tendencies toward disloyalty.[44]

The Decisions

On December 18, 1944, the Court released its *Korematsu* and *Endo* decisions. By a vote of 6 to 3, the Court upheld Korematsu's conviction; at the same time, it unanimously ordered Endo's release. Justice Black wrote the *Korematsu* majority's brief opinion accepting the government's claim that it should not consider the lawfulness of Fred Korematsu's *detention* in a relocation camp. The Court, it said, had to decide only whether the government could order Korematsu *excluded* from the West Coast, in effect forcing him to report to an assembly center. The Court held that the government could do so. It wrote that the exclusion order sufficiently resembled the curfew order that the Court in *Hirabayashi* had already upheld as lawful.[45]

The Court recognized that "exclusion from the area in which one's home is located is a far greater deprivation than constant confinement to the home from 8 p.m. to 6 a.m." But "exclusion from a threatened area, no less than curfew, has a definite and close relationship to the prevention of espionage and sabotage." Moreover, in *Hirabayashi* the Court accepted the military's finding that it was "impossible to bring about an immediate segregation of the disloyal from the loyal." The military based its "temporary exclusion" order here "on the same ground." Ultimately, the Court wrote, the "properly constituted military authorities" had found that the "urgency" of the situation "demanded that all citizens of Japanese ancestry be segregated from the West Coast temporarily." And because "Congress, reposing its confidence in this time of war in our military leaders—as inevitably it must—determined that they should have the power to do just this, . . . we cannot—by availing ourselves of the calm perspective of hindsight—now say that at that time these actions were unjustified."[46]

Justice Frankfurter wrote a concurring opinion repeating what he had said in *Hirabayashi,* namely, that the Court should determine whether the orders were " 'reasonably expedient military precautions' in time of war." He concluded that they were.[47]

Three justices filed dissenting opinions. Justice Roberts's opinion, in concluding that the exclusion orders were unconstitutional, undermined the majority's claim that the lawfulness of Korematsu's confinement was not before the Court. Justice Roberts pointed out that DeWitt's two March 1942 orders, taken together, required Korematsu both not to leave the West Coast and not to remain anywhere on the West Coast except for assembly centers, such as Tanforan Racetrack. What is that, asked Roberts, but "confinement" at a detention center, a "euphemism for a prison," from which no person was "permitted to leave except by Military Order"? In any event, had Korematsu reported to the assembly center, he would have been "removed to a Relocation Center," which Justice Roberts said was "a euphemism" for concentration camps.[48]

Justice Murphy examined the orders and found they had no adequate factual foundation. First, as explained in DeWitt's final report, they were based on a host of "questionable racial and sociological grounds not ordinarily within the realm of expert military judgment." Murphy said there was no evidence of "subversive activities," "teachings," and the like. He added that "every charge relative to race, religion, culture, geographical location, and legal and economic status has been substantially discredited by independent studies made by experts in these matters." He supported his conclusion with a series of footnotes that refer to studies about attendance at Japanese-language schools, dual citizenship, integration into American society, and religious practices. Murphy said that a "military judgment" to the contrary must rest on "racial and sociological" pieces of "misinformation, half-truths and insinuations" and did not warrant "the great weight ordinarily given the judgments based upon strictly military considerations."[49]

Second, Murphy said, the report did not clearly charge and did not prove that people of Japanese ancestry were responsible for "radio transmission," "night signaling," or three "minor isolated shellings." Third, the report nowhere described or verified any individual incident of hostility to Japanese-Americans that might justify removal for their own safety. Regardless, the "dangerous doctrine of protective custody" should not stand as "an excuse for the deprivation of the rights of minority groups." Fourth, the government did not explain why it could not treat these Japanese-Americans on an "individual basis," screening them for loyalty, as the British had done.[50]

Finally, Murphy wrote, there was no reason to think that the FBI and intelligence services "did not have the espionage and sabotage situation well in hand." After all, "not one person of Japanese ancestry was accused or convicted of espionage or sabotage after Pearl Harbor while they were still free."[51]

Justice Jackson also filed a dissent arguing that the Court could not possibly know whether relocation was justified in early 1942. The case, he said, showed the "limitation under which courts always will labor in examining the necessity for a military order." How, he asked, "does the Court know that these orders have a reasonable basis in necessity?" In "the very nature of things military decisions are not susceptible of intelligent judicial appraisal." The Court had "no real evidence before it." No "evidence whatever" as to need "has been taken by this or any other court." Thus the Court had "no choice but to accept General DeWitt's own unsworn, self-serving statement . . . that what he did was reasonable. And *thus it will always be* when courts try to look into the reasonableness of a military order." Hence, the Court was wrong to apply a standard that would consider whether "reasonable military grounds" supported the orders, for any such standard was inevitably meaningless in practice.[52]

Jackson's solution: Courts should not try to assess an order's reasonableness. They should instead simply refuse to enforce "an order which violates constitutional limitations" regardless. That refusal will not hurt the military effort, for any emergency that led to the military order would likely be over before a court could refuse to enforce the order. Moreover, the alternative, judicial acceptance of the order, would create a terrible precedent "that [would] lie[] about like a loaded weapon ready for the hand of any authority that can bring forward a plausible claim of an urgent need."[53]

Justice Jackson thus recommended what seems like a highly pragmatic approach: recognizing that generals may well act unconstitutionally when faced with an emergency, courts must later strike down their actions as unconstitutional, but only after the emergency has passed.

Lessons

To its long-lasting shame, the Court upheld exclusion orders based on racial and cultural stereotypes, which removed tens of thousands of American citizens from their homes and interned them in camps. The orders did not come accompanied with any system for individual loyalty screening. Nor could they be justified in terms of military necessity. Yet the Court held that these orders did *not* deprive these citizens of their "liberty . . . without due process of law." And, as Justice Jackson pointed out, the Court's holding came at a time when all military justification for the internment had vanished. The government was ready to free the Japanese-Americans regardless.[54]

Of course, the Court did order Endo released from confinement. But students of history do not think that *Endo* counterbalances *Korematsu.* The Court in *Endo* based its decision not on the Constitution but on statutes and regulations. It said the statutes and regulations that authorized the orders requiring Korematsu to report to a relocation center did not encompass later internment. It did not discuss whether the Constitution forbids internment. Hence, considering the two decisions together, the Court held that the Constitution permits Korematsu's confinement while leaving unanswered the question of the Constitution's relation to later internment.[55]

Why did the Court reach its *Korematsu* conclusion? The justices in the majority—many of whom were later part of the Court's unanimous *Brown v. Board of Education* decision—were not sympathetic to race-based decision making. Nor were they unsympathetic to claims for protection of individual liberty. The Frankfurter/Jackson dialogue suggests a better answer: The Court decided as it did because it could not find a way to protect individual liberties from invasion by the president without at the same time taking from the president discretionary powers that the war might require him to exercise.

Although the tension between Court and president is real, Justice Frankfurter's solution was not tenable. He wrote that military actions, if reasonable, do not violate the Constitution. Under that view, the Constitution grants the president broad authority to run the war. As Justices Jackson and Murphy observed, however, the Court cannot easily know what is reasonable. Furthermore, if the standard leads to a holding that Korematsu's forced relocation is lawful, then what is not? What constraint does it impose? As applied in *Korematsu,* Frankfurter's standard becomes essentially a license for the president to act virtually as he sees fit. The majority said that "legal restrictions which curtail the civil rights of a single racial group . . . are subject . . . to the most rigid scrutiny," but its actual ruling suggested the contrary.[56]

Justice Jackson's approach also suffers serious shortcomings. He argued that the military will act as it believes necessary and the Court can later strike down any actions that exceed ordinary constitutional limits. That approach seems both too broad and too narrow. It is too broad because its very realism suggests that the nation may well have to rely on its military taking *unconstitutional* actions to save the nation from invasion or destruction. That approach runs the danger of the military's and the president's taking the Court's statement itself as a permission to exercise wartime judgment as they wish and consequently exercising it in too broad a fashion. Furthermore, the statement, by encouraging the military or the president *not* to follow the Constitution (as the Court interprets it), undermines the very habits and customs needed to give the Constitution's promises practical effect. The approach is too narrow because its adoption of strict constitutional standards may sometimes stop a president or his advisers from taking actions they correctly conclude are necessary to save the nation. The president would obey the Court's constitutional interpretation at great peril to the nation. The Constitution, as Jackson later wrote, is not a "suicide pact."[57]

Justice Murphy, though right about the *Korematsu* case itself, did not offer a generally workable solution, for he did not directly consider the problem that concerned Frankfurter and the majority: How are courts to decide whether military orders are or are not reasonable? Murphy's approach of examining the factual underpinnings of the military orders threatened to enmesh the Court in case-by-case review of individual military orders—including orders issued in emergency circumstances. How would the Court decide future cases? Would military commanders fear that they needed legal advice and that they had to build court-type records before reaching military decisions? Perhaps fearing these consequences, the Court in effect chose to avoid this responsibility and defer to the president. The Court implicitly asked who has the ability and constitutional responsibility to manage a war—the Court or the president? This is certainly the question that Frankfurter addressed. If this is the question, the answer must be the president.

Might the Court have found a workable way to hold the president constitutionally accountable? Perhaps it could have developed a sliding scale in respect to the length of detention and the intensity of its examination of the circumstances. Perhaps it could have insisted that the government increase screening efforts the longer an individual is held in detention. Perhaps it could have required the government to have had in place from the beginning a plan for future screening. Perhaps it could have deemed critical the fact that the relocation was imposed within the United States itself during a period not of martial law but when ordinary civilian courts were fully operative. Perhaps, by focusing directly on these or similar possibilities, the Court might have written a legal rule that structured judicial review of military actions—ideally a rule that steered between burdensome, case-by-case judicial review and no review at all.

As it was, the Court majority understood the danger of excessive judicial interference in military affairs, but it did not satisfactorily address the problem of insufficient judicial involvement. If it had focused on the latter problem—telling the president even in wartime that the sky is not the limit—it might have found a way to maintain presidential accountability without undermining the president's need for broad discretionary wartime powers. Its mistake was focusing too heavily on the former.

WHAT HARM DID the *Korematsu* decision actually cause? The decision itself hurt the interned Japanese by validating their internment. It also affirmed Fred Korematsu's criminal conviction. The War Relocation Authority mitigated the harm to some degree when, the day before the Court announced its *Korematsu* and *Endo* decisions, it stated with unconscious irony that as of January 2, 1945, all "persons of Japanese ancestry whose records have stood the test of Army scrutiny" would be "permitted the same freedom of movement throughout the United States as other loyal citizens and law-abiding aliens."[58]

Fred Korematsu returned to the Bay Area, where he became a successful engineer and landscape architect. Eventually, a federal district court in San Francisco voided his original conviction. And the nation apologized, and in 1988 provided some monetary compensation, to those whom it had interned.[59]

History did not bear out Justice Jackson's prediction that the decision would create a bad legal precedent, a precedent that would lie in wait "like a loaded weapon" waiting to justify a future abusive act. The decision has been so thoroughly discredited that it is hard to conceive of any future Court referring to it favorably or relying on it. *Korematsu*'s impact as precedent likely consists of what it failed to do: make clear that there are at least some actions that the Constitution forbids presidents and their military delegates to take, even in wartime.[60]

Korematsu harmed the Court. It suggested that the Court was unwilling or unable to make an unpopular decision that would protect an unpopular minority. This suggests a failure to carry out what Hamilton saw as a primary function of the Court's exercise of judicial review. In general, the Court's ruling in this case has gone down as a judicial failure. *Korematsu* shows the practical need for the Court to assure constitutional accountability, even of the president and even in time of war or national emergency.

Chapter Fifteen

Presidential Power: Guantánamo and Accountability

THE SEPTEMBER 2001 terrorist attacks on the United States led to a war in Afghanistan, which was accused of harboring the terrorists who planned the attacks. It also led to the capture of suspected terrorists and terrorist sympathizers, the incarceration of several hundred suspected Al Qaeda or Taliban members and supporters at Guantánamo Bay, Cuba, and court cases growing out of that confinement. Between 2003 and 2007 the Court decided four of those cases. They involved detained persons who sought writs of habeas corpus to secure their release and raised questions involving the liberty of terrorist suspects and national security needs. They required the Court to consider its relationships with Congress and the president when security is at risk. And they presented the Court with a challenge similar to that presented in *Korematsu.* Is there a workable legal approach that can help the Court ensure constitutional fidelity when national security is endangered? I believe the Court adopted a more workable approach than in *Korematsu,* but history will ultimately decide whether the Court met that challenge appropriately. Here I can simply describe what the Court did, while emphasizing the Court's role in helping to make the Constitution work.

The basic facts are well-known. On September 11, 2001, Al Qaeda terrorists hijacked four commercial airliners and used them to destroy the World Trade Center and demolish a portion of the Pentagon. (Passengers brought down in Pennsylvania a fourth plane believed to be on its way to Capitol Hill.) The terrorist attacks killed approximately three thousand people, injured many thousands of others, and destroyed billions of dollars' worth of property. At the request of President Bush, Congress immediately authorized him to use "all necessary and appropriate force against those nations, organizations, or persons he determines planned, authorized, committed, or aided the terrorist attacks . . . or harbored such organizations or persons." The president sent American troops to Afghanistan to fight against that country's Taliban government as well as the Al Qaeda forces that the government had harbored.[1]

During the next several years American and allied forces captured and screened more than 10,000 suspected Al Qaeda or Taliban members. They sent about 750 individuals to the American naval base at Guantánamo Bay, Cuba. Most of those confined were citizens of Afghanistan, Saudi Arabia, or Yemen, and the rest came from among thirty different countries. In the early years most detainees were fighters from countries other than Afghanistan, and about one-third were Al Qaeda leaders or operatives. Many of those originally confined were released. In later years the population consisted primarily of Al Qaeda and Taliban leaders and operatives.[2]

As of late 2004 the government had freed or released to the care of other governments about 200 individuals, and about 550 remained in custody. As of late 2008 the number in custody had fallen to about 260, including 27 Al Qaeda leaders, 99 lower-level Al Qaeda operatives, 9 Taliban leaders, 14 lower-level Taliban operatives, 93 foreign fighters, and several others.[3]

Defense Department reports state that the inmates were initially housed in Camp X-Ray, a "spartan" facility with "simple" plywood interrogation rooms, built in the 1990s to house Cuban and Haitian refugees. Because of Camp X-Ray's "limited capacity and primitive conditions," military authorities soon built another facility, Camp Delta, which housed about six hundred detainees. Eventually, the authorities built a third "maximum security" facility, Camp 5, with room for about a hundred of "the most uncooperative individuals." Most detainees remained in custody for two to four years. About 10 percent were confined more than five years.[4]

A Defense Department document also explains why the department chose Guantánamo as a place for interrogation and confinement. Guantánamo was near the United States and under U.S. control. It also was secure and far from the Afghanistan battlefields. And most important, it "was considered a place where these benefits could be realized without the detainees having the opportunity to contest their detention in the U.S. courts."[5]

Guantánamo's inmates, aided by attorneys working free of charge, soon began to challenge this last assumption. The Defense Department did not permit any direct contact with the inmates, nor did it provide them with legal counsel, but it did release their identities. Civil rights groups and others then asked the detainees' friends or relatives to bring a lawsuit, under a law that permitted a suit on behalf of an individual held in custody, that is, as a "next friend." With legal representation provided by the interested groups, "next friends" brought petitions for writs of habeas corpus in the federal courts, claiming that the Constitution or laws of the United States entitled the inmate to release. Did the law permit such an inmate to file such a petition? If so, did it entitle the inmate to release? Four cases presenting these or similar questions made their way to the Supreme Court. (I joined the majority or plurality in all of these cases.)

Rasul

SHAFIQ RASUL, ELEVEN other Kuwaitis, and two Australians, all detained at Guantánamo, were the petitioners in the first case, *Rasul v. Bush,* which the Court decided in June 2004. Although the Defense Department said they were enemy combatants captured during fighting in Afghanistan, they argued that they were humanitarian aid workers who had been taken prisoner by mistake. They asked the federal district court to issue writs of habeas corpus requiring the Defense Department to release them or at least give them a better opportunity to prove they were not combatants. The question for the Court was whether a civilian court could even consider a Guantánamo prisoner's claim that the government was confining him unlawfully.[6]

The writ of habeas corpus provides a bedrock protection for an individual's freedom. The writ originated in England more than four hundred years ago and allows a court to review an individual's claim that the government, then the king, is confining that individual without the legal authority to do so. The Constitution underlines the importance of the writ by stating that the "privilege of the Writ of Habeas Corpus shall not be suspended, unless when in Cases of Rebellion or Invasion the public Safety may require it." The first Congress that met after the adoption of the Constitution enacted laws authorizing courts to issue writs of habeas corpus. The statute books have contained laws of this kind ever since.[7]

The *Rasul* case asked whether a civilian court has the power to issue a writ of habeas corpus on behalf of a Guantánamo prisoner. If not, neither the Supreme Court nor any lower civilian court could even consider the prisoners' claims of unlawful detention. The answer to the question turned on what seem highly technical matters. The congressional habeas corpus statute said that writs of habeas corpus "may be granted" by justices of the Supreme Court, by individual district courts, and by individual circuit judges, "*within their respective jurisdictions.*"[8]

These last four words make clear that a particular judge can issue a writ only within a particular geographic area. The word "jurisdiction" suggests that the area in question is one where the judge's court ordinarily exercises binding legal authority, say Washington, D.C., in the case of the federal district judge in question. How do these words apply when, as in the *Rasul* situation, the imprisoned person is held at Guantánamo Bay, but the jailer, namely, the government, operates, and is subject to being sued, within Washington, D.C.? Does the statute authorize a judge in Washington, D.C., to issue a writ on behalf of such a person, a person held by the military outside the United States?

Because the wording of the habeas corpus statute does not answer this question, the Court had to look elsewhere, and it found conflicting cases. On the one hand, several earlier cases suggested that the place that mattered was the place where the detained person was held, that is, Guantánamo, not the place where the government might be found, that is, Washington, D.C. Just after World War II the Court held in *Johnson v. Eisentrager* that federal courts did not have jurisdiction to consider the habeas corpus petitions filed in the United States by several German citizens who had been captured and were being held abroad. American forces had captured the Germans in China, and a military tribunal in Nanking had convicted them of war crimes. They were imprisoned in Germany at a prison managed by Allied forces, including Americans. When the Court decided that a court within the United States could not consider their habeas petitions, it referred to all these circumstances. It pointed out that the prisoner was an enemy alien who had never been to the United States. He had been captured abroad by military forces and convicted abroad of crimes committed outside the United States. And he was imprisoned outside the United States. In *Rasul* the government relied on this case. But after *Eisentrager* the Court decided another case in which it held that a Kentucky federal court could consider a habeas petition filed by a prisoner confined in a prison in Alabama. The Guantánamo petitioners relied on this case, arguing further that in the earlier case, *Eisentrager,* the court had based its conclusion on the presence of several factors, two of which were absent here. First, the Guantánamo petitioners had not been convicted of war crimes. Second, they were not being held *outside the United States.* Guantánamo, they said, was part of the United States.[9]

The Supreme Court agreed with this last argument. It held in *Rasul* that the prisoners could file their habeas petitions because for all practical purposes Guantánamo was part of the United States. The United States had leased Guantánamo from Cuba in 1903. But, as Justice Anthony Kennedy observed in a concurrence, the "lease is no ordinary lease." Although the lease says that Cuba retains "ultimate sovereignty," its term is "indefinite," and the lease cannot be abrogated unless the United States stops using Guantánamo as a naval base or otherwise consents to the abrogation. As long as the United States is present, the base is totally subject to American, and only to American, law.[10]

The Court made clear that precedent did not require it to decide in the government's favor. Precedent alone was too ambiguous to answer the question by itself; and, finding the legislative history of the habeas statute of little help, the Court tried to determine, hypothetically, what Congress *would have wanted* had it actually considered the matter. How far would Congress have wanted the habeas statute to reach? The Court's consideration of statutory purposes turned to more basic and practical questions.[11]

For the Court, the writ's basic critical role in protecting freedom argued strongly for a more expansive interpretation of the statute. The Court quoted Justice Jackson:

> Executive imprisonment has been considered oppressive and lawless since John, at Runnymede, pledged that no free man should be imprisoned, dispossessed, outlawed, or exiled save by the judgment of his peers or by the law of the land. The judges of England developed the writ of habeas corpus largely to preserve these immunities from executive restraint.

Given the constitutional importance of protecting individual rights, the writ's historic role in helping to do so, and the Constitution's own reference to that importance, the Court thought that Congress would likely have favored an expansive interpretation of the habeas statute—at least other things being equal.[12]

On this point the Court's six-member majority (which I joined) and the three dissenting justices disagreed. The dissenters thought that other things were not at all equal. They feared that an interpretation of the habeas statute that permitted the district court in this case to consider the Guantánamo prisoners' habeas petitions would also permit courts in other cases to consider petitions filed by other prisoners of war, including any equivalent to the millions of enemy combatants that the Allies imprisoned during World War II. If so, they asked, how could the military run the war?

The dissenting justices were concerned that the Court's holding read the habeas statute as extending to "aliens held beyond the sovereign territory of the United States and beyond the territorial jurisdiction of its courts." This, they thought, was a "breathtaking" expansion of habeas jurisdiction. If every prisoner of war could hire a lawyer and sue for release, how could army commanders organize a battle? How could inexpert federal courts oversee a significant "aspect of the Executive's conduct of a foreign war"?[13]

Although the Court majority did not deny the importance of these practical considerations, it also thought they did not require the dissenters' interpretation of the statute. Allowing Guantánamo prisoners to file habeas petitions need not interfere with the decisions of the president and the military during wartime or other national emergency. For one thing, as Justice Kennedy's concurrence pointed out, Guantánamo is *not* a foreign battlefield. It is "far removed from hostilities" and "is in every practical aspect a United States territory." To find that imprisonment at Guantánamo falls within the habeas "jurisdiction" of the federal courts tells us nothing about petitions filed under battlefield conditions, or other petitions filed concerning imprisonment outside the United States.[14]

In addition, the decision held only that a federal court *may consider* a habeas petition filed by a Guantánamo prisoner. It did not tell the court how to determine the merits of that petition. That court might take military needs, military expertise, and many other factors into account when it decided whether circumstances warranted *granting* the petition and *releasing* the prisoner. These matters were not before the Court, and its opinion said nothing about them.

Within the limits of the question before the Court—regarding the prisoners' right to *file* the petition—the Court gave greater weight to the importance of ensuring a prisoner access to the courts than to the risks of unwarranted interference with a president's congressionally authorized attempts to deal with a serious problem of national security. The detainees could file their habeas corpus petitions.

The upshot: The Court tried to interpret a silent statute consistently with a reasonable view of what Congress would have intended. It limited the president's power, but only to the extent that an individual detained at Guantánamo could file a habeas petition in federal court. It found a way to hold the president accountable to this limited extent while leaving much to be worked out later, perhaps by a district court, such as the extent to which foreign detainees have the same rights as American citizens. Furthermore, because the Court simply interpreted a statute, Congress would remain free to enact a new statute expressing a different view of its intentions—consistent with the Constitution.

HAMDI

ON THE DAY the Court decided *Rasul*, it also decided *Hamdi*. The facts of *Hamdi* were special. Yaser Esam Hamdi was an American citizen born in Louisiana. As a child he had moved with his family to Saudi Arabia, and as an adult he traveled to Afghanistan. Allied forces captured him during the fighting there and sent him to Guantánamo. But in light of his American citizenship, defense authorities transferred him to a navy prison in South Carolina.[15]

Hamdi's father filed a habeas corpus petition on his son's behalf in a federal district court in Virginia, claiming that he was simply a relief worker in Afghanistan. The government replied by producing a statement signed by an army official, which said that Hamdi had been "affiliated with a Taliban military unit," had "received weapons training," had "engaged in battle," and had "surrender[ed] his Kalashnikov assault rifle" to the allied forces who captured him.[16]

The district judge noted that the government's evidence consisted solely of hearsay and held that the evidence was not adequate. (The law often considers this kind of secondhand evidence less reliable than direct testimony and often bars its use at trial.) The court of appeals disagreed. It held that the evidence was sufficient to permit Hamdi's detention. Then the Supreme Court agreed to hear the case.[17]

Because Hamdi was imprisoned in South Carolina, no one doubted his right to *file* a habeas corpus petition in a federal court. As Justice O'Connor wrote in her opinion (which I joined), "All agree that, absent suspension, the writ of habeas corpus remains available to every individual detained within the United States." It is a "critical check on the Executive, ensuring that it does not detain individuals except in accordance with law." And, in petitioning for a writ of habeas corpus, "Hamdi was properly before [a federal] court to challenge his detention."[18]

At the same time, *Hamdi* presented fundamental questions about *how* the courts should handle these petitions. Hamdi's petition claimed that his detention violated the Constitution. The government responded that the Constitution permitted it to classify him as an enemy combatant and to hold him without filing formal charges until it decided whether further proceedings were warranted. The case presented the Court with two basic, related questions. First, does the Constitution permit the government to hold an American citizen as an enemy combatant? Second, if so, what procedures does the Constitution require the government to follow where the matter is contested? What evidence is necessary to determine who is telling the truth?

The Court answered the first question by holding, 5 to 4, that the Constitution did permit the government to hold enemy combatants during time of war and also to classify an American citizen as an enemy combatant. The Court pointed in support to a similar World War II case involving German sailors, some of whom had been born in America. Four of the five members of the majority in the *Hamdi* case (including me) added that the length of detention "may last no longer than active hostilities."[19]

Two dissenting justices agreed with the majority that the president could detain American citizens as enemy combatants, but they thought the president could do so only if Congress enacted a statute delegating this power, which, in their view, Congress had not done. Two other dissenting justices thought that the Constitution forbids the president to detain American citizens unless "criminal proceedings are promptly brought, or . . . Congress has suspended the writ of habeas corpus."[20]

The second question concerned Hamdi's claim that he was a relief worker, not an enemy combatant. What procedures did the Constitution require the government to follow, what evidence must it present, in order to resolve this claim? In answering these questions, the Court tried to reconcile its own constitutional role as a guardian of the Constitution's "fair procedure" requirements with the national security roles of Congress and the president. In doing so, a majority of the Court rejected the government's claim that it had provided Hamdi with fair procedures and provided sufficient evidence.

Justice O'Connor's opinion (for four members of the majority and which I joined) took as its "starting point" the "fundamental nature of a citizen's right to be free from involuntary confinement by his own government without due process of law." It added that " 'in our society liberty is the norm' and detention without trial 'is the carefully limited exception.' " It is "during our most challenging and uncertain moments that our Nation's commitment to due process is most severely tested; and it is in those times that we must preserve our commitment at home to the principles for which we fight abroad."[21]

Although the Constitution recognized that "core strategic matters of warmaking belong in the hands of those who are best positioned and most politically accountable for making them," it also recognizes the "time-honored and constitutionally mandated" role of courts. Unless "Congress acts to suspend it, the Great Writ of habeas corpus allows the Judicial Branch to play a necessary role in maintaining this delicate balance of governance, serving as an important judicial check on the Executive's discretion in the realm of detentions."[22]

Justice O'Connor continued:

> While we accord the greatest respect and consideration to the judgments of military authorities in matters relating to the actual prosecution of a war, and recognize that the scope of that discretion necessarily is wide, it does not infringe on the core role of the military for the courts to exercise their own time-honored and constitutionally mandated roles of reviewing and resolving claims like those presented here.[23]

Thus, a "judicious balancing" of interests was required. An approach that will work, even "in the enemy-combatant setting," requires the Court to ensure the "*core elements*" of procedural fairness, but otherwise allows the executive to "tailor" enemy combatant proceedings "to alleviate their uncommon potential to burden the Executive at a time of ongoing military conflict."[24]

The "core elements" of procedural fairness include the right of a "citizen-detainee" challenging his classification as an enemy combatant to "receive *notice of the factual basis for his classification, and a fair opportunity to rebut the Government's factual assertions before a neutral decisionmaker.*" As for other elements: military "exigencies" may sometimes demand "tailor[ing]" procedures to meet the needs of an "ongoing military conflict," perhaps to the point of using military tribunals, weakening hearsay rules, or applying pro-government assumptions. But, the plurality added, none of these matters need be decided now.[25]

In sum, the Court in *Hamdi* assured the president that, with congressional assent, he had authority during time of hostilities to take and to hold enemy combatants, including American citizens fighting against their country. At the same time, the Court exercised its constitutional role as guardian of the Constitution's procedural protections. It insisted on the application of the basic elements of procedural fairness while also seeking to ensure that the resulting procedures helped make democracy workable. In doing so, it was exceedingly practical. It took account of comparative institutional expertise, including practical considerations of workability in the particular military circumstances. It postponed any decision about particular detailed procedural requirements, and the flexibility of those requirements, leaving those for the time being to the lower courts.

Hamdan

After the Court decided *Rasul* and *Hamdi,* the Defense Department authorized Guantánamo detainees to obtain lawyers and file habeas corpus petitions. Almost all of them did. Meanwhile, the department created special military Combatant Status Review Tribunals, made up of three neutral commissioned officers, and gave each detainee the opportunity, with the help of a military representative, to contest his enemy combatant status before the tribunal. If the detainee later obtained new information, he could present it to the Administrative Review Board and explain why he no longer posed a threat (or why he never did) and why he should be released or transferred.[26]

At the same time, a presidential order subjected to trial before a "military commission"—a body not often used in the nation's history—any noncitizen who the military had reason to believe was a member of Al Qaeda or had "engaged or participated in terrorist activities aimed at or harmful to the United States." These special commissions, appointed by the military, allowed the individual before them fewer procedural protections than ordinary courts-martial or civilian courts provide defendants. For example, they could admit reasonably probative hearsay evidence; they could deny the detainee access to certain evidence; and they could exclude him from the proceeding when certain evidence was presented.[27]

In June 2006 the Supreme Court decided its third Guantánamo case, *Hamdan,* which concerned the president's authority to use these special military commissions. The case arose when military authorities brought charges before a special military commission claiming that Salim Ahmed Hamdan, who had been Osama bin Laden's personal driver and bodyguard, was a member of a conspiracy to attack civilians, engage in terrorism, and commit murder. The indictment charged that Hamdan had driven bin Laden to training camps, press conferences, lectures, and similar events, had arranged for the transportation of weapons, and had himself received weapons training.[28]

Hamdan filed a habeas petition in a federal district court. He argued that his confinement violated the law because he was confined pending trial before one of these commissions and the president lacked the legal authority to try him before such a commission. The district court agreed with Hamdan, but the court of appeals disagreed. The Supreme Court then consented to decide the question and held in Hamdan's favor, holding that the relevant statutes did not authorize the military to use these special commissions.

The case before the Court involved various questions of statutory interpretation. But the last sentence of the Court's opinion made an important general point. In "undertaking to try Hamdan and subject him to criminal punishment, the Executive is bound to comply with the rule of law that prevails in this jurisdiction." And it reaffirmed "the duty which rests on the courts, in time of war as well as in time of peace, to preserve unimpaired the constitutional safeguards of civil liberty."[29]

Nonetheless, the basic issue in the case was statutory, not constitutional, and the Court cautiously interpreted the relevant statutes. The key statute said the executive could use military commissions but only "with respect to offenders or offenses that [1] *by statute or* [2] *by the law of war* may be tried by military commissions." Because no "statute" gave military commissions authority to hear Hamdan's case, the determinative legal question was whether his case was one that a military commission could try "*by the law of war.*"[30]

Recognizing that the statute's language invited a historical investigation into what kinds of cases the "law of war" authorized commissions to try, the Court did just that. It concluded that the armed forces have used military commissions only where martial law has been declared, where civilian courts are not functioning, or where enemy battlefield combatants have violated the laws of war, say by committing atrocities. None of these circumstances was present in Hamdan's case. Hence the statute did not grant the president the power to try Hamdan before a military commission. Moreover, in the view of some justices, the government's basic charge, that Hamdan had conspired to help bin Laden commit terrorist acts, did not claim a violation of the "law of war."[31]

The Court pointed to another statute, which said that the military must (insofar as is "practicable") create procedures for military commissions and for courts-martial that are uniform and similar to those in ordinary courts. Where, asked the Court, is the procedural uniformity that this statute demands? Why can the commissions allow hearsay and exclude the defendant from certain proceedings in ways forbidden to courts-martial? Why is uniformity not "practicable"? The Court found no good answers to these questions, and it consequently held that the commissions' procedures violated the statute's uniformity requirement. The Court added that the commissions' unjustified use of nonuniform procedural rules could also violate an international treaty, the Fourth Geneva Convention, which required nations to try members of hostile armed forces in a "regularly constituted court" and to apply "all the judicial guarantees which are recognized as indispensable by civilized peoples."[32]

Three members of the Court dissented, reading the history differently. They also argued that Congress had authorized the commissions in the September 11 statute, which authorized the president to respond to the terrorist attacks with military force. They denied that the Geneva Convention applied. And they argued that, in any event, the Court should not have decided the case at that time, but considered the matter only if the commission convicted Hamdan. The remaining member of the Court, the chief justice, did not participate in the case because he had participated in the case earlier as a member of the court of appeals before his Supreme Court appointment.

For present purposes, the salient fact about the Court's decision is that it turned on the Court's interpretation of congressional statutes. The Court held that Congress had not issued the president a blank procedural check. The congressional statute that specifically mentioned commissions authorized the president to establish them only in certain circumstances—not present in Hamdan's case. Moreover, Congress had mandated certain procedural requirements, not satisfied when the military established Hamdan's commission, despite the statute's permission for special procedures when following regular procedures was not "practicable."

As in President Truman's steel seizure case, the Court insisted that the executive follow statutory requirements. It held that the executive had not done so, and hence its actions were unlawful. The Court, in examining the statute's requirement for the use of uniform procedures where "practicable," recognized the need for workable law. And it took account of the constitutional role of other branches of the government.

The majority pointed out that no emergency or other obstacle prevented the president from asking Congress to give him the authority he believed necessary. (Nor did the Court hold in advance whether or to what extent the Constitution might limit the use of any such later obtained authority.) As far as *Hamdan* is concerned, the Court simply limited the president's authority to act as he had *on his own,* without legislative authority. Insofar as the Court rested its holding upon statutes, it did not limit the president's ability, or that of the military, to act in time of hostilities.[33]

Boumediene

In November 2006, five months after the Court decided *Hamdan,* President Bush sent to Congress a proposed bill that would ratify his exercise of broad detention authority. And Congress then enacted a new law (as the Constitution permits, and expects, Congress to do when it disagrees with the Court's interpretation of a *statute*). The new law gave the president authority to establish the military commissions and also broadened the definition of "unlawful military combatant." Furthermore, the law forbade the courts to determine the lawfulness of detention by measuring it against Geneva Convention standards. And it provided, in respect to habeas corpus, that "[n]o court, justice, or judge shall have jurisdiction to hear or consider an application for a writ of habeas corpus filed by or on behalf of an alien" detained at Guantánamo.[34]

Thus, the new act made obsolete the Court's statute-based decision in *Rasul*. It thereby raised the constitutional question of whether Congress, acting by statute, could deprive the Guantánamo prisoners of the right to file a petition of habeas corpus. The question was not straightforward, because Congress had previously given the Court of Appeals for the District of Columbia Circuit explicit authority to review decisions of the Defense Department's Combatant Status Review Tribunals, including those about whether a detainee was an enemy combatant. The court of appeals could decide whether the tribunal's determination was "consistent with the . . . [Defense Department's] standards and procedures," and it could decide whether use of those procedures in the detainee's case "was consistent with the Constitution and laws of the United States of America." Did Congress, by granting this complicated authority, give the courts back with one hand the very kind of habeas corpus review it had just taken away with the other? If so, it did not deprive the Guantánamo detainees of any habeas corpus right.[35]

In June 2008, in the case of *Boumediene v. Bush,* the Court decided these questions. The case concerned a group of Guantánamo inmates taken prisoner in several different countries, including Afghanistan, Bosnia, and Gambia. Each detainee denied he was an enemy combatant, but in each case the status tribunal held that the detainee was an enemy combatant. The detainees all filed habeas corpus petitions in the federal district court for the District of Columbia. After the Court decided *Rasul* in 2004, the lower courts began processing those filings in batches and disagreed about the results, so the court of appeals started to review those disagreements. But then along came the new 2006 act, which the court of appeals interpreted as foreclosing any further consideration of the prisoners' petitions. The Supreme Court agreed to review that court of appeals decision.[36]

In *Hamdan* the Court had made clear that Congress could pass a new statute, directly authorizing special military commissions. But the Court had said nothing about habeas corpus. In particular, the Court did not, and it should not, promise Congress that it would simply approve as constitutional whatever statutory changes Congress chooses to make. Congress had made statutory changes, and they required the Court now to face a new issue—a constitutional issue: Did Congress's statutory habeas corpus changes exceed the Constitution's limits? Given the centuries-old importance of habeas corpus, the question of whether the Constitution itself granted Guantánamo prisoners the right to file the Great Writ was fundamental.

As previously noted, the Constitution says that Congress may "not . . . suspend[ ]" the "Writ of Habeas Corpus . . . unless when in Cases of Rebellion or Invasion the public Safety may require it." No one claimed that Congress had applied the "Rebellion or Invasion" exception to suspend the writ. Instead, the government argued that Congress had *not* suspended the writ of habeas corpus, because prisoners like those at Guantánamo had *never* had a basic, constitutionally protected right to file a petition seeking the writ in the first place. (Recall that in *Rasul* the issue was whether the detainees had a *statutory* right to file habeas petitions.) The government argued that when the founders wrote the Constitution in 1789, no court would have issued that writ at the request of a noncitizen held outside the country. Therefore, the Guantánamo prisoners had no constitutional right to the writ. Congress could not have *suspended* any such right, for it could not take away something the prisoners never had.[37]

The Court, by a vote of 5 to 4, rejected the government's argument. It held that the constitutional words "Writ of Habeas Corpus" did apply to Guantánamo's prisoners and that Congress had unconstitutionally suspended the writ. Thus one cannot characterize *Boumediene* as a case in which the Supreme Court followed congressional directions or implemented Congress's broader purposes. To the contrary, the Court invoked its ultimate judicial review power, holding that both Congress and the president had gone beyond the Constitution's boundaries. Nonetheless, in doing so, the Court took account of the concerns of the other branches, interpreting the Constitution in a way that reflected an awareness of practical realities. Indeed, the Court used a standard that, in determining the reach of the Constitution's habeas corpus guaranty, took account of "practical obstacles."[38]

In concluding that the writ of habeas corpus was available to the detainees, Justice Kennedy, writing for the Court, first considered the basic values underlying the Constitution's words. In 1215, King John signed the Magna Carta, in which he promised his barons that "[n]o freeman shall be . . . imprisoned . . . except . . . by the law of the land." For centuries in England the writ of habeas corpus had helped make a practical reality of King John's promise. From at least the seventeenth century, the writ allowed judges to ensure that neither the king nor other government officials could unlawfully imprison an individual. Because it prevented arbitrary imprisonment, Blackstone called habeas corpus "the BULWARK of the British Constitution." The Court wrote that the writ "protects the rights of the detained by affirming the duty and authority of the Judiciary to call the jailer to account." With this background in mind, the Court wrote that the framers of our own Constitution "viewed freedom from unlawful restraint as a fundamental precept of liberty, and they understood the writ of habeas corpus as a vital instrument to secure that freedom." That is why they included "specific language in the Constitution to secure the writ and ensure its place in our legal system."[39]

Second, the Court looked into historical practice. The English courts had considered a few petitions filed by aliens, including enemy aliens held in England, an African slave, and a group of Spanish sailors. The English judges had made clear that the writ covered Ireland, Canada, India, and the Channel Islands. But it did not cover Scotland or Hanover. The Court concluded that the historical evidence was too unclear, "too episodic, too meager," to decide whether the writ's scope was as limited as the government claimed.[40]

Third, the Court, taking a "practical approach," wrote that whether "a constitutional provision has extraterritorial effect depends on the 'particular circumstances, the practical necessities, and the possible alternatives,' " as well as whether "judicial enforcement . . . would be 'impractical and anomalous.' " The Court held that these considerations strongly supported application of the writ in this case. Guantánamo is "in every practical sense" part of the United States. Our forces at Guantánamo faced no threat from an armed enemy. Application of the writ would create no friction with a "host government." There was no reason to believe civilian courts and military forces could not work side by side. And the fact that Guantánamo had no civilian court system in operation meant that a habeas petition offered those detained there the best, possibly the only, way to obtain court review of their detention. In carrying out its role of safeguarding this basic constitutional protection of individual liberty, the Court did not ignore practical difficulties. Indeed, its opinion included the words "practical" or "impracticable" more than a dozen times. It held that it was not impractical to ensure the Guantánamo prisoners access to the writ of habeas corpus, and it held that the Constitution did so.[41]

The Court also had to consider a second government claim, namely, that the new act did not really suspend the writ because, by designating the court of appeals to review tribunal decisions, Congress had provided an adequate substitute for the writ of habeas corpus. The Court rejected this claim. The act did not explicitly give the appeals court the power to order a prisoner's release. Appellate court review could not easily make up for the tribunals' special pro-detention procedures, for example, the defendant's lack of a right to attend all proceedings and to see the evidence against him. The act did not give the appellate courts the power to hear evidence that came to light after the tribunal reached its decision, nor could the appellate courts review a prisoner's claim that the Defense Department should have convened, but did not, a tribunal in light of evidence that the prisoner had recently obtained. In any event, six years had passed and the prisoners still had not received habeas review, and the court of appeals' approach threatened even more delay. Anyway, Congress did not *want* a habeas equivalent—it had deliberately sought to limit judicial review.[42]

The dissenting justices concluded that the Court should not have decided the questions until after the court of appeals had decided the detainees' individual cases by applying the new act's standards. In any event, the Court should have given the appeals court an opportunity to cure any procedural defects by finding them contrary to the Constitution or laws of the United States, just as the new act gave that court the power to do. Moreover, in the dissenters' view, historical practice supported the government. In addition, the Court's "functional" test of the writ's scope would prove too difficult to administer in practice. It might well leave army field commanders uncertain as to whether courts would review their battle-specific decisions. And these potential consequences showed that the Court's interpretation was belied by the Constitution's delegation of the war powers to the president and Congress, not to the Court.

In examining the Guantánamo cases, I have not described at length the fierce arguments between majorities and dissenters. Nor have I considered how timing, personalities, the popularity of the war in Iraq, the approval ratings of the president, and similar matters might have psychologically influenced the parties' presentations to the Court or its decisions. I have focused instead on the way the Court tried to protect the individual rights of highly unpopular individuals in circumstances where the president's and Congress's constitutional powers to detain those individuals were particularly strong. And I have emphasized the Court's efforts to understand, and to respect, the role that other governmental institutions must play in wartime or where there is a special risk to national security.

In these four cases, the Court, aware of its role in protecting constitutional guarantees of liberty, recognized that the government's lengthy detention of an individual raised serious constitutional questions. It began by interpreting statutes in light of their purposes, always assuming those purposes were consistent with our constitutional traditions. It decided constitutional questions only where necessary and always answering those questions narrowly. It proceeded slowly, step-by-step, recognizing throughout the institutional need for the president, with congressional support, to manage wars and similar threats to national security. It recognized too that those threats will sometimes require special procedures that offer individuals less protection than normal. But it did not explicitly determine the precise nature of those procedures or when or where the Constitution permitted their use. Rather, where possible, the Supreme Court left exploration of these implications of its decisions to other institutions, including the lower courts, to work out. The Court's Guantánamo decisions seem to say, "Sufficient unto the day. . . ."

The strongest criticism of the Court's holdings, and one that the dissenters emphasized, is that the Court has not set forth clear criteria that would bind lower and future courts. It has created constitutional uncertainty about where the line is that presidents acting with congressional support may not cross. But what is the alternative? Although constitutional interpretations that did not restrain the president would have created more certainty, they would have come at the price of eliminating protections on which the Constitution insists. At the same time, a set of clear legal rules—a matrix of what and how and when and where and whom the Constitution protects—runs the risk of doing just what the critics seek to avoid, namely, interfering significantly with the powers of Congress and the president to protect the nation.

Where a serious threat to security exists, the need of the other branches to exercise broad discretionary power is great. But in the Guantánamo cases the Court nonetheless exerted a tug on the constitutional string. It made clear that the president can be held constitutionally accountable.

What was the practical value of the Court's holdings in these cases? The decisions did not secure speedy release of the Guantánamo prisoners, and many prisoners spent several years detained there, including some seventeen Uighurs who the government later said did not pose a threat to the United States. In part this long delay reflects the case-by-case way in which courts must work. In part it reflects the fact that after the Court's initial decisions, Congress responded with statutes supporting the president's actions.[43]

Still, the cases should slowly but surely bring about constitutional consideration by judges of the individual Guantánamo detainee cases, and the opinions may have considerable impact as precedent and as symbol. Rather than leaving a future executive administration free to act as it wishes, as the *Korematsu* Court effectively did, the Court left four cases for study by future presidential advisers. The cases counsel caution. They make clear that a president must take account of the Constitution, as interpreted independently by the Court. In that sense, in the Guantánamo cases, the law "held."

CONSIDER TOO THE fact that, controversial as the Court's Guantánamo decisions were, the president and the public nonetheless accepted them. In *Hamdan* a highly unpopular individual, bin Laden's driver, won his case, and the president of the United States lost. In *Boumediene* the Court set aside a congressional statute, but there was no strong public movement urging President Bush to ignore the Court's decisions. President Bush, unlike Andrew Jackson, expressed disagreement with the *Boumediene* decision but also said that he'd follow it: "We'll abide by the court's decision," adding, "that doesn't mean I have to agree with it."[44]

Widespread public acceptance of the Court's Guantánamo decisions may reflect in part political or other circumstances over which the Court had no control. But the way in which the Court decided the cases may have helped as well. The Court independently wrote decisions designed to safeguard constitutional protection of individual rights while also interpreting the Constitution in a workable way. The Court sought to respect the roles of other government branches. It sought to recognize the practical security needs that underlie enemy combatant detention. It proceeded cautiously, step-by-step. It decided the ultimate constitutional issue presented in *Boumediene* only after the Court had engaged in a dialogue with the other government branches through other case decisions over a period of several years.

Regardless, the other government branches thought it natural and appropriate to abide by the Court's decisions. That fact reflects two hundred years of American history. Americans today accept the Court's role as guardian of the law. They understand the value to the nation of following Court decisions, including those that protect unpopular minorities, even when they disagree with a Court decision and even when they may be right and the decisions may be wrong.

The public's acceptance is never a sure thing. It cannot be taken for granted. It must be transmitted through custom and understanding from one generation to the next. At the time of the Guantánamo cases, that hard-won custom of acceptance was strong enough for the Court, at a time of crisis, to exercise its distinctive power of judicial review. The Court could define and enforce constitutional, liberty-protecting limits. And the law held.

Conclusion

THE FRAMERS OF our Constitution sought to create a democracy that would protect our liberty, work in practice, and endure over time. They saw the need for an institution that would patrol the legal boundaries that the Constitution created. Alexander Hamilton thought the courts were best suited to exercise that power, not because judges necessarily make wiser decisions, but because lodging that power elsewhere was more dangerous. A president with sole responsibility for deciding whether his own acts complied with the Constitution would become too powerful. A Congress with that power would act too politically; it would too rarely strike down a statute that was popular. The judicial branch, however, lacked both "purse" and "sword." It was and is the "weakest" branch of government. And judges are expected to ignore political pressure when they decide cases.[1]

But can the Court exercise this power effectively? First, when courts issue decisions protecting those who are unpopular, will the public follow the decisions? In Hotspur's words, "Will they come when you do call for them?" The question is critical. *Active Liberty,* my previous book, pointed out that the Constitution's efforts to create democratic political institutions mean little unless the public participates in American political life. Similarly, the Constitution's efforts to assure a workable constitutional democracy mean little if the public freely ignores interpretations of the Constitution that it dislikes. In this book, Part I described a nation that has gradually come to place confidence in the

Court, accepting decisions with which it disagrees. And it provided examples of some of the ups and downs along the historical path that has led to this general acceptance.

Second, how can the Court write opinions that help the laws, including the Constitution, work well in practice? Part II described approaches that can help. It offered a practical approach to constitutional interpretation.

What does it mean for the Court to take a "practical" attitude toward legal interpretation? It means the Court will maintain strong workable relationships with other governmental institutions. It means the Court will take account of the constitutional role of other institutions, including their responsibilities, their disabilities, and the ways in which they function.

The concept of a workable Constitution is neither abstract nor ad hoc. We have seen examples of how that general idea helps shape more specific approaches to particular kinds of legal questions. Those approaches in turn can be useful when the Court faces difficult questions arising in different areas of law.

The approaches include those based on purposes and consequences, including the purpose of a reasonable legislator, where congressionally enacted statutes are at issue. They include comparative expertise, viewed in terms of a statute's objective, in respect to executive branch administrative action. They include subsidiarity in respect to interpreting federalism-related statutes. They include specialization in respect to the roles of the lower courts. They include stability in respect to the Court's relation through precedent to Courts of the past. As Part III pointed out, they include values and proportionality in respect to the interpretation of basic individual rights. And they include accountability in respect to the president and Congress in times of serious threats to national security, even if related practical and conceptual difficulties mean that the Court only sometimes tugs the accountability string.

These approaches do not make up a detailed theory of how to decide cases in general. They do not provide criteria for the evaluation of all cases. Nor will they prove useful in every case. They put to the side many factors that could affect how the Court does in fact decide cases—factors such as social or political context; the basic philosophical views of individual judges; contingent factual circumstances about the country that seem relevant at the time of decision; a consensus among bench, bar, and academy that earlier Court cases have gone "too far" in one direction and the Court should "pull back"; or new appointments to a Court perhaps made in order to change its direction. But simplification is necessary in order to describe the basic logic—the bones—of a few legal approaches that I believe can, should, and do play an important role when the Court decides. These approaches are consistent with one another. They form a coherent whole. And they can prove highly useful in resolving particularly difficult cases, area by area.

The approaches supplement other traditional legal tools, such as text, history, tradition, precedent, purposes, and consequences. They help to implement the Constitution's own basic objectives, such as maintaining our democratic institutions, protecting fundamental individual rights, securing a degree of equality, dividing and separating governmental powers, and ensuring a rule of law. But, importantly, they do so in a way that helps the Court apply unchanging constitutional principles to a world of continuous change. As a result, they help the Court produce legal interpretations that work better for those that the law seeks to serve. The ultimate benefit is that the public is more likely to understand and accept the Court's decisions as legitimately belonging to our democratic society. Thus, these approaches help to provide an affirmative answer to Hotspur's question. When the Court calls, the public will come. The Constitution's generally phrased promises will be kept in practice.

But a broader question still remains to be answered. As I said at the outset, when Benjamin Franklin was asked what kind of government the Constitutional Convention had created, his famous reply, "A republic, Madam, if you can keep it," challenges us to maintain the workable democratic Constitution that we have inherited. In a democracy, enduring institutions depend upon the enduring support of ordinary citizens. And citizens are more likely to support those institutions they understand. Thomas Jefferson pointed this out. Even under the "best forms" of government, he said, "those entrusted with power have, in time, . . . perverted it into tyranny"; the "most effectual means of preventing this" is "to illuminate . . . the minds of the people at large."[2]

So the broader question is, how do we "illuminate" those minds? How do we explain to the ordinary American why and how he or she should try to maintain a strong judiciary? The need is great. As we have seen, judicial independence forms one necessary part of a judicial institution that can help make the Constitution's promises effective. And, as Justice David Souter has pointed out, a

> populace that has no inkling that the judicial branch has the job of policing the limitations of power within the constitutional scheme, and no understanding that judges are charged with making good on constitutional guarantees even to the most unpopular people in society, that populace will hardly find much intuitive sense when someone trumpets judicial independence or decries calls to impeach judges who stand up for individual rights against the popular will.[3]

A public that does not understand the judiciary, its role in protecting the Constitution, and the related need for judicial independence may act in ways that weaken the institution. Where judicial elections take place, for example, as they do in many states, the electorate can vote against candidates who reach unpopular decisions, they can authorize litigants to contribute millions of dollars to judicial candidates, they can enhance the electoral importance of individual cases by limiting the length of judicial terms of office, and they can support ballot initiatives such as South Dakota's "jail for judges" who "wrongly" decide cases. Where judges are not elected, as in the federal system, voters can still communicate to legislators that when they help select judges, politics, not law, is what matters.[4] Indeed, as part of a 2000 survey asking whether judges decide cases on political or legal grounds, about two-thirds of respondents answered "legal"; five years later this number had dropped to about half.[5]

But explanation and widespread education are not easy to accomplish. People are busy going about their daily lives. And relevant concepts and reasons are not always easy to understand. Judicial independence, for example, is essentially a state of mind. Judicial independence was not present when a Soviet party boss would telephone a judge to tell him how to decide a case—on the unspoken penalty of the judge's being deprived of a decent apartment or good schooling for his children. How can we explain the isolation of a judge confronted with the task of independently deciding an unusually difficult case? Can we explain this quickly to our fellow citizens who live busy, pressured lives?

It takes time and continuous effort to communicate the nature and importance of our government institutions. Support for the judicial institution rests upon teaching in an organized way to generations of students about our history and our government. It grows out of knowledge of our Revolution, our founding documents, the Civil War, and eighty years of legal segregation. It rests upon an understanding of our Constitution, of how government works in practice, and of the importance of the students' own eventual participation to the Court's continued effectiveness.

There is cause for concern about the health of this kind of education. Compared with a generation ago, there seem to be fewer classes in civics and government, fewer town meetings where (in Justice Souter's words) "my concept of fundamental fairness began to form." Only twenty-nine states now require the teaching of civics or government as part of their public school curriculum. This decline may help explain the dismal statistics: that a vast majority of eighth graders are not proficient in civics; only one-third of all Americans can name the three branches of government (two-thirds can name a television judge on *American Idol*); only one-third of eighth graders can describe the historical purpose of the Declaration of Independence; and three-quarters of our population does not understand the difference between a judge and a legislator.

Still, pessimism is not the complete order of the day. Private citizens, foundations, corporate officials, legislative committees, leaders from across the political spectrum, and retired Supreme Court justices are hard at work developing teaching materials and encouraging the teaching of civics. No one has worked harder than Justice O'Connor to explain to the public the need for civics education, including education about how our judicial institutions work.

Lawyers, bar associations, and judges can do the same. They can speak to students about the law; they can arrange for visits to the courts; they can help the schools develop teaching materials. Lawyers and judges can meet with local groups and explain what law is, what our legal system is like, what courts do, how the legal system and the courts affect the lives of ordinary citizens. Their presence transmits a simple message: we work with the law and with the Constitution. Our democratic Constitution assumes a public that participates in the government that it creates. It also assumes a public that understands how government works. Without this public understanding, the judiciary cannot independently enforce our Constitution's liberty-protecting limits.

The stories this book sets forth are told from the point of view of one judge. I have drawn my own lessons from them. I hope they lead others to study the stories and ponder their lessons about our constitutional history. Then they too will be better able to help make our democracy work. I hope so.

That is why I have written this book.

Appendix A

Images

This book discusses legal cases and principles at length, but it is important to remember that these cases were decided by, and these principles have a profound effect on, human beings. My hope is that the following paintings and photographs will help the reader to make this connection—to recognize that behind each of the famous cases I have described are real issues that have confronted real people.

First, I have included a portrait of Chief Justice John Marshall, who did so much to shape our understanding of the Constitution, along with a copy of the order served on James Madison asking him to explain why he never delivered William Marbury his judicial commission. Of course, the controversy over Marbury's commission led directly to Chief Justice Marshall's decision in *Marbury v. Madison,* which established the Court's authority to engage in judicial review.

Second is a portrait of Chief John Ross, the Cherokee leader who fought so valiantly for his land, along with a painting of the Cherokee migration along the Trail of Tears, which the tribe traveled to Oklahoma after its eviction from Georgia.

Third, a well-known portrait of Dred Scott still leads us to think of his fortitude and humanity as he brought about a case the very vices of which helped awaken the nation to the need for slavery's abolition. And portraits of Chief Justice Roger Taney and Justice Benjamin Curtis represent the opposite sides of a deep division that would split not only the

Court in *Dred Scott v. Sanford,* but also the nation four years later in the Civil War.

Fourth, two photographs of the Little Rock integration tell us much without words. The first shows the failed efforts of one of the nine students to integrate the school in the face of strong opposition from those in the crowd. The second shows the world that, with the help of the 101st Airborne Division, the rule of law would carry the day. And a picture of the tombstone of Chief Ross's wife, who died on the Trail of Tears, reminds us that she, a symbol of a president's denial of the rule of law, lies only a mile from Little Rock High School, the scene of one of the law's greatest triumphs.

Fifth, I have included pictures of a sign directing individuals to World War II Japanese internment camps, and of a camp itself, providing a glimpse of the conditions in which these American citizens lived.

The final is a photograph of Thurgood Marshall and members of the Little Rock Nine sitting on the Supreme Court's front steps. This image suggests the distance our nation has traveled in making Chief Justice Marshall's vision of America, as set forth in *Marbury,* a practical reality.

This painting, which hangs in the United States Supreme Court, depicts John Marshall, the great chief justice who wrote the Court's opinion in *Marbury v. Madison.* *(Rembrandt Peale, Collection of the Supreme Court of the United States)*

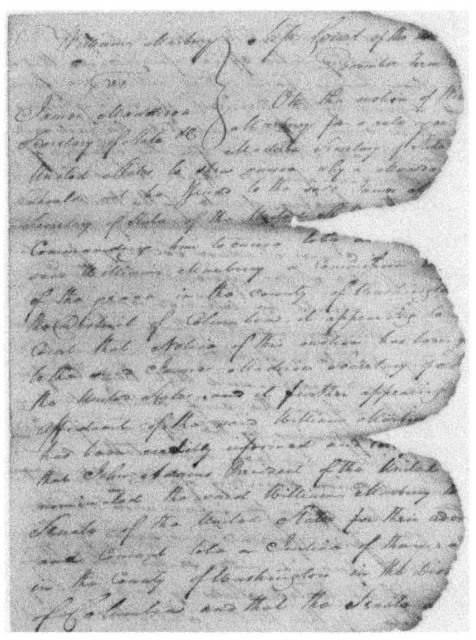

Before deciding *Marbury v. Madison,* the Court issued this show-cause order, in effect asking Secretary of State James Madison to respond to Marbury's claim. Madison did not respond. *(National Archives)*

Chief John Ross led the Cherokee Nation. He strongly opposed Georgia's efforts to seize the Cherokees' territory, and he encouraged Supreme Court litigation on the matter. *(Library of Congress)*

After the ultimate failure of the tribe's efforts to keep their land, they were forced to immigrate to the West. This painting depicts their involuntary journey along the Trail of Tears. *(The Granger Collection, New York)*

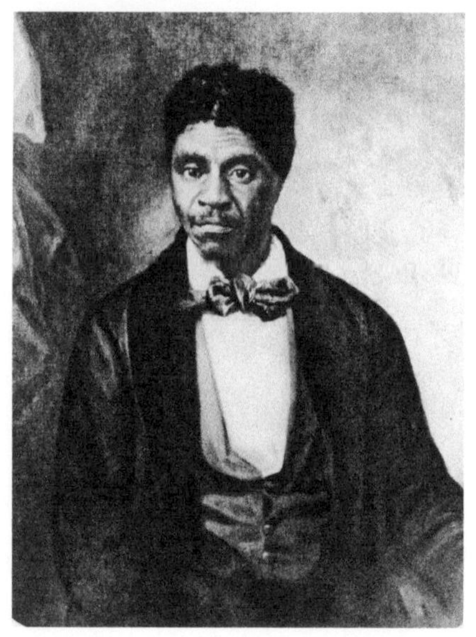

Dred Scott, who invoked the law in order to escape the bonds of slavery, became the subject of a Supreme Court case, now viewed as one of the Court's worst decisions. *(Hulton Archive/Getty Images)*

A native of Maryland and once Andrew Jackson's attorney general, Roger Taney wrote the Court's *Dred Scott* decision. *(George Peter Alexander Healy, Collection of the Supreme Court of the United States)*

A native of Massachusetts, Justice Benjamin Curtis wrote the principal dissenting opinion in *Dred Scott.* *(Gregory Stapko, Collection of the Supreme Court of the United States)*

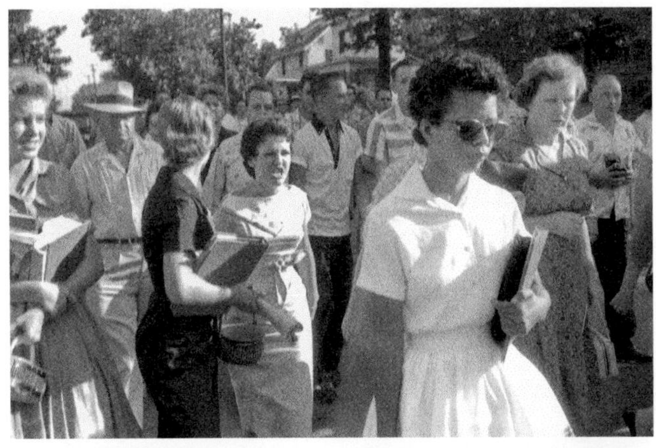

This famous photograph shows Elizabeth Eckford unsuccessfully attempting to enter Little Rock Central High School. *(Will Counts Collection: Indiana University Archives)*

Above: Members of the 101st Airborne Division escorting the Little Rock Nine into Central High School. *(Bettmann/Corbis)*

Right: Quatie Ross, the wife of Chief John Ross, lies buried where she died along the Trail of Tears. The trail symbolizes a defeat for the rule of law, but it is only a mile away from Little Rock Central High School, where, with the help of federal troops, the law won a great victory. *(Cindy Momchilov)*

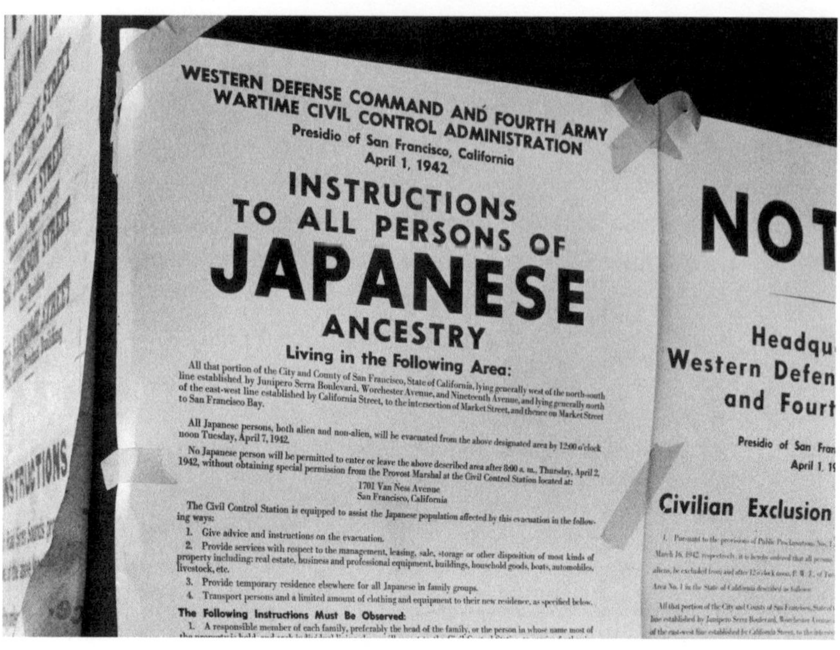

A notice ordering persons of Japanese ancestry to report for internment during World War II.
(Dorothy Lange/Time and Life Pictures/Getty Images)

This is one of the places to which those of Japanese ancestry had to report.
(Corbis)

Before he was appointed a justice of the Supreme Court, Thurgood Marshall argued as a lawyer for the plaintiffs (and won) the case of *Brown* v. *Board of Education.* Shown here, he sits on the Court's front steps with members of the Little Rock Nine.
(Bettmann/Corbis)

Appendix B

Background: The Court

THOSE NOT FAMILIAR WITH THE COURT MAY BE INTERESTED in certain essential background facts about how it functions and about the Constitution itself. The Court's membership changes slowly over time. The Court's nine members, each appointed by the president and confirmed by the Senate, serve "during good behavior," often for life. President Jefferson is remembered to have lamented the fact that Supreme Court judges never retire and they rarely die. In the recent past, the men and women who serve as justices have tended to come from professional judicial backgrounds. In the past, former senators, former governors, former cabinet members, and even a former president have served as justices, but more recently the men and women who serve on the Court have served as judges in lower courts (typically federal courts of appeals), and, like most federal judges, they have begun their judicial careers in midlife after previous legal experience, practicing or teaching law.[1]

The Court's decision-making role is more limited than many imagine. Its work focuses solely upon the interpretation and application of federal law. That law—the federal Constitution, congressional statutes, federal agency action—is itself limited, because the fifty states (each of which has a legislature, governor, and judicial system), not the federal government, are responsible for much of American law, including family law, property law, most tort law, business law, and criminal law. Perhaps 95 percent or more of all judicial proceedings take place in state courts.

Within the area of federal law itself, the Court hears only a handful of cases, mostly those that require the Court to resolve conflicts of interpretation among different lower courts. To put the caseload in perspective, consider that litigants file around forty-five million cases in all state and federal courts each year. Of these, I would guess that about eighty thousand to a hundred thousand may both raise a question of federal laws and reach the stage where a federal court of appeals or final state court decides that question. In about eight thousand of these cases, the losing litigant will ask the Supreme Court to hear the case. The Court in a year will fully hear and decide about eighty of those cases. Thus, those cases that the Court fully hears amount to a virtually invisible tip of a giant iceberg.[2]

These eighty cases, while few in number, are important in kind. Because the Court typically hears cases in which different lower courts have decided the same legal question in opposite ways, the Court's decision, resolving the conflict, will almost always have considerable legal significance. And, as the Court's history shows, decisions in some cases—for example, those involving desegregation or electoral reapportionment—have changed the life of our nation. In short, the Court comprises a small number of men and women of diverse views and backgrounds, appointed for life, who decide a small number of cases involving federal law. The Court's decisions are usually final and frequently have considerable legal and practical impact.

In reading this book, one needs to understand a few basic features of the Constitution. (I exhort readers who have not done so—and those who have not done so recently—to read the Constitution itself; it is an admirably concise document.) The document, adopted in 1789, almost immediately amended with a Bill of Rights, and subsequently amended a further seventeen times, establishes a federal government. From the time of its adoption, the Constitution with its Bill of Rights provided a framework for democratic government. The framework included an explicit delegation of powers to the federal government (reserving all others to the states); an allocation of governmental powers (among three branches, legislative, executive, and judicial); protections, particularly in the Bill of Rights, of certain individual liberties, including speech, press, religion, freedom from unreasonable searches and seizures, and the payment of compensation for the taking of private property, as well as guarantees of fair procedures for those threatened with criminal prosecution.

After the Civil War the nation adopted the Thirteenth, Fourteenth, and Fifteenth amendments, which ended slavery, guaranteed constitutional protection of individual liberties from infringement by the states, assured individual citizens fair and equal treatment, and sought to guarantee racial minorities the right to vote. Later amendments, among other things, assured the popular election of senators, extended suffrage to women, forbade the poll tax, and lowered the voting age to eighteen.

Moreover, Congress cannot set aside a Court interpretation of the Constitution simply by passing an ordinary law. Rather, unless the Court itself modifies or overturns a constitutional decision, that decision can be changed only by amending the Constitution. And the Constitution is difficult to amend, requiring the affirmative vote of two-thirds of each house of Congress plus approval by three-quarters of the states or the calling of a special national convention (which has never been done). In a word: The framework-creating document, namely, the Constitution, is brief, general, practical, and permanent.[3]

The Court's work has four important general features. First, specific, often determinative criteria normally govern the Court's decision about which cases to hear in full. These basic criteria do not rest upon the intrinsic interest of the legal questions in the case. Nor do they assume that the Supreme Court will reach a "better" decision than did the lower courts. As Justice Robert H. Jackson noted, we are not final because we are infallible; rather, we are infallible only insofar as our word is final.[4]

Neither do the criteria require the Court to examine each petition (asking the Court to hear a case) in order to decide whether the lower courts decided the case correctly. Basic fairness does not require such an examination. Each litigant has previously received a trial and taken an appeal. And in any event, a Supreme Court bench of only nine judges could not fully consider and evaluate the soundness of eight thousand lower-court decisions each year.

As Chief Justice William Howard Taft, a former president of the United States, explained, the basic criterion for hearing a case is the need for federal law to be uniform throughout the nation. If all lower courts have reached similar conclusions about the meaning of a statutory or constitutional phrase, the law is already uniform. And there is normally no need for the Court to hear the case. If, however, the lower courts disagree, with some applying the law one way and others a different way, then there is a need for the Court to hear the case—to achieve national uniformity. We may also grant a petition for hearing if there is some other particular need for a single, authoritative court decision—for example, when a lower court has held a federal statute unconstitutional. But still, disagreement among the lower courts is the most commonly used criterion.[5]

Second, in carrying out its responsibilities to interpret statutes and the Constitution, the Court typically must decide how to apply a word or phrase in a document to a particular set of circumstances. To do so, the judges must interpret that word or phrase, that is, explain its meaning. Does the word "costs," for example, in a statute that awards "costs" to a parent (who successfully shows that a school board must provide a better education to his disabled child) include the expense of hiring an expert witness? Does the Fourth Amendment's language prohibiting "unreasonable searches and seizures" require police to obtain a search warrant for a car whose driver they have properly arrested and already restrained?[6]

Third, when deciding a typical case, each justice will read the same set of ten to fifteen (or more) briefs (legal documents of thirty to fifty pages each containing arguments) filed by the parties and other interested persons. Those persons can include the federal government, state governments, law enforcement officials, businesses, labor unions, environmental associations, public interest associations, and so forth. After reading the set of briefs, the justices will hear an hour-long oral argument, giving them an opportunity to ask the lawyers questions. Within a few days, the justices will discuss the case in a private conference and reach a preliminary decision. The chief justice, if he sides with the majority (or, if he doesn't, then the most senior justice in the majority), will assign one justice to write a draft opinion (usually fifteen to thirty pages) explaining the Court's legal conclusion and its reasons. The draft opinion's author circulates the draft internally; other justices make suggestions; and eventually every justice joins the draft or writes a concurrence (an opinion agreeing in the result but for different or additional reasons) or a dissent or joins a concurrence or a dissent written by another justice. When all have written or joined, the work is done. The opinion upon which at least five members of the Court have agreed is the Court's majority opinion. (Where a justice is disqualified from hearing a case and the Court then divides 4 to 4, the lower-court decision is automatically affirmed.) All opinions are then released to the public and eventually published. About 30 percent of the decisions are unanimous. About 25 percent are closely divided (5–4). However closely divided and controversial a decision may be, the justices maintain good personal relations with one another.

Fourth, when considering the Court's interpretation of the Constitution, one needs to keep in mind that the Constitution sets forth a framework for government. It sets boundaries within which other government bodies must act. The boundaries not only structure government but also set limits upon its authority, explicitly defining, and thereby protecting, individual liberties that government cannot infringe. The Court, in a sense, patrols those boundaries, deciding when an action by a state or federal government falls outside the bounds and lies in forbidden territory. The legal questions about where the boundaries lie may be difficult. When, for example, does a law affecting speech (say, restricting political campaign contributions) fall outside the boundary that the First Amendment puts in place? When does a law prohibiting abortion fall outside the boundary's limits? Nonetheless, remember that difficult boundary-defining decisions constitute but a tiny part of the vast number of government decisions (embodied in laws, ordinances, rules, and regulations) that determine the kinds of communities, cities, states, and nation that Americans seek to maintain. The Constitution assumes that Americans will make these latter decisions, the vast bulk of government decisions, democratically through the direct or indirect actions of elected officials.

Within this basic decision-making framework the issues that this book discusses arise. How has the public come to accept the Court's decision-making role as legitimate—to the point where it will typically follow even Court decisions with which it strongly disagrees? What can the Court do to merit the public's confidence in the institution and to help maintain it?

Acknowledgments

SOME PORTIONS OF THIS BOOK HAVE PREVIOUSLY APPEARED AS lectures at the University of Oklahoma (the Henry Family Lecture), the Rehnquist Center at the University of Arizona, Yale University, the New York Public Library, the American Academy in Berlin (the Cutler Lecture), and the Supreme Court Historical Society.

I should like to thank Charles Nesson, with whom I worked in the 1970s at Harvard bringing together materials that evolved into the chapters about the Cherokee Indians and *Korematsu*. Similarly, material that Charles Ogletree gathered for a seminar about *Dred Scott* at Harvard in 2007 helped me write the chapter on that case. I owe a great intellectual debt to my teachers and my colleagues at Harvard Law School, who helped teach me how to think about law, for example, Paul Freund, Al Sacks, Henry Hart, Ben Kaplan, Louis Jaffe, John Hart Ely, Richard Stewart, and Charles Fried; to judges and legal scholars, such as Arthur Goldberg, Ronald Dworkin, Michael Boudin, and Richard Posner; and to many others as well.

I should like especially to thank Michael Bosworth for his great help with this book, for tirelessly devoting much time and effort to reading manuscripts and making enormously constructive comments. I also thank my friends, former law clerks, and others who have had the patience to read ever-changing manuscripts and the willingness to provide structural insights, numerous helpful comments, and useful suggestions. They include Georges de Ménil, Lois de Ménil, Strobe Talbott, Lisa Bressman, Sally Rider, Paul Gewirtz, and Elizabeth Drew.

They include as well members of my own family: Joanna, Chloe, Nell, and Michael.

I thank my research assistants at Yale for their helpful footnoting work: Hunter Smith, Elina Tetelbaum, Thomas Schmidt, and Benjamin Ewing.

And, of course, I very much thank my editor, Pat Hass, for her continuous encouragement, her perseverance, and her fine editing work.

Notes

Introduction

1. Gordon S. Wood, *Empire of Liberty* 468 (2009).

2. Stephen Breyer, *Active Liberty* (2005).

Chapter One / Judicial Review

1. For a description of the "Commonwealth model" of judicial review and its operation in Canada, the U.K., New Zealand, and elsewhere, see Janet L. Hiebert, *Parliamentary Bills of Rights: An Alternative Model?* 69 Mod. L. Rev. 7, 11–16 (2006); Stephen Gardbaum, *The New Commonwealth Model of Constitutionalism,* 49 Am. J. Comp. L. 707 (2001).

2. See, e.g., David Johansen & Philip Rosen, Parliamentary Information and Research Service Background Paper BP-194E, *The Notwithstanding Clause of the Charter* 10–13 (2008), www.parl.gc.ca/information/library/PRBpubs/bp194-e.pdf (describing limited usage, outside of Quebec, of the "notwithstanding clause" of the Canadian Charter).

3. Reference to the "people drunk" and the "people sober," common among constitutional law scholars, may find its origin in an ancient discussion of an appeal from Philip drunk to Philip sober. See Valerius Maximus, *Facta et dicta memorabilia,* bk. 6, ch. 2 (A.D. 32).

4. James Madison, Speech in Congress Proposing Constitutional Amendments (June 8, 1789), in James Madison, *Writings* 437, 449 (Jack N. Rakove ed., 1999).

5. Federalist 78 (Alexander Hamilton).

6. 1 *The Records of the Federal Convention* 97 (Max Farrand ed., 1966) (Madison's notes, June 4, 1787); *id.* at 109 (Pierce's notes, June 4, 1787); Speech of James Wilson at Pennsylvania Ratifying Convention, in 2 *Documentary History of the Ratification of the Constitution* 451 (Merrill Jensen et al. eds., 1976); Saikrishna B. Prakash & John C. Yoo, *The Origins of Judicial Review,* 70 U. Chi. L. Rev. 887, 952 (2003). For a book with an excellent history of judicial review at the founding and in the early Republic, see Larry D. Kramer, *The People Themselves* (2004).

7. Federalist 78 (Alexander Hamilton).

8. *Id.;* Federalist 81 (Alexander Hamilton).

9. Federalist 78 (Alexander Hamilton); Federalist 81 (Alexander Hamilton).

10. Federalist 78 (Alexander Hamilton); Federalist 81 (Alexander Hamilton).

11. Federalist 78 (Alexander Hamilton).

12. *Calder v. Bull,* 3 U.S. (3 Dall.) 386, 398–99 (1798) (Iredell, J., concurring in judgment).

13. James Iredell to Richard Spaight (Aug. 26, 1787), in 2 *Life and Correspondence of James Iredell* 172, 175 (Griffith J. McRee ed., 1858).

14. James Iredell, *To the Public* (1786), reprinted in *id.* at 145, 146; Iredell, *supra* note 14 at 173.

15. *Id.* at 175.

Chapter Two / Establishing Judicial Review

1. *Marbury v. Madison,* 5 U.S. (1 Cranch) 137 (1803).

2. See Louise Weinberg, *Our* Marbury, 89 Va. L. Rev. 1235, 1255–57 (2003) (describing the Court's business around the time of *Marbury* as modest in volume and importance and noting the onerous circuit-riding duties of the justices); 1 Charles Warren, *The Supreme Court in United States History* 171–74 (1922); John A. Garraty, Marbury v. Madison: *The Case of the "Missing" Commissions,* Am. Heritage (June 1963), at 6, 84.

3. Garraty, *supra* note 2, at 7; Warren, *supra* note 2, at 185–215; Gordon S. Wood, *Empire of Liberty* 415–20 (2009); see generally *id.* at 400–68.

4. Thomas Jefferson to Spencer Roane (Sept. 6, 1819), in *The Essential Jefferson* 250, 252 (Jean M. Yarbrough ed., 2006) (emphasis added); Larry D. Kramer, Marbury *at 200: A Bicentennial Celebration of* Marbury v. Madison, 20 Const. Comment. 205, 224 (2003).

5. 4 *The Documentary History of the Supreme Court of the United States* 292–94 (Maeva Marcus & James R. Perry eds., 1992).

6. Mark Tushnet, *Introduction to Arguing* Marbury v. Madison 3–4 (Mark Tushnet ed., 2005); Weinberg, *supra* note 2, at 1264–65; *id.* at 1287–93. On the impeachment of Justice Chase, see William H. Rehnquist, *Grand Inquests* 15–113 (1992).

7. Warren, *supra* note 2, at 200–201.

8. See Susan Low Bloch, *The* Marbury *Mystery: Why Did William Marbury Sue in the Supreme Court?* 18 Const. Comment. 607 (2001); Weinberg, *supra* note 2, at 1303–10 (2003); Judiciary Act of 1789, ch. 20, § 13, 1 Stat. 73 (emphases added).

9. Garraty, *supra* note 2, at 86.

10. *Marbury,* 5 U.S. at 163.

11. *Id.* at 164–66 (emphasis added).

12. *Id.* at 173. But see William W. Van Alstyne, *A Critical Guide to* Marbury v. Madison, 1969 Duke L.J. 1, 14–16 (suggesting that Marshall may have been wrong to assume that the Judiciary Act intended to grant the Supreme Court original jurisdiction).

13. U.S. Const. art. III, § 2 (emphasis added); *Marbury,* 5 U.S. at 176.

14. *Marbury,* 5 U.S. at 176–78.

15. *Id.* at 177–78.

16. U.S. Const. art. III, § 2; *id.* art. III, § 3; *id.* art. I, § 9; *id.* art VI; 1 Stat. 76 § 8; *Marbury,* 5 U.S. at 179–80. On the oath of office, see Supreme Court of the United States Office of the Curator, Information Sheet, Text of the Oaths of Office for Supreme Court Justices (Aug. 10, 2009), www.supremecourtus.gov/about/textoftheoathsofoffice2009.pdf.

17. See, e.g., Warren, *supra* note 2, at 249–52 (quoting contemporary newspapers criticizing the *Marbury* opinion for reaching the merits). This criticism of Marshall's opinion (Jefferson claimed it should be ignored as an "extrajudicial opinion") has remained a common one. See letter from Jefferson to George Hay, June 20, 1807, in *The Works of Thomas Jefferson,* ed. Paul L. Ford, vol. 10 (New York: Putnam, 1905).

18. If a modern reader criticizes Marshall for failure to abide by jurisdictional rules, then why not defend him as I have done? For historical detail, see Bruce Ackermann, *The Failure of the Founding Fathers* (2005).

19. *Marbury,* 5 U.S. at 180 (second emphasis added); see Larry D. Kramer, *The People Themselves* 125–26 (2004) (arguing that though Marshall "was daring in finding a way to introduce judicial review into [*Marbury*], he [was not] equally bold and imaginative in developing the doctrine").

Chapter Three / The Cherokees

1. For a lengthier treatment of the events underlying the Cherokee cases, the reader is directed to the following sources that inform this account: Jill Norgren, *The Cherokee Cases: Two Landmark Federal Decisions in the Fight for Sovereignty* 11–86 (2004); Grace Steele Woodward, *The Cherokees* (1963); Annie Heloise Abel, *The History of Events Resulting in Indian Consolidation West of the Mississippi,* in 1 Annual Report of the American Historical Association for 1906, 233–450 (1908); Wilson Lumpkin, *The Removal of the Cherokee Indians from Georgia* (1907); Ulrich Bonnell Phillips, *Georgia and State Rights,* in 2 Annual Report of the American Historical Association for the Year 1901, 66–86 (1902); 2 John P. Kennedy, *Memoirs of the Life of William Wirt* 240–64, 290–97 (1850). The early secondary sources, even those sympathetic to the Cherokees, present a somewhat benighted view of their subject; in other respects, however, they are valuable, detailed historical accounts.

2. Phillips, *supra* note 1, at 70; see generally *id.* at 69–86 (describing the presidents' resistance to Georgia's demands).

3. *Id.* at 68–71; Woodward, *supra* note 1, at 139–46 (describing the Cherokee nation's establishment of a newspaper, schools, and a court system); *id.* at 157–91 (describing the leadership of Chief John Ross); Kennedy, *supra* note 1, at 245–46 (quoting an 1825 letter from a Cherokee man describing the Cherokee nation, including its public roads, villages, manufacturing, agriculture, religion, schools, and plans for a national library and museum); Samuel Carter III, *Cherokee Sunset* 103 (1976).

4. Phillips, *supra* note 1, at 72–73, 84; Woodward, *supra* note 1, at 158–60.

5. Abel, *supra* note 1, at 379, 375–81; Woodward, *supra* note 1, at 160.

6. Phillips, *supra* note 1, at 66–67; Norgren, *supra* note 1, at 26; U.S. Const. art. VI, cl. 2 (emphasis added).

7. Kennedy, *supra* note 1, at 253–59 (quoting letters from Wirt describing the Cherokees' case and his fears that Georgia might not obey an adverse decision of the Supreme Court); Phillips, *supra* note 1, at 63 (quoting Georgia's governor, George Troup); see generally *id.* at 39–65 (describing the acquisition of the Creeks' land); see also Lumpkin, *supra* note 1, at 42–43 (account of Lumpkin, Georgia's governor from 1831 to 35, describing the "problem" for Georgia presented by the Cherokees);

Joseph C. Burke, *The Cherokee Cases: A Study in Law, Politics, and Morality,* 21 Stan. L. Rev. 500, 508 (1969) (describing Wirt as an advocate).

8. Kennedy, *supra* note 1, at 256 (quoting letter from Wirt); Norgren, *supra* note 1, at 61–62, 97–98; Phillips, *supra* note 1, at 75–77.

9. *Cherokee Nation v. Georgia,* 30 U.S. (5 Pet.) 1 (1831); U.S. Const. art. III, § 2, cl. 2; Kennedy, *supra* note 1, at 293.

10. *Cherokee Nation,* 30 U.S. at 15–20; George Gilmer to S. S. Hamilton (June 20, 1831), in 2 Indian Removal Records, S. Doc. No. 23–512, at 22, 25.

11. *Worcester v. Georgia,* 31 U.S. (6 Pet.) 515, 537, 542 (1832); Phillips, *supra* note 1, at 78–81 (describing Worcester's arrest and trial); Abel, *supra* note 1, at 396–403 (same); Samuel A. Worcester to George R. Gilmer (June 10, 1831), in 27 Missionary Herald 250, 251 (1831) ("I have the pleasure of sending to your excellency a copy of the Gospel of Matthew, of a hymn-book, and of a small tract . . . of excerpts from scripture" all translated into Cherokee).

12. *Worcester,* 31 U.S. at 541.

13. *Id.* at 548–54; *id.* at 575; *id.* at 557.

14. *Id.* at 561–62.

15. *Id.* at 562 (emphasis added).

16. 2 Charles Warren, *The Supreme Court in United States History* 216–17 (1922).

17. *Id.* at 215–16; *id.* at 228; Lumpkin, *supra* note 1, at 104.

18. Lewis Cass to William Reed (Nov. 14, 1831), in Robert Sparks Walker, *Torchlights to the Cherokees* 285, 285–86 (1931); Andrew Jackson, Veto Message—Bank of the United States (July 10, 1832), reprinted in *The Statesmanship of Andrew Jackson* 154, 163–64 (Francis Newton Thorpe ed., 1909); Warren, *supra* note 16, at 217; *cf. id.* at 219 (characterizing it as "a matter of extreme doubt" whether Jackson ever uttered his famous dictum); *id.* at 229.

19. An ordinance to nullify certain acts of the Congress of the United States, purporting to be laws and imposts on the importation of foreign commodities, South Carolina (Nov. 24, 1832); Warren, *supra* note 16, at 234.

20. Andrew Jackson, Anti-nullification Proclamation (Dec. 10, 1832), in *The Statesmanship of Andrew Jackson, supra* note 18, at 232, 238 (emphasis removed); Warren, *supra* note 16, at 234–38.

21. Warren, *supra* note 16, at 235–37; Norgren, *supra* note 1, at 127–28.

22. Norgren, *supra* note 1, at 136–37.

23. Woodward, *supra* note 1, at 193–94; Norgren, *supra* note 1, at 134–36; *id.* at 143; Charles C. Royce, *The Cherokee Nation* 164 (1975).

24. Royce, *supra* note 23, at 162.

25. Woodward, *supra* note 1, at 193–94.

Chapter Four / Dred Scott

1. *Scott v. Sandford,* 60 U.S. (19 How.) 393 (1857).

2. *Id.* at 397–98. For a more comprehensive account of the facts of *Dred Scott,* see Don E. Fehrenbacher, *The* Dred Scott *Case* (1978), especially 240–49.

3. James F. Simon, *Lincoln and Chief Justice Taney* 13 (2007) (quoting Wirt); *id.* at

9; *id.* at 11 (quoting Taney's opposition to slavery as expressed in oral argument at the trial of an abolitionist); *id.* at 16–17 (quoting Taney's views on citizenship rights of the "African race" as expressed in a legal opinion to Secretary of State Edward Livingston).

4. 1 Benjamin R. Curtis, *A Memoir of Benjamin R. Curtis, LL.D.* 249–51 (Benjamin R. Curtis ed., 1879).

5. U.S. Const. art. I, § 9, cl. 1; *id.* art. V; *id.* art. I, § 2, cl. 3, amended by U.S. Const. amend. XIV, § 2.

6. See Mark A. Graber, Dred Scott *and the Problem of Constitutional Evil* 124–27 (2006) (describing how, despite expectations, population growth in the Northwest greatly surpassed that in the Southwest).

7. See generally Fehrenbacher, *supra* note 2, at 250–83 (describing Dred Scott's litigation in the Missouri courts and the federal circuit court); *id.* at 264 (quoting the Missouri Supreme Court opinion).

8. *Id.* at 281–82; *id.* at 293; Austin Allen, *Origins of the* Dred Scott *Case* 148–49 (2006).

9. Fehrenbacher, *supra* note 2, at 288–90; Simon, *supra* note 3, at 117–19; Fehrenbacher, *supra* note 2, at 314–21.

10. *Scott,* 60 U.S. at 403; *id.* at 427.

11. U.S. Const. art. III, § 2; *Scott,* 60 U.S. at 407; *id.* at 413–17; *id.* at 419–21.

12. U.S. Const. art. IV, § 2, cl. 1; *Scott,* 60 U.S. at 423–25; *id.* at 426.

13. *Scott,* 60 U.S. at 572–76 (Curtis, J., dissenting); *id.* at 582; *id.* at 580.

14. *Id.* at 574–75.

15. *Id.* at 580.

16. For an account of the complex interaction between state and federal law in *Dred Scott,* see Allen, *supra* note 8, especially 52–67, 139–59.

17. *Scott,* 60 U.S. at 598–600 (Curtis, J., dissenting).

18. *Id.* at 432 (majority opinion); U.S. Const. art. IV, § 3, cl. 2; *Scott,* 60 U.S. at 451–52; U.S. Const. art. IV, § 2, cl. 3, amended by U.S. Const. amend. XIII.

19. *Scott,* 60 U.S. at 452.

20. *Id.* at 611–19 (Curtis, J., dissenting); *id.* at 616.

21. *Id.* at 624–26.

22. *Id.* at 626–27.

23. Fehrenbacher, *supra* note 2, at 312–13; *id.* at 417 (quoting *New York Tribune*); 3 Charles Warren, *The Supreme Court in United States History* 27 (1922).

24. Report of the Joint Committee on *Dred Scott* (Apr. 9, 1857), reprinted in 3 *Southern Slaves in Free State Courts* 279, 280–81 (Paul Finkelman ed., 2007).

25. Frederick Douglass, The *Dred Scott* Decision: Speech Delivered Before the American Anti-slavery Society (May 11, 1857), in 2 *The Life and Writings of Frederick Douglass* 407, 411–12 (Philip S. Foner ed., 1950).

26. Abraham Lincoln, Speech in Reply to Douglas, Chicago, Ill. (July 17, 1858), in *Abraham Lincoln: His Speeches and Writings* 385, 397 (Roy P. Basler ed., 2d ed. 2001); Abraham Lincoln, The *Dred Scott* Decision, Speech at Springfield, Ill. (June 26, 1857), in *id.* at 352, 362; Abraham Lincoln, First Debate with Stephen Douglas, Ottawa, Ill. (Aug. 21, 1858), in *id.* at 428, 458.

27. Fehrenbacher, *supra* note 2, at 574–75; *id.* at 568.

28. Graber, *supra* note 6, at 15–16 (quoting sources).

29. *Scott,* 60 U.S. at 407; *id.* at 574 (Curtis, J., dissenting).

30. Abraham Lincoln, First Inaugural Address (Mar. 4, 1861), in *Abraham Lincoln: His Speeches and Writings, supra* note 26, at 579, 585–86.

31. See Harriet Beecher Stowe, *Uncle Tom's Cabin* (1852).

Chapter Five / Little Rock

1. See, e.g., Michael Klarman, Brown v. Board of Education *and the Civil Rights Movement* 3–53 (2007) (detailing the legally sanctioned segregation in place in the South prior to 1954); *Brown v. Board of Education,* 347 U.S. 483, 493, 495 (1954) (*Brown I*); U.S. Const. amend. XIV, § 1.

2. Martin Luther King, Jr., *MIA Mass Meeting at Holt Street Baptist Church* (Dec. 5, 1955), in 3 *The Papers of Martin Luther King, Jr.* 71, 73 (Clayborne Carson et al. eds., 1997).

3. For cases decided during the NAACP's step-by-step litigation campaign, see, for example, *Missouri ex rel. Gaines v. Canada,* 305 U.S. 337 (1938); *Sipuel v. Board of Regents of University of Oklahoma,* 332 U.S. 631 (1948) (per curiam); *Sweatt v. Painter,* 339 U.S. 629 (1950); and *McLaurin v. Oklahoma State Regents,* 339 U.S. 637 (1950). See generally Richard Kluger, *Simple Justice: The History of* Brown v. Board of Education *and Black America's Struggle for Equality* (1975; rev. ed. 2004) (tracing the history of desegregation lawsuits leading up to *Brown*). For desegregation of the armed forces, see EO 9981, 13 Fed. Reg. 4313 (July 26, 1948).

4. *Brown I,* 347 U.S. at 495–96 (stating that remedial questions would be addressed in a subsequent opinion after further argument); *Brown v. Board of Education,* 349 U.S. 294 (1955) (*Brown II*).

5. Brief for Appellants in Nos. 1, 2, and 3 and for Respondents in No. 5 on Further Reargument at 28–30, *Brown II,* 349 U.S. 294; Brief for the United States on the Further Argument of the Questions of Relief at 6, 22–29, *Brown II,* 349 U.S. 294; *id.* at 25. For a more detailed treatment of the executive branch's participation as amicus curiae in *Brown II,* see David A. Nichols, *A Matter of Justice: Eisenhower and the Beginning of the Civil Rights Revolution* 66–74 (2007).

6. *Brown II,* 349 U.S. at 299–301. See generally Paul Gewirtz, *Remedies and Resistance,* 92 Yale L.J. 585, 609–28 (1983) (discussing "all deliberate speed" and the Court's efforts to factor white resistance into its remedial approaches in *Brown II* and subsequent cases).

7. Nichols, *supra* note 5, at 118; Southern Manifesto, 102 Cong. Rec. 4515–16 (1965); Tony A. Freyer, *Little Rock on Trial:* Cooper v. Aaron *and School Desegregation* 38–39 (2007).

8. Klarman, *supra* note 1, at 154; Freyer, *supra* note 7, at 36–39, 68–73.

9. Nichols, *supra* note 5, at 116–18; Freyer, *supra* note 7, at 29–30.

10. Although the Civil Rights Act of 1957 was the first civil rights legislation Congress passed since 1875 (see Klarman, *supra* note 1, at 128), the bill that made it through the Senate was significantly weaker than the bill President Eisenhower proposed. See Nichols, *supra* note 5, at 143–68; *id.* at 112–15; Freyer, *supra* note 7, at 152.

11. Nichols, *supra* note 5, at 66–69 (discussing school integration in the District of Columbia); *id.* at 118; Paul E. Wilson, *A Time to Lose: Representing Kansas in* Brown v. Board of Education 198–202 (1995); Daniel A. Farber, *The Supreme Court and the Rule of Law:* Cooper v. Aaron *Revisited,* 1982 U. Ill. L. Rev. 387, 392 (listing cities that issued statements of intent to comply with *Brown*); Virgil T. Blossom, *It Has Happened Here* 9–24 (1959) (offering a first-person account of Little Rock's preparations for compliance with *Brown*).

12. Farber, *supra* note 11, at 392–93 (stating that Little Rock's elected officials were "mostly moderates," that the "city had little history of racial violence," and that the public transportation had been desegregated before the events giving rise to *Cooper v. Aaron*); Freyer, *supra* note 7, at 17–22 (discussing Little Rock's reaction to a 1952 study decrying the conditions at black students' schools and describing later reaction to the *Brown* decision); Blossom, *supra* note 11, at 11–12 (providing the Little Rock School Board's May 1954 statement concerning *Brown*).

13. Freyer, *supra* note 7, at 27–28; see also *Cooper v. Aaron,* 358 U.S. 1, 8 (1958); Blossom, *supra* note 11, at 21–24.

14. *Aaron v. Cooper,* 143 F. Supp. 855 (E.D. Ark. 1956); *Aaron v. Cooper,* 243 F.2d 361 (8th Cir. 1957); Freyer, *supra* note 7, at 78–79 (discussing the selection of the Little Rock Nine).

15. *Cooper,* 358 U.S. at 8–9 (discussing the state constitutional amendments and legislation passed in Arkansas in the wake of *Brown*); Freyer, *supra* note 7, at 80–81 (detailing the Capital Citizens' Council protests against Little Rock's desegregation plans).

16. Freyer, *supra* note 7, at 81; see also *id.* at 63–66 (discussing Faubus's economically liberal policies and primary victory over his segregationist opponent); *id.* at 81–88, 98–99 (describing the pressure placed on Faubus); *id.* at 99–112 (discussing the reasons that Faubus ultimately chose to defy federal authority).

17. Nichols, *supra* note 5, at 170; Freyer, *supra* note 7, at 90–112 (discussing rising political pressure in Little Rock leading up to integration); *id.* at 105 (describing Faubus's public comments); *id.* at 90 (quoting threats aimed at Bates).

18. Freyer, *supra* note 7, at 104–6, 108.

19. *Id.* at 112–13.

20. *Id.* at 114.

21. *Id.* at 115.

22. *Id.* Will Counts, at the time a twenty-six-year-old photographer for the *Arkansas Democrat,* took the famous photograph of Eckford. See *Will Counts, 70; Noted for Little Rock Photo,* New York Times, Oct. 10, 2001, at D8. The photograph and numerous other pictures Counts shot of the events surrounding the integration of the Little Rock schools can be found in his book *A Life Is More Than a Moment: The Desegregation of Little Rock's Central High* (2007).

23. Freyer, *supra* note 7, at 115–16, 119–20.

24. Nichols, *supra* note 5, at 176–83.

25. *Id.* at 182–83, 186–87.

26. *Id.* at 189–91.

27. *Id.* at 67.

28. *Id.* at 186. For a discussion of Eisenhower's reservations about expanding federal authority over traditional state functions, see *id.* at 141, 153–55, 176; and Freyer, *supra* note 7, at 41–46.

29. Nichols, *supra* note 5, at 198 (recounting Eisenhower's belief, detailed in a presidential address, that "the overwhelming majority of the people in the South—including those of Arkansas and of Little Rock—are of good will, united in their efforts to preserve and respect the law even when they disagree with it").

30. *Id.* at 136; Freyer, *supra* note 7, at 42.

31. Nichols, *supra* note 5, at 6 (describing Eisenhower's youth in Abilene, Kansas); *id.* at 8–13 (discussing Eisenhower's experience with black soldiers during World War II); *id.* at 42–43 (discussing Eisenhower's desegregation of the armed forces); *id.* at 34–40 (discussing Eisenhower's desegregation of federal contracting); *id.* at 26–29, 33–34, 40–41, 66–69 (discussing the desegregation of the District of Columbia). But see Alan L. Gropman, *The Air Force Integrates, 1945–1964* 149–53 (1985) (describing Eisenhower's approach to civil rights as "passive"); Everett Frederic Morrow, *Black Man in the White House: A Diary of the Eisenhower Years by the Administrative Officer for Special Projects, the White House, 1955–1961* 298–300 (1963) (describing Eisenhower's stand on civil rights as "lukewarm"). See also *Report: Tuskegee Airmen Lost 25 Bombers,* USA Today, Apr. 1, 2007.

32. Nichols, *supra* note 5, at 191–96 (describing Eisenhower's decision to send federal troops to Little Rock).

33. *Id.* at 192.

34. *Id.* at 195.

35. *Id.* at 197, 199.

36. Freyer, *supra* note 7, at 133; Blossom, *supra* note 11, at 120–24.

37. Nichols, *supra* note 5, at 200.

38. *Id.* at 202, 212–13; Freyer, *supra* note 7, at 138–40.

39. Nichols, *supra* note 5, at 222.

40. Freyer, *supra* note 7, at 142–44; *Aaron v. Cooper,* 163 F. Supp. 13, 17–21, 28 (E.D. Ark. 1958).

41. *Cooper,* 163 F. Supp. at 32; *Aaron v. Cooper,* 257 F.2d 33 (8th Cir. 1958), *cert. granted,* 358 U.S. 1 (1958); Freyer, *supra* note 7, at 151.

42. Freyer, *supra* note 7, at 152–57.

43. *Id.* at 169–70, 175; *Cooper v. Aaron,* 358 U.S. 1 (1958).

44. *Cooper,* 358 U.S. at 4, 18.

45. *Marbury v. Madison,* 5 U.S. (1 Cranch) 137 (1803) (emphasis added); *Cooper,* 358 U.S. at 18.

46. *Cooper,* 358 U.S. at 19. For an extensive discussion of the opinion-drafting process in *Cooper v. Aaron,* see Freyer, *supra* note 7, at 169–201; and Tony A. Freyer, Cooper v. Aaron *(1958): A Hidden Story of Unanimity and Division,* 33 J. Sup. Ct. Hist. 89 (2008).

47. *Cooper,* 358 U.S. at 15; *id.* at 6.

48. Freyer, *supra* note 7, at 174–75.

49. *Cooper,* 358 U.S. at 6 (citing *Brown II,* 349 U.S. at 300–301); *id.* at 4–7; *id.* at 25–26 (Frankfurter, J., concurring).

50. *Id.* at 19–20 (emphasis added); Gewirtz, *supra* note 6, at 627–28, 676–77, 681.

51. Freyer, *supra* note 7, at 203.

52. *Id.* at 205–7.

53. *Id.* at 208–9.

54. *Id.* at 203–4; Gary Smith, *Blindsided by History,* Sports Illustrated, Apr. 9, 2007.

55. Freyer, *supra* note 7, at 232; see also Smith, *supra* note 54.

56. Freyer, *supra* note 7, at 205; Jack Bass & Walter De Vries, *The Transformation of Southern Politics: Social Change and Political Consequence Since 1945* 89–90 (1995).

57. Felicia R. Lee, *Return to a Showdown at Little Rock,* New York Times, Sept. 25, 2007; American Youth Policy Forum, *Expanding Advanced Placement Participation and Building Public Will in Little Rock, AR* www.aypf.org/tripreports/2007/TR110707.htm (accessed Jan. 28, 2010).

Chapter Six / A Present-Day Example

1. *Cf. Roe v. Wade,* 410 U.S. 113 (1973); *Planned Parenthood v. Casey,* 505 U.S. 833 (1992); *Wallace v. Jaffree,* 472 U.S. 38 (1985).

2. *Bush v. Gore,* 531 U.S. 98 (2000).

3. U.S. Const. amend. XII; U.S. Const. art. II, § 1; Fla. Stat. § 103.011 (2000).

4. *Bush,* 531 U.S. at 100–101.

5. *Id.* at 112–22 (Scalia, J., concurring) (expressing concern that the Florida Supreme Court had established a system for appointment of electors, in contravention of U.S. Const. art. II, § 1's requirement that the state legislature do so); *id.* at 110 ("[I]t is obvious that the recount cannot be conducted in compliance with the requirements of equal protection and due process without substantial additional work").

6. *Id.* at 158 (Breyer, J., dissenting). I agreed with the majority, however, that there should be a uniform standard for all counties.

7. The author was present to hear Senator Reid's remarks.

Chapter Seven / The Basic Approach

1. *Cf. Maryland v. Craig,* 497 U.S. 836 (1990) (holding that a child witness may testify via closed-circuit television); *Crawford v. Washington,* 541 U.S. 36, 56 n. 6 (2004) (considering whether the use of a dying statement in a criminal prosecution violates the Sixth Amendment).

2. *Youngstown Sheet & Tube Co. v. Sawyer,* 343 U.S. 579, 634 (1952) (Jackson, J., concurring).

3. U.S. Const. amend. II (emphasis added). See James Lindgren, *Fall from Grace: "Arming America" and the Bellesiles Scandal,* 111 Yale L.J. 2195 (2002) (describing the controversy surrounding Michael Bellesiles's book *Arming America*).

4. U.S. Const. art. I, § 3, cl. 1, amended by U.S. Const. amend. XVII, § 1; U.S. Const. art. I, § 8, cl. 3.

5. See, e.g., *Giles v. California,* No. 07–6053, slip. op. (U.S. June 25, 2008) (admitting into evidence the unconfronted testimony of the murder victim under a doctrine of forfeiture by wrongdoing).

6. Gordon S. Wood, *Empire of Liberty* 457 (2009).

7. Learned Hand, *The Spirit of Liberty: Papers and Addresses of Learned Hand* 120 (1959).

8. Federalist 51 (James Madison) (emphasis added).

9. *Plessy v. Ferguson,* 163 U.S. 537 (1896).

10. Ken Gormley, *Archibald Cox: Conscience of a Nation* 46 (1999).

11. Justice Ruth Bader Ginsburg, *A Tribute to Sandra Day O'Connor,* 119 Harv. L. Rev. 1239, 1244 (2006).

12. U.S. Const. art. I, § 2, cl. 2; *U.S. Term Limits, Inc. v. Thornton,* 514 U.S. 779 (1995).

Chapter Eight / Congress, Statutes, and Purposes

1. Ségolène de Larquier, *La SNCF en fait baver aux escargots,* Le Point, Apr. 6, 2008; *Escargots sans billet: La SNCF va rembourser le propriétaire verbalisé,* La Dépêche, June 4, 2008.

2. *Cf. Ali v. Federal Bureau of Prisons,* 552 U.S. 214 (2008) (emphasis added).

3. Einer R. Elhauge, Interpreting Statutes: Ordinary English, Canons, and Conventions (Feb. 29, 2008) (unpublished manuscript on file with author).

4. *Cf. Zuni Public School District No. 89 v. Department of Education,* 550 U.S. 81, 93–95 (2007).

5. *Cf. Small v. United States,* 544 U.S. 385 (2005) (holding that a statute prohibiting firearm ownership by any individual "convicted in any court" of certain crimes did not apply to a person convicted in Japanese court); *Nixon v. Missouri Municipal League,* 541 U.S. 125, 132 (2004) (" '[A]ny' " means "different things depending upon the setting").

6. *Ali,* 552 U.S. (Breyer, J., dissenting).

7. *Arlington Central School District Board of Education v. Murphy,* 548 U.S. 291, 303 (2006); Brief of Respondents at 8, *Arlington Central School District Board of Education v. Murphy* (U.S. Mar. 28, 2006) (No. 05–18).

8. Brief of Respondents, *supra* note 7, at 9–10.

9. *Id.* at 10–11.

10. *Murphy,* 548 U.S. at 294.

11. *Id.* at 297.

12. *Id.* at 313–16 (Breyer, J., dissenting).

13. *Id.* at 308–13 (emphasis added).

14. See generally J. Gordon Christy, Federal Statutory Interpretation: The Gordian Knot Untied (Mar. 12, 2009) (unpublished manuscript on file with author) (defending reliance on statutory purposes in interpreting statutes as the only correct method of statutory interpretation).

15. See, e.g., Sherman Anti-trust Act, 15 U.S.C. § 1 (2006) ("Every contract, combination in the form of trust or otherwise, or conspiracy, in restraint of trade or commerce among the several States, or with foreign nations, is declared to be illegal");

Armed Career Criminal Act, 18 U.S.C. § 924(e) (2006) (providing minimum sentences for multiple "violent felony" or "serious" drug crime offenses).

16. For a classic statement of the criticism that Congress, as an institution consisting of multiple individuals, cannot have an intent, see Max Radin, *Statutory Interpretation,* 43 Harv. L. Rev. 863 (1930). For an equally classic response, see James M. Landis, *A Note on Statutory Interpretation,* 43 Harv. L. Rev. 886 (1930).

17. *Zadvydas v. Davis,* 533 U.S. 678 (2001).

18. *Id.* at 684.

19. *Id.* at 685–86.

20. 8 U.S.C. § 1231(a)(6) (1994) (emphasis added); *Zadvydas,* 533 U.S. at 689.

21. U.S. Const. amend V; *Zadvydas,* 533 U.S. at 690–92.

22. *Zadvydas,* 533 U.S. at 701.

23. *Id.* at 689 (citing *Crowell v. Benson,* 285 U.S. 22, 62 [1932]).

Chapter Nine / The Executive Branch, Administrative Action, and Comparative Expertise

1. U.S. Const. art. II, § 1, cl. 1.

2. See *President's Committee on Administrative Management, Report with Special Studies* (1937) (characterizing administrative agencies as a "headless 'fourth branch' " of government).

3. Bureau of Labor Statistics, U.S. Department of Labor, *Career Guide to Industries, 2010–11 Edition* (2009), www.bls.gov/oco/cg/home.htm.

4. James M. Landis, *The Administrative Process* 46 (1938); Federalist 51 (James Madison).

5. See M. J. C. Vile, *Constitutionalism and the Separation of Powers* 277–80 (1st ed. 1967) (tracing the history of the idea of public administration as an apolitical science).

6. See 5 U.S.C. § 706; see, e.g., *Service v. Dulles,* 354 U.S. 363, 388 (1957).

7. See Fed. R. Civ. P. 52(a)(6); see *Jackson v. Virginia,* 443 U.S. 307, 318–19 (1979); see 5 U.S.C. § 706.

8. *International Brotherhood of Electrical Workers, Local Union No. 68 v. National Labor Relations Board,* 448 F.2d 1127, 1142 (D.C. Cir. 1971) (Leventhal, J., dissenting).

9. See Stephen Breyer, *Judicial Review of Questions of Law and Policy,* 38 Admin. L. Rev. 363, 365–67 (1986) (describing two opposing views toward agency decisions of law—one "deferential" and another "independent"); *id.* at 371–72 ("[T]he 'delegation' way of looking at deference . . . suggests that Congressional intent to make agency decisions of law binding is really a question of *how much* deference Congress intended courts to pay to the agency's decisions, a matter of degree, not kind").

10. 5 U.S.C. § 706(2)(a).

11. *National Labor Relations Board v. Labor Services, Inc.,* 721 F.2d 13, 14–15 (1st Cir. 1983); *cf.* Breyer, *supra* note 9, at 383 ("When writing an administrative law case book in the late 1970s, the authors could find only a handful of cases that faced so directly an agency policy decision and held it 'arbitrary'; by the time the second edition was published in 1985, they found many more").

12. *Cf. National Labor Relations Board v. Hearst Publications,* 322 U.S. 111 (1944); see

Chevron, U.S.A. v. Natural Resources Defense Council, 467 U.S. 837, 844 (1984) (noting that legislative delegation to an agency may be implicit, in which case a court must defer to a reasonable interpretation by the agency).

13. See Breyer, *supra* note 9, at 370 (noting that courts have inferred legislative intent and looked to whether an agency has special expertise when deciding whether to defer to an agency's interpretation of a statutory provision).

14. *Chevron,* 467 U.S. at 840–42; *id.* at 856–58; *id.* at 866.

15. *Id.* at 842–44.

16. *Massachusetts v. Environmental Protection Agency,* 549 U.S. 497, 505–6 (2007); *id.* at 528–30; 42 U.S.C. § 7521(a)(1); 42 U.S.C. § 7602(g).

17. 19 U.S.C. 1500(b); *United States v. Mead Corp.,* 533 U.S. 218, 225–27 (2001); *id.* at 229–34.

18. *Mead,* 533 U.S. at 233.

Chapter Ten / The States and Federalism

1. *New State Ice Co. v. Liebmann,* 285 U.S. 262, 280–311 (1932) (Brandeis, J., dissenting).

2. Bernard Bailyn, *The Ideological Origins of the American Revolution* 55 (1967) (quoting James Madison); see U.S. Const. preamble; U.S. Const. amend. X.

3. See Federalist 45 (James Madison).

4. *New State Ice Co.,* 285 U.S. at 311 (Brandeis, J., dissenting).

5. See Chantal Millon-Delsol, *L'état subsidiaire* 13 (1992).

6. See, e.g., art. 5, Consolidated Version of the Treaty on European Union, O.J. C 115/13, at 18 (2008). For a recent, general discussion of subsidiarity in European Union law, see Theodore Konstadinides, *Division of Powers in European Union Law* (2009).

7. Case 90/86, Criminal Proceedings Against Zoni, 1988 E.C.R. 4285.

8. U.S. Const. art. I, § 8.

9. *United States v. Lopez,* 514 U.S. 549, 551 (1995).

10. For cases treating such issues, see, for example, *Wickard v. Filburn,* 317 U.S. 111 (1942); and *Gonzales v. Raich,* 545 U.S. 1 (2005).

11. *Lopez,* 514 U.S. at 551; U.S. Const. art. I, § 8, cl. 3; see *Lopez,* 514 U.S. at 558–59; see *id.* at 560–61 (citing *Wickard,* 317 U.S. at 128); see *id.* at 606–7 (Souter, J., dissenting).

12. *Lopez,* 514 U.S. at 551 (majority opinion); *id.* at 564–65.

13. That is the position I took in my dissent. *Id.* at 619–22 (Breyer, J., dissenting).

14. 18 U.S.C. § 922(q)(2)(A).

15. U.S. Const. art. I, § 8, cl. 3.

16. See *C & A Carbone, Inc. v. Clarkstown,* 511 U.S. 383, 401–2 (1994) (O'Connor, J., concurring); see, e.g., *Camps Newfound/Owatonna, Inc. v. Town of Harrison,* 520 U.S. 564, 595 (1997) (striking down a Maine statute that excluded, from its property tax exemption for charitable organizations, organizations operated principally for the benefit of nonresidents); see also *Wyoming v. Oklahoma,* 502 U.S. 437, 461 (1992) (striking down an Oklahoma law that discriminated against out-of-state coal producers).

17. See, e.g., *Wyoming*, 502 U.S. at 454–55 ("[W]hen the state statute amounts to simple economic protectionism, a 'virtually *per se* rule of invalidity' has applied" [citing *Philadelphia v. New Jersey*, 437 U.S. 617, 624 (1978)]).

18. *Cf. Wyeth v. Levine*, 129 S. Ct. 1187, 1191 (2009); *cf.* also *Altria Group, Inc. v. Good*, 129 S. Ct. 538, 541 (2008).

19. *New State Ice Co.*, 285 U.S. at 271; *id.* at 273–77; Brief of the Appellee at 17, *New State Ice Co.*, 285 U.S. 262 (No. 463); *New State Ice Co.*, 285 U.S. at 281 (Brandeis, J., dissenting); *id.* at 310–11.

20. *Parents Involved in Community Schools v. Seattle School District No. 1*, 551 U.S. 701, 709–11 (2007).

21. *Id.* at 715–16.

22. *Id.* at 711–12; *id.* at 812–13 (Breyer, J., dissenting).

23. *Id.* at 709–11 (majority opinion); *id.* at 782 (Kennedy, J., concurring in part and concurring in the judgment); *id.* at 832–35 (Breyer, J., dissenting); *id.* at 823–29, 855–58; *id.* at 836; *id.* at 803.

24. *Id.* at 866; *id.* at 849 (citing *Brown v. Board of Education* [*Brown II*], 349 U.S. 294, 299 [1955]).

25. *Id.* at 862.

Chapter Eleven / Other Federal Courts

1. See Robert C. LaFountain et al., National Center for State Courts, *Examining the Work of State Courts* (2007); and Statistics Division, Administrative Office of the U.S. Courts, *2008 Annual Report of the Director: Judicial Business of the United States Courts* (2009).

2. See Fed. R. Civ. P. 52(a)(6).

3. See, e.g., *Graver Tank & Manufacturing Co. v. Linde Air Products Co.*, 336 U.S. 271, 275 (1949) ("A court of law, such as this Court is, rather than a court for correction of errors in fact finding, cannot undertake to review concurrent findings of fact by two courts below in the absence of a very obvious and exceptional showing of error"); see also Sup. Ct. R. 10; *United States v. Reliable Transfer Co., Inc.*, 421 U.S. 397, 401 n. 2 (1975).

4. *Brown v. Allen*, 344 U.S. 443, 540 (1953) (Jackson, J., concurring).

5. *Horne v. Flores*, 129 S. Ct. 2579, 2588 (2009); *id.* at 2610 (Breyer, J., dissenting).

6. *Id.* at 2610–12.

7. *Id.* at 2590–92 (majority opinion); *id.* at 2612 (Breyer, J., dissenting) (noting that the district court hearing produced an evidentiary record of 1,684 pages); *id.* at 2608.

8. *Id.* at 2594–98 (majority opinion); *id.* at 2607; *id.* at 2608 (Breyer, J., dissenting).

9. *Flores v. Arizona*, 480 F. Supp. 2d 1157, 1160 (D. Ariz. 2007) ("There is no doubt that [the school district] is doing substantially better than it was in 2000"), *rev'd sub nom.*, *Horne v. Flores*, 129 S. Ct. 2579 (2009).

10. See generally Stephen J. Carroll et al., RAND Institute for Civil Justice, *Asbestos Litigation* xxiv (2005), www.rand.org/pubs/monographs/2005/RAND_MG162.pdf; *id.* at 45–48.

11. See *id.* at 45–48.

12. See generally Fed. R. Civ. P. 23; Fed. R. Civ. P. 23(b)(3); Fed. R. Civ. P. 23(c)(2)(b).

13. *Amchem Products, Inc. v. Windsor,* 521 U.S. 591, 602–4 (1997).

14. *Georgine v. Amchem Products, Inc.,* 157 F.R.D. 246, 315–16 (E.D. Pa. 1994), *vacated,* 83 F.3d 610 (3d Cir. 1996), *aff'd sub nom., Amchem Products, Inc. v. Windsor,* 521 U.S. 591 (1997); 157 F.R.D. at 334–35.

15. *Amchem,* 521 U.S. at 597 (holding that the class certification failed to meet the requirements of the federal rules); *id.* at 622–27; *id.* at 625.

16. *Georgine,* 157 F.R.D.

17. *Amchem,* 521 U.S. at 633 (Breyer, J., concurring in part and dissenting in part) (citation omitted); *id.* at 598 (majority opinion) (quoting *Report of the Judicial Conference Ad Hoc Committee on Asbestos Litigation* 2–3 [1991]); *Ahearn v. Fibreboard Corp.,* 162 F.R.D. 505, 509 (E.D. Tex. 1995) (citing RAND studies); *id.* at 530; *Ortiz v. Fibreboard Corp.,* 527 U.S. 815, 866 (1999) (Breyer, J., dissenting) (citing *Cimino v. Raymark Industries Inc.,* 751 F. Supp. 649, 651 [E.D. Tex. 1990]).

Chapter Twelve / Past Court Decisions

1. *Brown v. Board of Education,* 347 U.S. 483 (1954); *Plessy v. Ferguson,* 163 U.S. 537, 540 (1896); *id.* at 552.

2. *Brown,* 347 U.S. at 495.

3. U.S. Const. amend. XIV, § 1.; see *Sweatt v. Painter,* 339 U.S. 629, 635–36 (1950) (holding that state provision of racially segregated law schools violated equal protection); see also *McLaurin v. Oklahoma State Regents,* 339 U.S. 637 (1950) (holding that segregated treatment based on the race of a student pursuing a doctorate in education violated equal protection); see also EO 9981, 13 Fed. Reg. 4313 (July 26, 1948) (ordering equality of treatment and opportunity in the armed services).

4. *Brown,* 347 U.S. at 492–96; see *Brown v. Board of Education* (*Brown II*), 349 U.S. 294, 298 (1955) ("All provisions of federal, state, or local law requiring or permitting [racial] discrimination [in public education] must yield to this principle [that such discrimination is unconstitutional]").

5. See generally Henry M. Hart Jr. & Albert Sacks, *The Legal Process* 568–69 (William N. Eskridge Jr. & Philip P. Frickey eds., 1994).

6. See, e.g., *Leegin Creative Leather Products, Inc. v. PSKS, Inc.,* 551 U.S. 877, 923–26 (2007) (Breyer, J., dissenting).

7. *Id.* at 925.

8. *Id.* at 924.

9. *Id.*

10. *Id.*

11. *Id.* at 926; *Miranda v. Arizona,* 384 U.S. 436, 444 (1966); *Dickerson v. United States,* 530 U.S. 428, 443–44 (2000).

12. See *Citizens United v. Federal Election Commission,* No. 08-208 (Jan. 21, 2010), overruling *Austin v. Chamber of Commerce,* 494 U.S. 652 (1990) and *McConnell v. Federal Election Commission,* 540 U.S. 93, 205–09 (2003).

13. See U.S. Const. art. V.

14. See *Northern Securities Co. v. United States,* 193 U.S. 197, 400 (1904) (Holmes, J., dissenting); Jeffrey Rosen, *The Supreme Court: The Personalities and Rivalries That Defined America* 115 (2006).

15. *New York v. Belton,* 453 U.S. 454, 462–63 (1981); *cf. Arizona v. Gant,* 129 S. Ct. 1710, 1723–24 (2009) (holding that *Belton*'s acceptance of warrantless vehicle searches incident to arrest is confined to cases in which the arrestee is in reaching distance of the passenger compartment or it is reasonable to believe the vehicle contains evidence related to the offense of arrest).

16. Consider, from the 2006–7 term, the following cases: *Leegin,* 551 U.S.; *Parents Involved in Community Schools v. Seattle School District No. 1,* 551 U.S. 701 (2007); *Federal Election Commission v. Wisconsin Right to Life, Inc.,* 551 U.S. 449 (2007); *National Association of Home Builders v. Defenders of Wildlife,* 551 U.S. 644 (2007); *Hein v. Freedom from Religion Foundation, Inc.,* 551 U.S. 587 (2007); *Bowles v. Russell,* 551 U.S. 205 (2007); *Uttecht v. Brown,* 551 U.S. 1 (2007); *Ledbetter v. Goodyear Tire and Rubber Co.,* 550 U.S. 618 (2007), superseded by statute, Lilly Ledbetter Fair Pay Act of 2009, Pub. L. No. 111–2, 123 Stat. 5 (2009); and *Gonzales v. Carhart,* 550 U.S. 124 (2007).

Chapter Thirteen / Individual Liberty

1. See Hugo L. Black, *The Bill of Rights,* 35 N.Y.U. L. Rev. 865, 874 (1960).

2. *Schenck v. United States,* 249 U.S. 47, 52 (1919).

3. 541 U.S. 267, 272, 355(2004).

4. *Davis v. Bandemer,* 478 U.S. 109 (1986).

5. See *Kyllo v. United States,* 533 U.S. 27 (2001).

6. *Grutter v. Bollinger,* 539 U.S. 306, 353–54 (2003) (Thomas, J., concurring in part and dissenting in part); *Gratz v. Bollinger,* 539 U.S. 244, 301 (2003) (Ginsburg, J., dissenting).

7. See generally Alec Stone Sweet & Jud Matthews, *Proportionality Balancing and Global Constitutionalism,* 47 Colum. J. Transnat'l L. 72, 97–159 (2008) (tracing history of proportionality analysis and its use by courts around the world); *cf. Ysursa v. Pocatello Education Association,* 129 S. Ct. 1093, 1103–4 (2009) (Breyer, J., concurring in part and dissenting in part) (arguing for and applying a proportionality analysis in the First Amendment context).

8. *District of Columbia v. Heller,* 128 S. Ct. 2783 (2008).

9. *Id.* at 2797–99.

10. *Id.* at 2826–27, 2831–36 (Stevens, J., dissenting); *id.* at 2847 (Breyer, J., dissenting); U.S. Const. art. 1, § 8.

11. *Heller,* 128 S. Ct. at 2801–2.

12. *Id.* at 2870 (Breyer, J., dissenting).

13. *Id.* at 2846 (Stevens, J., dissenting) ("Until today, it has been understood that legislatures may regulate the civilian use and misuse of firearms so long as they do not interfere with the preservation of a well-regulated militia").

14. *Id.* at 2817–18.

15. *Cf. id.* at 2865 (Breyer, J., dissenting). Compare also the approach of Eugene

Volokh, *Implementing the Right to Keep and Bear Arms for Self-Defense: An Analytical Framework and a Research Agenda*, 56 UCLA L. Rev. 1443 (2009), who attempts to translate the right to keep and bear arms into "workable constitutional doctrine."

16. *Heller*, 128 S. Ct. at 2865–66 (Breyer, J., dissenting).

17. *Id.* at 2854–59 (discussing the empirical studies provided in amicus briefs).

18. *Id.* at 2859 ("[T]he question here is whether [the empirical arguments] are strong enough to destroy judicial confidence in the reasonableness of a legislature that rejects them").

19. *Id.* at 2861–64.

20. *Id.* at 2864.

21. *Id.* at 2865.

22. *Id.* at 2865–67.

Chapter Fourteen / The President, National Security, and Accountability

1. *Ex parte Merryman*, 17 F. Cas. 144 (1861).

2. Abraham Lincoln, Message to Congress in Special Session (July 4, 1861), in *Abraham Lincoln: Speeches and Writings, 1859–1865* 253 (Don E. Fehrenbacher ed., 1989).

3. *Youngstown Sheet & Tube Co. v. Sawyer*, 343 U.S. 579 (1952); *id.* at 635–40 (Jackson, J., concurring).

4. *Korematsu v. United States*, 323 U.S. 214 (1944); see, e.g., Mark Tushnet, *Defending* Korematsu?*: Reflections on Civil Liberties in Wartime*, 2003 Wis. L. Rev. 273, 296 ("*Korematsu* seems now to be regarded almost universally as wrongly decided").

5. EO 9066, 7 Fed. Reg. 1407 (Feb. 19, 1942).

6. Peter Irons, *Justice at War* 6–7 (1983); Jacobus tenBroek, Edward N. Barnhart & Floyd W. Matson, *Prejudice, War, and the Constitution* 70 (1954).

7. Irons, *supra* note 6, at 7; *id.* at 60; *id.* at 40–43; tenBroek et al., *supra* note 6, at 83–84.

8. See Irons, *supra* note 6, at 27, 41–42, 58–59; Edward Sanpei, "A Viper Is a Viper Whenever the Egg Is Hatched," 12–13 (1972) (unpublished manuscript on file with author).

9. Dorothy Swaine Thomas & Richard S. Nishimoto, *The Spoilage: Japanese-American Evacuation and Resettlement During World War II* 5 (1969).

10. Irons, *supra* note 6, at 51–52, 56–57; *id.* at 53–55 (discussing constitutional concerns among Justice Department officials); see also tenBroek et al., *supra* note 6, at 357–58 n. 65.

11. TenBroek et al., *supra* note 6, at 111–12; Irons, *supra* note 6, at 60–62.

12. EO 9066; Act of March 21, 1942, 56 Stat. 173, 18 U.S.C. § 97a; Irons, *supra* note 6, at 65–66.

13. Irons, *supra* note 6, at 70; *id.* at 73.

14. *Id.* at 73–74; *id.* at 320.

15. *Id.* at 268–77; tenBroek, *supra* note 6, at 170–84.

16. Civil Liberties Act of 1988, 50 U.S.C. app. § 1989b (2006); Irons, *supra* note 6, at 367.

17. Irons, *supra* note 6, at 87–93.
18. *Id.* at 154–59 (describing the trial and sentencing of Hirabayashi).
19. *Id.* at 175, 182, 184–85.
20. *Id.* at 186–92.
21. *Id.* at 198–202.
22. *Id.* at 206–12.
23. *Id.* at 202–4, 208.
24. *Id.* at 197–98, 211–12, 225–26.
25. *Hirabayashi v. United States,* 320 U.S. 81 (1943).
26. *Id.* at 100–105.
27. *Id.* at 93; *id.* at 101–2.
28. *Id.* at 96, 103.
29. *Id.* at 100, 96, 98, 99.
30. *Id.* at 102.
31. *Id.* at 106 (Douglas, J., concurring); *id.* at 110–12 (Murphy, J., concurring); *id.* at 114 (Rutledge, J., concurring).
32. Irons, *supra* note 6, at 93–94.
33. *Id.* at 98–99.
34. *Id.* at 153, 227, 268.
35. *Id.* at 278–79.
36. *Id.* at 280–84.
37. *Id.* at 280–81.
38. *Id.* at 286.
39. *Id.* at 290–91.
40. *Id.* at 268–73.
41. *Id.* at 99–103.
42. *Id.* at 298–99.
43. *Id.* at 307–8.
44. *Id.* at 315; *id.* at 305–6.
45. *Korematsu,* 323 U.S.; *Ex parte Endo,* 323 U.S. 283 (1944); *Korematsu,* 323 U.S. at 222; *id.* at 218.
46. *Korematsu,* 323 U.S. at 218; *id.* at 219; *id.* at 223–24.
47. *Id.* at 225 (Frankfurter, J., concurring).
48. *Id.* at 230–31 (Roberts, J., dissenting).
49. *Id.* at 236–37 (Murphy, J., dissenting); *id.* at 237 n. 7; *id.* at 240; *id.* at 237–39 nn. 4–12; *id.* at 239–40.
50. *Id.* at 238–39; *id.* at 238 n. 10; *id.* at 241, 242 n. 16.
51. *Id.* at 241.
52. *Id.* at 244–46 (Jackson, J., dissenting) (emphasis added).
53. *Id.* at 246–48.
54. U.S. Const. amend. XIV.
55. *Ex parte Endo,* 323 U.S. at 297 ("[W]e do not come to the underlying constitutional issues which have been argued").
56. *Korematsu,* 323 U.S. at 216.
57. *Terminiello v. Chicago,* 337 U.S. 1, 37 (1949) (Jackson, J., dissenting).

58. Irons, *supra* note 6, at 345.

59. *Korematsu v. United States,* 584 F. Supp. 1406 (N.D. Cal. 1984); Civil Liberties Act of 1988, 50 U.S.C. app. § 1989b (2006).

60. *Korematsu,* 323 U.S. at 246 (Jackson, J., dissenting).

Chapter Fifteen / Presidential Power

1. Authorization for Use of Military Force, § 2(a), 115 Stat. 224 (2001).

2. A. T. Church III (Vice Admiral, U.S. Navy) to the Secretary of Defense, memorandum, Re: Report on DoD Detention Operations and Detainee Interrogation Techniques, Mar. 7, 2005, at 100 (hereinafter Church Report); Laurel E. Fletcher et al., Human Rights Center, University of California, Berkeley, *Guantánamo and Its Aftermath* 29 (Nov. 2008); Benjamin Wittes et al., Governance Studies, Brookings Institution, *The Current Detainee Population of Guantánamo: An Empirical Study* 2 (Dec. 16, 2008).

3. Church Report, *supra* note 2, at 100; Wittes et al., *supra* note 2, at 2.

4. Church Report, *supra* note 2, at 101–3; Fletcher et al., *supra* note 2, at 29, 31 fig. 2.

5. Church Report, *supra* note 2, at 99; see also Jack Goldsmith, *The Terror Presidency* 108 (2007).

6. *Rasul v. Bush,* 542 U.S. 466 (2004).

7. See *id.* at 473–74; U.S. Const. art. I, § 9, cl. 2.

8. 28 U.S.C. § 2241(a).

9. *Johnson v. Eisentrager,* 339 U.S. 763 (1950); *Braden v. 30th Judicial Circuit Court of Kentucky,* 410 U.S. 484 (1973); see *Rasul,* 542 U.S. at 475–76.

10. *Rasul,* 542 U.S. at 483; *id.* at 487 (Kennedy, J., concurring).

11. See *id.* at 480–81.

12. *Id.* at 474 (quoting *Shaughnessy v. United States ex rel. Mezei,* 345 U.S. 206, 218–19 [1953] [Jackson, J., dissenting]).

13. *Id.* at 497–99 (Scalia, J., dissenting).

14. *Id.* at 487 (Kennedy, J., concurring).

15. *Hamdi v. Rumsfeld,* 542 U.S. 507, 510 (2004).

16. *Id.* at 511–13.

17. *Id.* at 513–14.

18. *Id.* at 525.

19. *Id.* at 516–21.

20. *Id.* at 545–52 (Souter, J., concurring in part and dissenting in part); *id.* at 573 (Scalia, J., dissenting).

21. *Id.* at 531 (plurality opinion); *id.* at 529 (citations omitted); *id.* at 532.

22. *Id.* at 531, 535–36.

23. *Id.* at 535.

24. *Id.* at 529 (citing *Mathews v. Eldridge,* 424 U.S. 319 [1976]); *id.* at 535; *id.* at 533 (emphasis added).

25. *Id.* at 533–34 and n. 2 (emphasis added).

26. Detainee Treatment Act of 2005, 119 Stat. 2739; Paul Wolfowitz (Deputy Secre-

tary of Defense) to the Secretary of the Navy, memorandum, Re: Order Establishing Combatant Status Review Tribunals, July 7, 2004, www.defenselink.mil/news/Jul2004/d20040707review.pdf.

27. Military Order of November 13, 2001: Detention, Treatment, and Trial of Certain Non-Citizens in the War Against Terrorism, 66 Fed. Reg. 57,833; *Hamdan v. Rumsfeld,* 548 U.S. 557, 568 (2006).

28. *Hamdan,* 548 U.S. at 569–70.

29. *Id.* at 635; *id.* at 588 (quoting *Ex parte Quirin,* 317 U.S. 1, 19 [1942]).

30. Uniform Code of Military Justice (UCMJ), art. 21, 10 U.S.C. § 821 (emphasis added).

31. *Hamdan,* 548 U.S. at 595–97; *id.* at 612.

32. UCMJ, art. 36, 10 U.S.C. § 836; *Hamdan,* 548 U.S. at 623; *id.* at 633–35, 639–41 (Breyer, J., concurring).

33. *Hamdan,* 548 U.S. at 636.

34. Military Commissions Act, 28 U.S.C. §2241(e) (Supp. 2007).

35. Detainee Treatment Act of 2005 § 1005(e), 119 Stat. 2739.

36. *Boumediene v. Bush,* 128 S. Ct. 2229 (2008).

37. U.S. Const. art. I, § 9, cl. 2.

38. *Boumediene,* 128 S. Ct. at 2259.

39. *Id.* at 2244–47; 4 William Blackstone, *Commentaries* 438.

40. *Boumediene,* 128 S. Ct. at 2251 (quoting *Reid v. Covert,* 354 U.S. 1, 64 [1957] [Frankfurter, J., concurring in result]).

41. *Id.* at 2255 (quoting *Reid,* 354 U.S. at 74–75 [Harlan, J., concurring in result]); *id.* at 2261.

42. *Id.* at 2271–74.

43. See Adam Liptak, *Judge Orders 17 Detainees at Guantánamo Freed,* New York Times, Oct. 21, 2009, at A14.

44. Linda Greenhouse, *Justices, 5–4, Back Detainee Appeals for Guantánamo,* New York Times, June 13, 2008, at A1.

Conclusion

1. Federalist 78 (Alexander Hamilton).

2. Thomas Jefferson, *A Bill for the More General Diffusion of Knowledge,* in *Jefferson: Political Writings* 235 (Joyce Appleby & Terence Ball eds., 1999).

3. David Souter, *Remarks on Civic Education* (ABA Opening Assembly, Aug. 1, 2009), www.abanet.org/publiced/JusticeSouterChallengesABA.pdf.

4. See Stephen Breyer, *Serving America's Best Interests,* Daedalus (Fall 2008), at 139; Sandra Day O'Connor, Op-Ed, *The Threat to Judicial Independence,* Wall Street Journal, Oct. 1, 2006 (discussing the JAIL 4 Judges ballot initiative).

5. David Souter, *Striking the Balance: Fair and Independent Courts in a New Era* (Luncheon Remarks, May 20, 2009); Sandra Day O'Connor, *Education: A Big Idea in Today's America* (Remarks at the Seattle Public Library Town Hall, Sept. 14, 2009); Breyer, *supra* note 4, at 139.

Appendix B

1. See Thomas Jefferson to the New Haven Merchants (July 12, 1801), in 34 *The Papers of Thomas Jefferson* 554, 556 (Barbara B. Oberg et al. eds., 2007) ("how are vacancies to be obtained? those by death are few, by resignation none"). Although in this letter Jefferson was referring to holders of public office generally, his remarks have widely been remembered as relating to Supreme Court justices. For biographies of the current members of the Court, see www.supremecourtus.gov/about/biographies current.pdf.

2. 28 U.S.C. § 1257 allows the Supreme Court to review state court decisions that raise a question of federal law and are "rendered by the highest court of a State in which a decision could be had." Other statutory provisions provide for review of federal court rulings. For statistics on the caseloads of federal and state courts, see Robert C. LaFountain et al., National Center for State Courts, *Examining the Work of State Courts* (2007); and Statistics Division, Administrative Office of the U.S. Courts, *2008 Annual Report of the Director: Judicial Business of the United States Courts* (2009).

3. Article V of the Constitution sets out the procedures by which the Constitution may be amended.

4. *Brown v. Allen*, 344 U.S. 443, 540 (1953) (Jackson, J., concurring in judgment).

5. See, e.g., William Howard Taft, *Three Needed Steps of Progress*, 8 A.B.A. J. 34, 35 (1922) ("The use of the Supreme Court is merely to maintain uniformity of decision for the various courts of appeal"). Supreme Court Rule 10 lists the most important factors that the Court considers when deciding whether to hear a case.

6. *Cf. Arlington Central School District Board of Education v. Murphy*, 548 U.S. 291 (2006) (holding that the word "costs" in the Individuals with Disabilities Education Act does not include expert witness fees); *Arizona v. Gant*, 129 S. Ct. 1710 (2009) (holding unconstitutional the police search of a vehicle after the driver's arrest).

Index

Page numbers in *italics* refer to illustrations.

A NOTE ABOUT THE AUTHOR

STEPHEN BREYER is an associate justice of the United States Supreme Court. He is a resident of Cambridge, Massachusetts, and Washington, D.C.

A NOTE ON THE TYPE

THIS BOOK was set in Minion, a typeface produced by the Adobe Corporation specifically for the Macintosh personal computer, and released in 1990. Designed by Robert Slimbach, Minion combines the classic characteristics of old-style faces with the full complement of weights required for modern typesetting.

Composed by North Market Street Graphics,
Lancaster, Pennsylvania
Printed and bound by Berryville Graphics,
Berryville, Virginia
Designed by Virginia Tan